V12 VANTAGE
WWW.ASTONMARTIN.COM

CW00553824

Official fuel consumption for V12 Vantage in mpg. (Manual) Urban 11.6, Extra-Urban 24.1, Combined 17.3, CO_2 Emissions 388 g/km

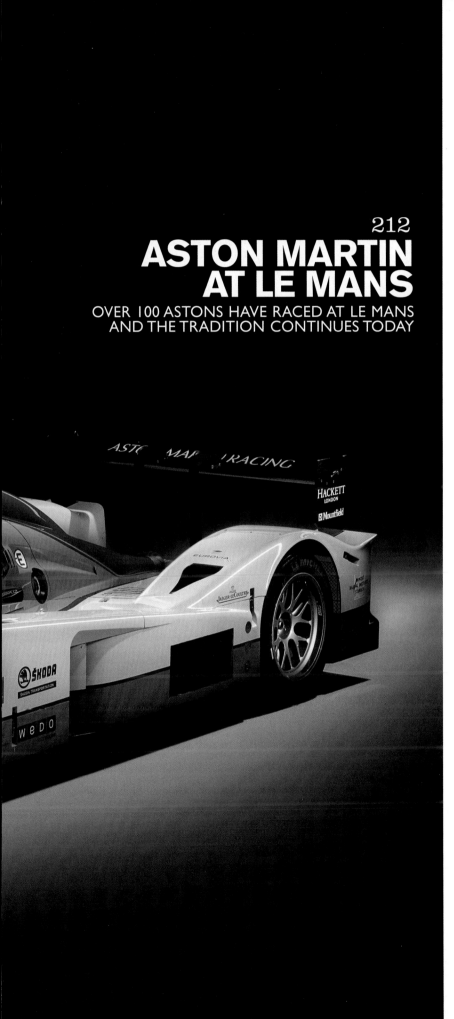

212
ASTON MARTIN AT LE MANS
OVER 100 ASTONS HAVE RACED AT LE MANS AND THE TRADITION CONTINUES TODAY

CONTENTS
Aston Martin 2009

The 40 year shine

For 40 years Autoglym has provided the final gleaming finish to Aston Martins. This legendary DB6, once owned by a former Beatle, not only started life with an Autoglym shine but, having been painstakingly restored by the factory, has once again received the latest treatment from Autoglym.

Today, Aston Martin uses Autoglym polishes and conditioners both inside and out, on all the cars entering the Works Service at Newport Pagnell. The long relationship they have had with Autoglym is a testament to the trust they place in the products.

Proven over 40 years, Autoglym will also bring a lasting shine to your vehicle.

BY APPOINTMENT TO
HER MAJESTY THE QUEEN
SUPPLIER OF CAR CARE PRODUCTS
AUTOGLYM, LETCHWORTH, ENGLAND

BY APPOINTMENT TO
H.R.H. THE PRINCE OF WALES
SUPPLIER OF CAR CARE PRODUCTS
AUTOGLYM, LETCHWORTH, ENGLAND

AUTO GLYM

Product and local stockist information, telephone +44 (0)845 130 4536 or visit our website, www.autoglym.com.

EDITORIAL

Aston Martin 2009

We've never had it so good

HAS THE ASTON MARTIN world ever had it better? The classic models are riding high on a wave of appreciation for the DB4, 5 and 6; a new, credible James Bond is back in an Aston; and the company returned to Le Mans this year, achieving a brilliant fourth place (and highest-placed petrol car) in the world's toughest race.

Within two weeks of that great Le Mans event we took a first drive in the earliest known surviving Aston Martin, the 1921 A3, just out of an extensive restoration. And from that point we have virtually every significant Aston Martin ever made, right through to the One-77 and the proposals for a new 'commuter' Aston.

You want the Aston Martin Bond 007 cars? Check. The 1959 Le Mans-winning DBR1 (and an exclusive double interview with the winning drivers, Carroll Shelby and Roy Salvadori)? Check. All the DB models, from rarely-seen DB1 to current flagship DBS? Check. The latest Le Mans car? Check. You get the picture...

Yes, this is a marque with a rich and varied history, but what's so good is that the latest Astons don't rely on that history for their core appeal. They sound incredible, look fantastic and perform superbly. Read on....

David Lillywhite

'The latest Aston Martins don't rely on history for their core appeal'

Editorial office
Octane, 1 Tower Court, Irchester Road,
Wollaston, Northants NN29 7PJ, UK
Tel: +44 (0)207 907 6585. Fax: +44 (0)1933 663367
Email: info@octane-magazine.com
Website: www.octane-magazine.com

Advertising office
Octane Media Advertising Dept, 19 Highfield Lane,
Maidenhead, Berkshire SL6 3AN, UK
Tel: +44 (0)1628 510080. Fax: +44 (0)1628 510090
Email: ads@octane-magazine.com

Managing editor:	David Lillywhite
Art editor:	Rob Gould
Designer:	Dean Lettice
Production:	Nigel Grimshaw
	Sarah Bradley
	Ben Field
Advertising director:	Sanjay Seetanah
Advertising sales:	Samantha Snow
	Sue Farrow
Advertising production:	Anisha Mogra
	Kerem Kolcak
Publisher	Geoff Love
Newstrade director	Martin Belson
Marketing manager	Alex Seeberg
Managing director	Ian Westwood
Group finance director	Ian Leggett
COO	Brett Reynolds
CEO	James Tye
Chairman	Felix Dennis

Licensing
To license this product, please contact Winnie Liesenfeld on
+44 (0) 20 7907 6134 or email winnie_liesenfeld@dennis.co.uk

Magbook

MAGBOOK

The "Magbook" brand is a trademark of Dennis Publishing Ltd.

Aston Martin: The Complete Story is published under licence from Octane Media Ltd, a subsidiary company of Dennis Publishing Limited, United Kingdom. All rights in the licensed material belong to Felix Dennis, Octane Media or Dennis Publishing and may not be reproduced, whether in whole or in part, without their prior written consent. Octane is a registered trademark.

Repro by Octane Repro **Printed by** BGP, Bicester

Distribution Seymour, 2 East Poultry Avenue,
London EC1A 9PT. Tel: +44 (0)20 7429 4000

Periodicals Postage paid @ Emigsville, PA.
Postmaster: send address corrections to Octane Media c/o 3330
Pacific Ave, Suite 404, Virginia Beach, VA 23451

Aston Martin: The Complete Story ISSN 1906-372 is published by Octane Media Ltd.

♻ recycle
When you have finished with this magazine please recycle it.

The text paper used within this magazine is produced from sustainable forestation, from a chain of custody manufacturer

CONTRIBUTORS

NICK TROTT
PROBABLY the new car journalist most *au fait* with current Astons, Nick describes the latest models in a series of features, from p8.

SHELBY & SALVADORI
TWO LEGENDS in one room. Writer Paul Chudecki recorded the lively recollections of Aston's 1959 Le Mans winners, p58.

RICHARD HESELTINE
WITH HIS great knowledge of both Le Mans and Aston Martin, who better to document the company's 24Hr efforts (p212)?

MARK DIXON
THE FASCINATING variations on the DB4 theme, including GT and Bertone Jet, is brilliantly told by Mark, starting p64.

GEORGE BAMFORD
ACE PHOTOGRAPHER and Bond fanatic George was responsible for the amazing shots of the 007 Astons, p186.

Aston Martin
TODAY

Today, the supremely-talented team of craftsmen at Aston Martin share a modern space equipped with high-tech gadgetry and a lonely robot. Between them they continue to respectfully build on the company's glorious history...
Words: Nick Trott

IN 1915, the first car registered Aston Martin by Lionel Martin and Robert Bamford's Kensington-based business chuffed along with a 1.5-litre, four-cylinder Coventry Simplex side-valve engine. It was fast by 1915 standards, but its nickname (the Coal Scuttle) did it no favours. Ninety four years later, Aston Martin is putting the finishing touches to a machine that's more space shuttle than coal scuttle – the spectacular £1.2million One-77 hypercar. In one rich cocktail of carbon fibre and aluminium, this car represents what Aston Martin is today, where it has come from, and the extraordinary journey it has been on.

We wonder what Lionel Martin and Robert Bamford would make of the One-77, and indeed of Aston Martin Lagonda of today. The 700+bhp One-77 would undoubtedly fascinate the pair, but we'd wager the fascination would only last a fleeting moment before they blasted off in the direction of the nearest hillclimb, eyes on stalks and tongues wrapped around the sides of their heads.

Today, Aston Martin produces approximately 4500 cars a year; between 1915 and 1920 the coal scuttle was the only Aston Martin built. The company is owned by a consortium of two international investment houses, Investment Dar and Adeem Investment, led by David Richards of Prodrive. Since taking control of Aston Martin from Ford in 2006, and with assistance from Richard's Prodrive empire, Aston Martin has emerged as not only a major player in the sports car market, but also in the world of motorsport. Aston Martin Racing, a small corner of the Prodrive empire, has won the GT1 class at Le Mans twice and is embarking on an ambitious plan to win the race outright with a trio of LMP1 prototypes developed jointly with British motorsports manufacturer Lola. This year – its first with the car – the Lola Aston Martins finished a creditable fourth overall.

The current Aston Martin road car range consists of the DB9, the DBS and the V12 and V8 Vantage. All except the V12 Vantage are available in soft-top Roadster guise (although rumour has it a V12 Vantage Roadster

Above
For all the high-tech machinery now employed on Aston's production line, these cars are still very much hand built by artisans.

will be available soon), and all are built on Aston Martin's lauded vertical horizontal (VH) chassis architecture. This bonded aluminium platform does more for Aston Martin than simply provide a stable anchorage for the oily bits; it delivers an adaptable and cost-effective 'long-life' platform for a series of models. A backbone then, not only for the cars but for the company, too.

Testament to the engineering integrity and longevity of VH is that in its fifth year the platform is about to spawn another new model: the Rapide. This four-door sports coupé is the fourth new model based on the Vertical Horizontal chassis since 2004 and sees Aston Martin go head-to-head with a raft of sporting four doors including Bentley's Continental Flying Spur, Porsche's new Panamera and Maserati's Quattroporte. The Rapide will be manufactured by Magna-Steyr in Austria; the first time an Aston Martin will be manufactured outside the UK.

2009 has also seen the return of the Lagonda brand in the bold form of

'The VH chassis is a backbone not only for the cars but for the company, too'

Below
The spectacular heart and soul of the DB9 and DBS is this gigantic 5935cc, 48-valve V12 engine.

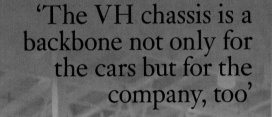

a giant V12-powered sports SUV shown early this year at the 79th Geneva International Motor Show. The Lagonda's dramatic styling divided opinion at Geneva, but Aston Martin Chief Executive Dr Ulrich Bez expects Lagonda to achieve greater sales in markets where Aston Martin does not have a major foothold – nations, in other words, where demand for practical luxury cars outstrips that of sports-coupés or GTs. These territories include Russia, the Middle East, South America, India and China.

Until production of the Rapide begins in Austria later this year, all Aston Martins are currently assembled at a purpose-built facility at Gaydon in Warwickshire. However, since 2004 all Aston Martin engines have been built at a separate building in Ford's Neihl engine plant in Germany and in 2008 Aston Martin opened a dedicated test centre at the famous Nürburgring in Germany. One of Aston Martin's particular triumphs in recent years has been to retain its essential Britishness, despite increasing assistance from overseas. Aston Martin's product development director Ian Minards, himself a Yorkshireman, believes this is a result of the design and engineering integrity being British.

The Gaydon headquarters, opened in 2004, is ultra-modern but the hand-crafted culture is strictly maintained. Gaydon comprises a spectacular customer atrium, complete with a full-size cutaway DBS and various other models. Adjacent to the atrium are a series of smaller rooms where customers can study paint and trim options and view a virtual version of the their intended specification on flat screens. As you would expect the coffee is first rate and you choose from a variety of classic furniture to sit on, including Mies Van Der Rohe Barcelona chairs.

In the production area, the cars are constructed in a series of work stations. Once a technician has finished with the car at one work station, it is moved to the next. The pace is slow by mass-production standards – each car takes around 200 man-hours to build and there is just one robot in the entire facility.

Below
Accurate measuring in the coordinate measuring machine area leads to perfection in production. Aston Martin now uses the very latest LY-90 CNC horizontal-arm measuring machines.

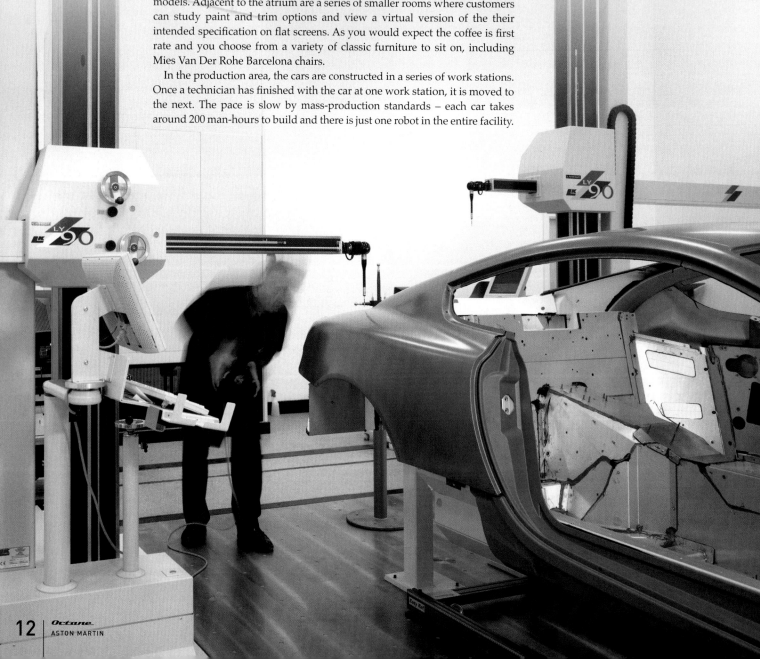

'The only robot at Aston Martin
is based in the chassis bonding
area and is affectionately known
as James Bonder'

This robot, based in the body-in-white chassis bonding area, is affectionately nicknamed James Bonder.

Other areas within Gaydon include the paint shop, where each Aston Martin takes 50 hours to finish, and the CCM (coordinate measuring machine) shop. In the CCM area, tolerances are checked and each chassis assessed before the cars are sent to the final assembly area. It is a clean, relaxed and surprisingly quiet production facility – thanks in part to the lack of production robots.

The Gaydon headquarters expanded in 2007 when Dr Bez formally opened the bespoke design centre adjacent to the main building. This studio, Aston's first stand-alone design facility, took just six months to build and a remarkable 12 months from conception to realisation. Inside this high-ceilinged structure, Aston Martin's designers – led by Sheffield-born Marek Reichman – draw, carve and programme the Astons of the future. Equipped with three-axis milling machines, vehicle lifts and a galleried area that enables viewing from all angles, the design centre is a thoroughly modern and complete

Above
Entire engine and drivetrain is assembled as one piece before fitting to the chassis.

facility. The cherry on top is a presentation area complete with a turntable and visual and sound pyrotechnics from audio partner Bang & Olufsen.

As Aston Martin approaches its centenary, the business finds itself in an unusual scenario. After years of turmoil it now has strong financial backing from its investors, a superb production facility, dedicated design and test centres, the kudos of the James Bond association and last, but by no means least, a superb range of cars. However, the global economic crisis has strangled consumer spending worldwide and luxury car sales have hit a wall. In these tough times, Aston Martin can only continue to do what it has done since the 1915 – build supremely desirable cars.

The One-77 seems a risky proposition in the current climate. However, not only is the One-77 a bold, forward-reaching talisman for a company that could sit back and ride out the recession, it's also a car to celebrate when it is becoming uncustomary to celebrate the car. Lionel Martin and Robert Bamford would approve.

Aston Martin: The current line-up

DB9

Introduced in spring 2004, the DB9's fabulous curves wrapped over the brilliantly-conceived, hi-tech bonded aluminium (VH) aluminium chassis presented a bold manifesto for a company as it struggled to reassert itself after years in the wilderness.

The design paid tribute to the car it replaced, the DB7, but was in another league in terms of performance, technology and engineering. For instance, the DB9 bodyshell is 25% lighter than the DB7 but the structure has more than double the torsional rigidity. Matched to Aston's sublime all-alloy, quad overhead camshaft, 48-valve, 5935cc, V12 engine, the DB9 became an instant hit. Now, five years later, the DB9 has surpassed the DB7 as the most successful Aston Martin of all time and the pioneering chassis has proved its adaptability by underpinning every Aston introduced since 2004.

Vantage

For many people, the entry-level V8 Vantage is the most sublime of the current Aston Martins. Launched at the Geneva Motor Show in 2005 and based on a concept study first shown at the 2003 North American International Auto Show, the V8 has since gone on to sell more than 10,000 worldwide.

Available initially as a 4.3-litre 380bhp V8 coupe with a manual gearbox, the engine has grown to 4.7-litres and 420bhp. A Sportshift clutchless manual gearbox with paddle-shift is available as an option, as is a soft-top Roadster. A race-ready GT4 version has recently gone on sale, as has the extraordinary 510bhp V12 Vantage coupé – a car that won its class on its debut at the 2009 Nürburgring 24-hour race with a team of drivers including Aston Martin chief executive Dr Ulrich Bez.

DBS

Until the One-77 makes its debut in 2010, the DBS maintains its status as the flagship of the Aston Martin range.

Initially dismissed by critics as simply a DB9 with a extrovert bodykit, the DBS's personality is in fact more focused and raw than its GT-led brother thanks in part to a 510bhp version of the 48-valve V12 engine and a keener, more responsive chassis set-up.

Instant kudos was guaranteed in 2006 when Daniel Craig's James Bond drove a DBS in *Casino Royale*. Bond also does a thorough job of making car enthusiasts wince in the latest film, *Quantum of Solace*, when he comprehensively wrecks his DBS in the film's spectacular opening sequence.

Today, two versions of the DBS are available: the coupé and an open Volante model. Both utilise the latest lightweight carbon ceramic matrix (CCM) brakes technology and both reach 191mph flat out. Yet more sophistication was added to the range in 2009 with the addition of a Touchtronic six-speed automatic gearbox with steering-wheel mounted paddleshift. And for those who find themselves bored by listening to that glorious V12 (a scenario almost impossible to imagine), the DBS is available with an extraordinarily theatrical Bang & Olufsen BeoSound audio system. Why theatrical? Well, not only does the hi-fi consist of 13 individual speakers, two of them emerge silently from the dash when the driver switches on the ignition.

ASTON MARTIN

**Power
Beauty
Soul**

Broughtons
Cheltenham
01242 232 667
www.broughtons.co.uk

Charles Hurst Limited
Belfast
02890 381 721
www.charleshurstgroup.co.uk

Grange Brentwood
Brentwood
01277 249 555
www.grange.co.uk

Grange Exeter
Exeter
01392 678 044
www.grange.co.uk

Grange Welwyn
Welwyn Garden City
01707 280 868
www.grange.co.uk

Harwoods
Chichester
01243 836 500
www.harwoods.uk.com/
astonmartin

HWM
Walton on Thames
01932 240 611
www.hwmastonmartin.co.uk

Jacksons (C.I.) Ltd
Jersey
01534 497 777
www.jacksonsci.com

**JCT600 Aston Martin
Brooklands**
Leeds
08448 443 101
www.jct600.co.uk

Lancaster Cambridge
Cambridge
08704 103 848
www.lancasterplc.com/
cambridge/astonmartin

Lancaster Reading
Reading
0118 9658 500
www.lancasterplc.com/
reading/astonmartin

Lancaster Sevenoaks
Sevenoaks
08704 137 316
www.lancasterplc.com/
sevenoaks/astonmartin

Murray Motor Company
Edinburgh
01314 422 800
www.jmgroup.co.uk/murray/
aston_martin.htm

Stratstone Amersham
Amersham
01494 788 360
www.stratstone.com

Stratstone Cardiff
Cardiff
02920 695 700
www.stratstone.com

Stratstone Derby
Derby
01332 258 787
www.stratstone.com

Stratstone Hagley
Stourbridge
01562 888 380
www.stratstone.com

Stratstone Of Mayfair
London
020 7235 8888
www.stratstone.com

Stratstone Tyne & Wear
Tyne & Wear
0191 5123 500
www.stratstone.com

Stratstone Western Avenue
London
0208 752 8720
www.stratstone.com

Stratstone Wilmslow
Wilmslow
01625 548 802
www.stratstone.com

Stratton Motor Company Ltd
Norwich
01508 530 491
www.strattonmotor
company.com

WWW.ASTONMARTIN.COM

STON MARTIN was founded in 1914 by two individuals who had a passion for beautiful and fast cars. Lionel Martin and Robert Bamford were based in London selling and modifying Singers from a small workshop in Henniker Place, Callow Street off the Fulham Road while regularly making the 90-mile round trip to hillclimb events at Aston Hill, near Aston Clinton, in Buckinghamshire.

It was at these hillclimbs where the Bamford and Martin Singers, driven by Lionel Martin himself, established a firm reputation for performance and quality and it was at these hillclimbs that the pair crystallised their ambitions to become an independent car manufacturer. Just over a year after Bamford and Martin Ltd incorporated their business in Kensington the first Aston Martin was registered in March 1915.

Based on a 1908 Isotta-Fraschini chassis (designed by Ettore Bugatti), the car was fitted with a Coventry-Simplex engine. Bamford and Martin described the vehicle as: 'A quality car of good performance and appearance: a car for the discerning owner driver with fast touring in mind, designed, developed and built as an individual.' Ninety four years later, the Aston Martins of 2009 resonate with the same principles established by Bamford and Martin from their small workshop in Kensington.

The Coal Scuttle was a limited edition in the truest sense – the first Aston Martin was indeed the only Aston Martin manufactured for five years. The company closed its shutters for the duration of

the First World War and returned again in 1919 with its second car – named 'Bunny'. Again powered by a Coventry-Simplex engine, this vehicle was Aston Martin's first production road car and retailed at a costly £850.

By now Aston Martin was receiving financial assistance from Count Louis Zborowski – a colourful motoring pioneer who inspired Ian Fleming to write *Chitty Chitty Bang Bang*. Despite building his own Chitty series of aero-engined 23-litre Mercedes-Maybachs, Count Zborowski was funding the construction of two Aston Martin racing cars. On May 24th 1922, one of them – believed to be Bunny – broke ten world speed records at Brooklands, clocking an average of 76.04mph. Despite this success, Robert Bamford chose to sell his interest in the company to Lionel Martin. A year later the third Aston Martin, chassis number A3, lapped Brooklands at 84.5mph despite its tiny 1.5-litre 11hp four-cylinder side-valve engine.

Lionel Martin left Aston Martin in 1925. He was bought out by Lord Charnwood who by now owned a substantial holding in the company. With fellow directors Augustus Cesare Bertelli and William Somerville Renwick on board, the trio formed Aston Martin Motors and moved to new premises in Feltham, Middlesex with Bertelli's brother, Enrico, providing coachbuilding services from an adjacent bodyshop. A new range of cars was shown at the 1927 Motor Show at Olympia and in 1930 E Bertelli styled a fixed head coupe for Whitby ship owner, WS Headlam. This car is considered one of the most beautiful in Aston Martin's history,

Aston Martin HISTORY

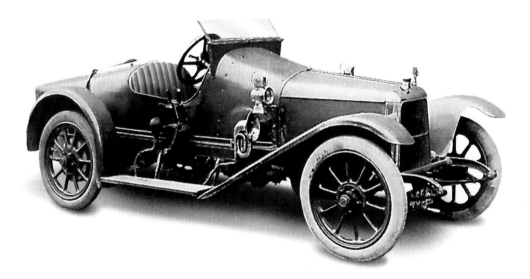

From its humble origins, through glorious race victories, James Bond and onto its current owner David Richards the Aston Martin story is one of passion, beauty and determination...
Words: Nick Trott

Below
Aston Martin founders
Lionel Martin (left) and
Robert Bamford sold
their interests in the
company early in its
history. Down the years,
many other owners and
investors have followed
their example

and survives to this day.

The Italian-born 'Bert' Bertelli proved to be a talented engineer and businessman and by 1929 had navigated the company through dire financial straits to produce the superb International, Le Mans and the Ulster models. In 1932, Bertelli and Pat Driscol won the Biennial Cup in the Le Mans 24-hour race – the first of many successes at the great endurance event for the British motor manufacturer.

The Ulster, in particular, became one of the most popular racing cars of the 1930s, but once again Aston Martin was faced with financial hardships and the company was taken over by Sir Arthur Sutherland. A pattern was emerging.

In 1936, Aston Martin turned its attention away from the racetrack and towards the touring market. The 2-litre 15/98 model was considered more mainstream but proved extremely successful and despite a period of uncertainty as World War Two approached, 140 Aston Martins found buyers in 1937 – the highest pre-war production figure. Arguably more significant was the Aston Martin being developed behind the scenes as World War Two shook Europe. The car was called the Atom and although it never made production this sophisticated prototype, featuring an early type of spaceframe construction, aluminium body panels and independent front suspension, became the basis for the subsequent range of post-war Astons.

The next chapter in the extraordinary story of Aston Martin came in 1947 when industrialist David Brown answered an advertisement in *The Times* for an unnamed 'high class motor business'. The company was floundering in the wake of World War Two and Brown, who had prospered from the family tractor business, offered £20,000 for the company having driven, and been impressed by, the advanced Atom prototype. Brown bought the struggling Lagonda business too and merged the companies to form Aston Martin Lagonda – the name by which it is known today – and immediately turned his attention to developing new models.

Based on the Atom and sporting the earliest example of the distinctive grille-shape still used today, the Two Litre Sports (retrospectively named the DB1) made its debut in 1948. Powered by a Claude Hill four-cylinder engine, the Two Litre Sports was considered underpowered and just 16 found owners.

A version of this car won the 1948 Spa 24-hour race but by now David Brown was looking at six-cylinder powerplants and a return to Le Mans. The following year both ambitions had been realised.

The DB2 superseded the DB1 in 1949 and David Brown led Aston Martin back to Le Mans with a trio of DB2s. The familiar Claude Hill four-cylinder engine powered two of the cars, but all eyes were on the third car, registration UMC 66. Like the four-cylinder cars, UMC 66 was based on a short-wheelbase chassis with slippery bodywork by Frank Feely, formerly of Lagonda. However, this new car wailed along the Mulsanne straight under the power of a new 2.6-litre Willie Wilson-designed inline six-cylinder engine. Another famous name in British motoring, WO Bentley, supervised Wilson during the design of this new engine. UMC 66 retired early with water pump failure, but it would evolve into the development prototype for the production DB2.

Right
In 1947, tractor magnate David Brown answered a newspaper advert, stumped up £20,000 and saved Aston Martin

'Models like the DB3 proved to a thorn in the side of Ferrari on road and track'

The DB2 became not only one of Aston Martin's most successful racing cars but also one its most popular road cars. The production DB2 met the world for the first time at the 1950 New York Motor Show, a suitably glamorous occasion.

For a company that built just one car during its first five years, Aston Martin was inundated with orders for the new car following George Abecassis and Lance Macklin's fifth overall at the 1950 Le Mans 24-hour race. The three cars that raced at Le Mans were the first three cars off the production line and the race team was managed by John Wyer, who went on to experience further success with Ford and Porsche in the 1960s.

The DB2 saw production for three years with 410 reaching customers around the world. Its main competitor was the XK120/140/150 series from Jaguar, but the Aston carried a higher price and greater rarity value. The most desirable DB2s proved to be the drophead coupe and the 123bhp Vantage – the first time this famous model name was used on an Aston Martin. The Vantage cost £100 more than the standard 107bhp DB2 but its larger carburettors and 8.2 to 1 compression ratio made it a formidable performer.

Riding high on the success of the DB2, David Brown stabilised Aston Martin with the purchase of Tickford Motor Bodies – a Newport Pagnell coachbuilder established as Salmon & Sons in 1820 and famous for its skilled workforce. Production gradually transferred from Feltham to Newport Pagnell and further success in motorsport came when the DBR1 won the World Sports Car Championship in 1959.

An overall victory at Le Mans came the same year and subsequent models such as the DB4GT proved to be a thorn in the side of Ferrari on road and track. However, storm clouds were on the horizon for Aston Martin as the company struggled to turn racing success into commercial success. Jaguar in particular was proving more adept at marketing its sporting road cars and despite Brown's investment, he withdrew Aston Martin from motorsport in 1964 and turned his attention to the road car business. Fortuitously, the producers for a certain popular film franchise phoned Brown the same year with a proposal that would prove the biggest marketing opportunity the company would ever receive.

James Bond drove a DB5 in *Goldfinger* and *Thunderball*. Two cars were provided to Eon Productions, both running 4-litre engines and Silver Birch paintwork. Extras not available on the standard options list included extending rams, .30 calibre Browning machine guns, a radar scanner, smoke screen cartridge, revolving number plates and retractable tyre slashers. As a result the DB5 instantly became one of the most recognisable and desirable cars in the world.

Above
The new Aston Martin facility at Gaydon
Above right
Dave Richards (left) and Dr Ulrich Bez, the two men in charge of Aston Martin's future

'Aston Martin had success while Ford suffered with increasing financial woes'

Aston Martin soon added the Kamm-tailed DB6 and a convertible Volante version to the line-up then introduced a larger four-seat car, the William Towns-designed DBS, in 1967. It was David Brown's intention to fit a new V8 engine to the DBS but it wasn't ready.

David Brown sold Aston Martin in 1972, the same year the Aston Martin Vantage was introduced. Despite its credentials the Vantage couldn't return Aston to profit in a world gripped by the horrors of the fuel crisis.

Company Developments initially took charge before North Americans Peter Sprague and Canadian George Minden injected some stability. A new Lagonda was introduced; a wedgy, angular William Towns-designed four-door saloon that shocked the Aston Martin faithful. The Lagonda had a troubled debut, with just 16 cars built during the first two years of production due to problems with the sophisticated electronics.

Aston Martin Lagonda changed hands again in 1981 when Pace Petroleum and CH Industrials took charge with Victor Gauntlett at the helm. Gauntlett was a perfect match for Aston Martin. With backing from Greek Livanos shipping family he increased production at Newport Pagnell and embarked on resurrecting Aston Martin's former collaboration with Italian styling house Zagato. The result was the limited-edition Zagato coupé and drophead – two of the fastest cars in the world at the time.

Gauntlett also took Aston Martin back to Le Mans twice, with mixed success, and oversaw production of the Aston Martin Virage – the first all-new Aston Martin for 20-years. This V8-powered coupé cost £135,000 but despite the huge price tag the order book soon filled. Gauntlett had moulded the company to the extent that

it generated interest from the Ford Motor Company and in 1987 decided to sell 75% to the North American car giant. Gauntlett's sale to Ford is thought to have ensured the company's survival.

Ford began investing in Aston Martin almost immediately. New design, research and manufacturing facilities were created and by the time it acquired 100% of the business in 1994 another all-new model was already in production. The beautiful DB7 achieved instant acclaim all over the world and particularly in North America where the Volante model was in great demand. A V12 version was announced in 1999; shortly afterwards former BMW, Porsche and Ford engineer Dr Ulrich Bez took over as CEO.

Bez's arrival reinvigorated the company and with the V12 Vanquish of 2001, Aston Martin was yet again on a high. A purpose-built manufacturing facility was completed in 2003 at Gaydon and shortly afterwards what would become the biggest selling Aston Martin in history, the DB9, was introduced. The V8 Vantage came next, followed by the DBS. In 2006, the 30,000th Aston Martin rolled off the production line at Gaydon and a year later Aston Martin Racing won the GT1 class at Le Mans with the V12-powered DBR9. A year later, they repeated the victory.

Aston Martin's ascendancy proved inversely proportional to the increasing financial woes suffered by the Ford Motor Company. In 2007, Ford sold its crown jewel to a consortium led by David Richards of British motorsport business Prodrive.

Today, Richards, a former World Rally Champion co-driver, and Dr Bez, a keen amateur racer, now control Aston Martin. Two men who above all else have a passion for beautiful, fast cars. Does that sound familiar?

WE PUT 24 WATCHES IN ONE.

REVERSO SQUADRA WORLD CHRONOGRAPH.
Jaeger-LeCoultre Calibre 753/1000®
First-ever automatic movement with chronograph and 24 time zones on two
faces, especially created for the swivel case of the legendary Reverso.

HAVE YOU EVER WORN A REAL WATCH?

JAEGER-LECOULTRE

Aston Martin A3

MEET THE ANCESTOR

**It's the oldest Aston Martin in the world and, following
a painstaking restoration to original condition, this
former racing car is now back on the road**

Words: Keith Adams   Photography: Matthew Howell

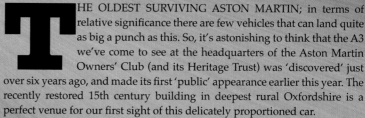

'To understand
the importance
of A3 one has to
learn every nuance
and drink in the
exquisite detailing'

THE OLDEST SURVIVING ASTON MARTIN; in terms of relative significance there are few vehicles that can land quite as big a punch as this. So, it's astonishing to think that the A3 we've come to see at the headquarters of the Aston Martin Owners' Club (and its Heritage Trust) was 'discovered' just over six years ago, and made its first 'public' appearance earlier this year. The recently restored 15th century building in deepest rural Oxfordshire is a perfect venue for our first sight of this delicately proportioned car.

From a distance the A3 is a pretty, if unassuming, pre-war special. It's easy to imagine walking past this car at a show without giving it a second glance; first impressions can be deceptive, especially from 20 paces or more.

To fully understand the importance of A3 one has to delve deeply into its history and learn every nuance. Do this and *then* take a closer look. Drink in the exquisite detailing; take time to touch, feel and caress it. And then, like a lightning bolt, the revelation strikes – you're in the presence of something very special. Pretty, yes. Unassuming, certainly not.

Although A3 was originally built in 1921, the history of Aston Martin goes back somewhat further. In 1913-'14, Bamford and Martin Limited started a healthy business modifying 10hp Singers at their premises at Henniker Place, Callow Street off the Fulham Road, London. Their cars proved popular due to their excellent hillclimb and race performance and vindicated Lionel Martin's trenchant view that a lightweight race car also makes a great touring car.

These lessons were incorporated in the very first Aston Martin, which appeared in October 1914. The new marque was created by combining Lionel's surname with Aston Hill, the Buckinghamshire hillclimb at which

The car, which subsequently became known as the 'Coal Scuttle', majored on quality of construction and enjoyed serious longevity. It racked up 15,000 competitive miles and placed Aston Martin firmly on the map. In 1920 the company built its second car, registered AM270, at its new premises in Kensington. It was powered by a new 1486cc engine designed by ex-Coventry Simplex man HV Robb, with competition in mind, and its beefed-up chassis was used in the next three prototypes.

And this is where our car comes in. Built on the third of those chassis, registered as AM273 and initially bearing the chassis number 'No.3', it first appeared in 1921 and has outlived its contemporaries. A3 was considered a pre-production car and ended up covering many 'development' (racing) miles, mostly at Brooklands. As a hack-cum-sports racer, B&M had no qualms about changing its configuration.

What is also known about A3 is that, depending on the event being entered, it could be powered by the company's first single-overhead-camshaft 16-valve engine, the later twin-cam 16v or, most frequently, a racing version of the sidevalve engine. The mix-and-match nature of A3 didn't finish there: two bodies were used during this period, a streamlined racing style and a more conventional sports item.

By 1923, their reputation established, B&M had finally got their cars to market, offering a choice of two- or three-seat tourers, as well as a long-chassis four-seater. Despite the competition pedigree, the last option proved the most popular with the affluent buyers being courted by the company at the time – although many customers subsequently chose to rebody their cars to suit their lifestyles.

As for A3, it was retired from development duties after two years and sold to its first private owner, Captain JC Douglas. The car was given a new engine (while the factory retained the racing sidevalve) and was re-registered XN2902 – no doubt to flatter the company's new-car sales figures – and Douglas continued to take to the tracks with his new acquisition. For the sake of simplicity, the engine and chassis were given the same number, 1918.

However, after decades out of the public eye the car resurfaced when its then-current owner, Mr Turner, decided to offer it for sale at Bonhams. (The annual Aston Martin Works Service sale seemed like the logical place.) Andy Bell, owner of Aston Martin specialist Ecurie Bertelli, is only too familiar with A3. 'I've known about this car for a very long time,' he says. 'It had been in my workshop several times during the previous years. At what I thought was my last contact with the car, I got it MoT'd so Mr Turner could offer it for auction.'

In the run up to the sale in late 2002, Stewart Skilbeck from Bonhams made contact with Neil Murray, one of the AMHT's founder trustees and a pre-war car historian. 'During his examination of the car, Stewart discovered, stamped in the end of the chassis dumb-irons, the inscription "No.3". This suggested that the car was, as had always been suspected, an earlier car that had been re-registered,' Neil recalls.

But there were further giveaways: 'Closer examination of the chassis confirmed this belief because it was of the first type with the less-than-substantial chassis side members, which were prone to breaking behind the gearbox crossmember,' Neil continues.

Despite its emerging provenance as a pre-production car, A3 failed to sell. Andy comments: 'We were advised that pre-war cars often struggle to sell at Newport Pagnell, and that it would do better at the Goodwood Festival of Speed sale. However, once again, the car failed to meet its reserve and consequently find a buyer.'

Neil was soon back in contact with A3, though. 'I received a call from

Right
AM273, A3 or 1918 as it looked when sold in 1923. The performance and agility of Lionel Martin's lightweight race car continue to impress today.

'After decades out of the public eye the car resurfaced at Bonhams'

'A3 had been conclusively proven to be the oldest surviving Aston Martin'

Right
A3 pictured at
Brooklands in 1926,
when its fifth owner, Mr
Malabar, modified the
bodywork to feature a
lower scuttle line.

John Lunn to find out more about the car he had just bought by private treaty, post-Goodwood. I was able to prove its provenance to his satisfaction, and when I asked him what were his plans, he suggested that he was going to tidy it up and use it, and then, maybe, sell it on.'

For the Aston Martin historian, this was the opportunity of a lifetime. 'I suggested that I could bring him an instant profit if we could agree a price acceptable to both him and the Trust. All this despite not yet having agreement from the Trustees to actually purchase the car!'

But it was a foregone conclusion that the AMHT would say yes. After all, A3 had been conclusively proven to be the oldest surviving Aston Martin. 'Fortunately for the health of my bank balance, the Trustees agreed to make the purchase – and in early 2003 I was able to collect it from Mr Lunn's storage in Putney,' Neil says.

Purchasing A3 was going to be a huge financial undertaking, and fund-raising activities were initially planned. But, subsequently, a staunch supporter of both the AMOC and AMHT, a person the Trust describes as a 'generous benefactor', financed the restoration.

It's here that Andy gets excited: 'In 2006 we were commissioned to undertake A3's restoration and Neil would end up acting as a historical consultant throughout the process.' A good job, too: 'Quite a lot had been changed over the years, making the restoration as much about detective work as fitting new – in period – parts.'

The car, as it came into AMHT's ownership, wore a three-seater body that had been installed during the mid-1930s, and which probably

incorporated elements of the earlier 'Malabar' body (Mr Malabar was the fifth owner). To make the restoration even more awkward, A3 had been given front-wheel brakes and an axle from a Morris, as well as sundry other modifications introduced by various owners.

'We had a brief to restore A3 back to the two-seater sports configuration it was originally in when sold to Captain Douglas. Because it was a prototype, that meant Sankey wheels – and, of course, you can't get them anymore, so we had new ones cast in aluminium.'

That's typical of the attention to detail that went into the restoration, a real labour of love. Jim Young rebuilt the engine and Ecurie Bertelli outsourced many of the individual jobs. 'We're based near Newport Pagnell and there's an absolute wealth of ex-Aston Martin expertise on our doorstep. We used an antique furniture restoration shop based next door for the body frame, so I could keep a close eye on them; Alan Pointer at Body Lines and I managed the creation of the body frame and, being Aston trained, we were able to create this sports body by eye, saving us £5000 by not having to use a buck,' Andy says.

»

Below
Aston Martin A3 has been beautifully, intelligently and sympathetically restored – just like AMHT's new HQ in Oxfordshire.

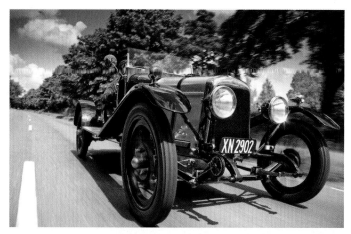

'What really stops you when you see A3 is how small and perfectly proportioned it is'

Clockwise from top left
Period instrumentation is
exquisite to behold; A3 is
still light and nimble on
the road; 1389cc engine
was rebuilt by Jim Young.

The frame had to be right, as it's this that determines the shape of the body. You can see the results clearly, too – A3's exquisitely curvaceous tail section, which took three attempts to get right, belies the fact that it's mounted on a flat crossmember.

A closer look reveals that this elevated level of detail abounds all over A3. The brass nuts have been aged using a tumbler, the wood is to original specification and the instrumentation is as it came from the factory and has been refurbished to the highest standard. The distinctive bulge in the offside to accommodate the brake pedal is also beautifully made and pleasurable to look at.

But what really stops you dead in your tracks when you see A3 for the first time is just how small and perfectly proportioned it is. The cycle wings are delicate, the bodywork fits like tailored glove and, despite it being an early '20s car, A3 sits low and has a purposeful stance.

Climbing into the snug cockpit you're ensconced in a tight cabin that affords a wonderful legs-outstretched driving position, perfect for competition. It's not so rosy for the passenger, in a seat that was intended for the pilot's mechanic – it may be mounted further back, but let's just say that any pair riding A3 should be intimate friends.

Typically for a racer of this era, the pedal layout is alien to those brought up on more modern cars: the centre-mounted throttle is on the left-hand side of the steering column (although it will soon be modified with a U-shaped piece for drivers who prefer the opposite) and takes some time to get used to. Firing up the engine with its button is simple enough, once the fuel system is primed, and little effort is needed to make it burst into life. Most impressively, it quickly settles down into a smooth, even and quiet idle.

When Andy takes the helm it's clear he truly loves the car he's about to take for a run through Oxfordshire's leafiest country lanes. 'The steering is light and accurate, and the acceleration is surprisingly brisk.

It's a wieldy car and far more accessible than you'd expect – but then this is a true thoroughbred,' he says.

Andy obviously knows the car well and soon sets a cracking pace appropriate to such an accomplished lightweight competition car. The steering has millimetric accuracy and on one blind bend an oncoming truck pitches us into an emergency avoidance that truly reveals A3's dynamic abilities, Andy skilfully placing the car between hedge and unyielding behemoth with microns to spare. Try that with a Bentley of the same vintage…

The pedal layout is actually not a handicap, either, because in reality you do your stopping with the substantial brake lever mounted outside the snug cabin. However, it doesn't quite pull up the car as smartly as one might wish and it's little wonder that subsequent production models sold to enthusiasts featured drums all round.

Our ride soon has us in awe of what B&M achieved with its diminutive racer and makes clear why buyers were clamouring to get hold of an Aston Martin throughout 1920 and '21. There isn't a trace of excess anywhere to be found on A3, just a whole lot of 'less is more'. It could be argued that the Aston Martins that followed diluted these principles, becoming fatter while admittedly a whole lot faster. A continued and successful presence in motor sport, along with first-class production standards, means the immaculate bloodline remains intact.

A3 is now the pride of AMHT's fleet and is utterly priceless thanks to the expertise of Neil Murray and Andy Bell's restorative genius. A more suitable home for such an important vehicle is impossible to think of – it's beautifully renovated for the years to come. △

Thanks to Andy Bell of Ecurie Bertelli, www.ecuriebertelli.com, +44 (0)1234 240024, Neil Murray, and the Aston Martin Heritage Trust, www.amheritage.org, +44 (0)1865 400414.

L'INSTANT
TAITTINGER

CHAMPAGNE
TAITTINGER
Ancienne Maison Fourneaux Forest et Cie
FONDÉE à Reims EN 1734
FRANCE
BRUT RESERVE
ÉLABORÉ PAR TAITTINGER, REIMS FRANCE

*Vitalie Taittinger,
who works for the
family Champagne house*

*Champagne Taittinger is widely stocked in UK hotels, restaurants and bars, as well as retailers
such as ASDA, Majestic Wine Warehouse, Oddbins, Sainsbury's, Tesco, Threshers, Waitrose,
www.everywine.co.uk and many independent wine merchants*

www.champagnetaittinger.co.uk

This 1923 Sidevalve is thought to be
the oldest surviving production Aston
Martin – and it's a long way from home

Words & photography: William Edgar

SIDEVALVE
IN SIDEWAYS
COUNTRY

ROGER HIGGINS AT THE WHEEL, we trundle along to the accompaniment of a mechanical concerto that's sporadically interrupted by a lively *Haaa-HAAA!* from he who drives. I'm squeezed tight in what might be misconstrued as a monoposto, despite these two seats. We've been at it about an hour, Higgins and I, touring a bucolic area called Happy Canyon in Southern California's Santa Ynez Valley, where coincidentally Universal Studios rolled in several years ago to shoot a buddy film called *Sideways*. About the time the movie opened in London, the 1923 Aston Martin Sidevalve in which we're travelling was having its first thrash along these grape-lined roads. Its new owner, Three Creek Vineyard proprietor Higgins, is a British ex-pat who retired here to be an organic vintner after a varied career that took him all the way from Leeds to California's Silicon Valley. »

From handcrank to exhaust tip, Higgins' Aston is a thoroughly splendid apparatus, invited to last year's Pebble Beach Concours d'Elegance and Los Angeles' neighbouring Palos Verdes show. Historians readily know its Lionel Martin Series chassis number 1920. Aficionados swoon over its rarity. Romantics dream themselves driving it on Brooklands' Home Banking, goggles strapped tight, dust and leaves swirling behind. But the sheer reality is that it's arguably the oldest surviving production Aston Martin.

Earlier in the day, Higgins lifted the bonnet to unveil the engine that powered Astons like this one to 85mph over 80 years ago. It's a four-cylinder, 1486cc, sidevalve unit with a cast iron block and head, fed by a pair of brass $1^1/_8$in SU carburettors.

Enamoured more with fun than austere data, this owner's description of his Aston's stopping power could be said to define unceremonious. 'The brake pedal,' Higgins makes clear, 'actually pulls all these bits of wire – and the brakes may or may not come on in any given order. You plan ahead. Like Bugattis of the era, the accelerator is in the middle, brake on the right, clutch on the left. You end up using the outside handbrake most of the time to slow it down.'

Reiterating my sentiment that its cockpit shuns comfort prompts Higgins to delve into times gone by. 'Mechanics back then traditionally came from the working class and were small,' he says. 'The wealthy who owned these cars got much better food and nutrition, and they were bigger and stronger. So it had the little seat for the riding mechanic… and the big seat for the well-nourished driver.'

The 'little' seat, predictably, is mine. But first I'm asked to lend a hand – two, really – with the starting procedure. Serving as chokes, my open palms cover the SU throats while Roger (actually, the electric starter he's installed) spins this elderly 1.5-litre four to life, ushering up sounds akin to waking a percussion ensemble. Nonetheless, for Aston enthusiasts the racket is divine. My hands smelling of petrol and Higgins seated behind old number 1920's substantial steering wheel, we're soon off and away on a serpentine road that descends the Higgins Hill. More than just grapevines thrive in this dry, rocky soil. 'We've got rattlesnakes,' he says. 'Our foreman found one in his boot left outside last night.' Ahead, a vulture's broad, swoopy shadow crosses the road.

The Aston now transports us at an escalating pace. Going only half of what this car will do, it feels like we've found a casual limit at 40mph. Ranch fences and shade trees stream past, the day blurs to years gone by, and we are in 1923 again.

When this Aston was built – in that jazz-age decade long before PG Wodehouse's Bertie Wooster drove himself and Jeeves on TV to Totleigh Towers and elsewhere in one – the Aston Martin Company was a cramped little workshop at 53 Abingdon Road, Kensington. The time was both blithe and turbulent: America's marathon dancing had turned to mania, Hitler's putsch flopped, the song *Yes, We Have No Bananas* hit big time… and Carroll Shelby was still a baby. In Britain, where open-air touring cars were much in favour, those few editions produced by Aston Martin were coveted for their looks and performance.

Historians of the marque know Lionel Martin and business partner Robert Bamford conceived their firstborn machine of various components, giving birth in 1913 to a cobbled-together tester dubbed *The Hybrid*. Higgins' chassis number 1920, supposedly the tenth Bamford and Martin creation, was handbuilt in 1923 and first bought by Captain JC Douglas, a noted racer who promptly humiliated himself by driving it headlong into a roadside bollard.

Left and below
Twin-carb conversion was carried out in 1960s; engine puts out 45bhp, good for more than 80mph top speed.

Above and right
Cockpit designed for 1920s physiques; long chassis originally had four-seat body, now a two-seater.

'IT WAS FIRST BOUGHT
BY CAPTAIN JC DOUGLAS,
WHO PROMPTLY DROVE
IT HEADLONG INTO A
ROADSIDE BOLLARD'

A string of UK ownerships followed, eventually bringing number 1920 to be restored in 1965 by PN Delves-Broughton, who often raced and showed the car over a span of five years. Later it was sold to the American Ken Griffin, who kept it in the States until 1984, when it was bought by German Aston collector Andreas Rossbach. Three years on, the engine exploded before the grandstands at the Nürburgring. For 14 more years, the broken car sat unrepaired.

Meanwhile, Roger Higgins had bought a 1940 Type-C Aston Speed Model, one of only eight built. It earned third in class at Pebble Beach, after which Higgins sold it. 'I never liked it much as a car,' he reflects now. 'It was heavy to drive, and at the end of a long rally you needed to lie around a swimming pool for days just to recover.'

If Higgins wanted another Aston, he also knew where to go for it. 'No-one in their right mind,' he insists, 'would dream of buying a pre-war Aston without first calling Andy Bell at Ecurie Bertelli on Stilebrook Road in Olney, Bucks.' Bell, a psychology scholar and acclaimed authority in Aston Martin restoration, is also a delightful raconteur. Of Captain Douglas' ungainly crash, Bell relates: 'He was at a party with Count Zborowski and, driving back through London fairly pissed, he and his wife hit a bollard, *smack*, straight into the middle of the radiator, and the whole car folded around this bollard. The damage pushed the engine back, it pushed the gearbox back, and the gearbox pushed the torque tube back – and it broke the back axle.' At that time the car had a four-seater body on it, before Delves-Broughton replaced it with two-seater coachwork: common practice with these cars.

Bell reveals more. 'Quite a few Sidevalves were built as tourers, and a surprising number as saloons, and they have all been changed.' He points out that there's only one Sidevalve left with its original body: a 16-valve racing car in Bell's shop at the time of our chat. 'Some of

them were changed within a year or two of sale,' he continues. 'People very quickly decided they wanted to copy the racing bodies, or have open two-seaters.'

According to Bell, who knows Higgins' car intimately through his workshop's 1000-hour restoration of it seven years ago, number 1920 'was originally a long-chassis four-seater tourer' and 'in the range of the cars that Aston made, it was fairly ordinary'. Ordinary is a rather peculiar term for something so rare, but it must be taken as relative to what was being built then and there, all those years ago.

'Our brief was to rebuild it very much as we found it,' says Bell. 'In other words, to the two-seater form in which Delves-Broughton rebuilt it in the 1960s. We didn't shorten the chassis; it still was a long chassis. What Delves-Broughton tried to do was to produce a copy of the short-chassis Strasbourg GP cars, a similar sort of pointed-tail Strasbourg. It has the Strasbourg body but on a long chassis.

'Normally on a Sidevalve, there would be a single carburettor, but I'm pretty sure that when Delves-Broughton made the body he made that inlet manifold and fitted the two carburettors. It seems to work quite well.

'Until we did Roger's, no-one had rebuilt a Sidevalve for decades. But they are beginning to come out and about now, and to be recognised as the beautiful little cars that they really are. They are jewel-like, so beautifully made. They genuinely are a sort of English Bugatti. Perhaps not conceived with the artistry of Bugatti, but as far as quality and performance are concerned they are really up there, as good a light car as you could possibly find.'

As the sun sets low in the west here in Sideways Country, it's difficult for me to recall a finer time spent with a vintage car. Roger Higgins is an epic car guy, who has certainly come a long way from Leeds. △

MORE AND MORE classic car drivers are opting for discreet improvements to overcome what are now seen as mechanical disadvantages; ones that were not a hindrance in a less technically sophisticated world, when traffic was minimal in comparison with our congested modern roads.

Simon Gulliford is one such owner. He hadn't intended to buy a 1950s car, but when he attended Bonhams' annual auction at Aston Martin's Newport Pagnell works in 2004 he couldn't resist. The model he chose was a 1955 DB2/4, prepared by Cobham, Surrey-based Aston specialist Trinity Engineering. Previous owner Barry Weir had taken Simon's Aston to fifth overall and first in the historic sports car class on the Round the World Rally in 80 Days, back in

Adding lightness

In order to use his newly-acquired Aston Martin DB2/4 as often as possible, one owner commissioned a clever five-speed gearbox conversion that transformed the car Words: Paul Chudecki Photography: Ian Dawson

2000. It was clearly a good buy…

'I went to bid for an old brochure or an interesting part, but then I saw this car,' explains the 47-year-old retired marketing consultant, who also owns a DB9 and a Sunbeam Tiger. 'It had over £95,000-worth of bills and I paid £28,000 for it. I think it's fantastic – an aesthetically gorgeous machine to look at.

'I'm a great believer that if you've got an old car you should drive it a lot and get the maximum enjoyment from it. But with that truck-like gearbox, it felt as though I needed to brace my feet on the bulkhead to get it into gear. Driving it in traffic was such hard work. And my intention was to take it for long European runs and use it on holiday.

'I realised I needed to change the gearbox. Fortunately, I also knew that, thanks to the modifications which had already been made to the engine, it would easily pull a higher top gear.'

Simon approached Tim Butcher at Trinity with the suggestion that a Borg-Warner T5 gearbox, which he'd

Clockwise from above
Aston grips strongly, despite roll; useful rear hatch; car is ideal cross-country tool; driving gloves surely de rigueur...

'THE SHEER EVERYDAY PRACTICALITY OF THE DUNDROD CONVERSION AND ITS INVISIBLE INSTALLATION ARE HARD TO ARGUE AGAINST'

fitted to his Tiger, might go in the Aston. But this would have necessitated changing the rear axle, so Trinity arrived at a compromise that would also be reversible.

'Simon had no specific preference other than to use a modern five-speed 'box, and he left the entire project to us,' says Tim. 'But because of the way the gearbox sits in the chassis, with the main cross-brace in the centre, it's necessary to have a short unit. That precluded anything that was an easy fit, and there wasn't a 'box on the market that would go straight in.

'In the end we used the casing and gears from a modern manufacturer but we had to make our own adaptor plates and machine the bellhousing that's original to the car. The most important factor was that the transmission had to look original from under the bonnet.'

Adapting the new 'box to the DB2/4 necessitated modifying the tail-shaft in order for the output shaft to be located in the right plane, and using a smaller and lighter propshaft. The original coil-spring clutch assembly was replaced with a lightweight diaphragm unit (capable of handling up to 240bhp) with hydraulic rather than mechanical activation.

Rather aptly, fitment of the new gearbox package is known as the Dundrod Conversion, a reference to George Abecassis' retirement from the 1951 Tourist Trophy race when his works DB2 failed with transmission problems. Inclusive of parts and labour, the Dundrod Conversion costs £7500 plus VAT and the job can be done within a fortnight.

The DB2/4 had been in full rally trim when Simon bought it: roll cage, Recaro front seats, supplementary fuel tank,

Facing page
Rear suspension has been raised slightly to maintain a level stance when under acceleration.

sump guard, fire extinguisher system, harder spring/damper rates and a special exhaust system with greater ground clearance. 'We've returned it nearer to road spec,' explains Tim. 'We replaced the rear and front seats and took all the heavy bits off. The suspension is marginally stiffer than standard but the ride height is still sensible. I like to run these models with a bit of rake so that the back is higher and when you're on the power the car remains level.'

Remaining in rally trim, however, is the venerable twin-overhead-cam six-cylinder engine. 'It's a standard three-litre motor with slightly lower compression – we weren't sure the countries the car would be going through would have quality fuel – and larger valves, standard carburettors but with altered jetting, and a special exhaust manifold and silencers which are now altered at the rear to make it more road friendly. It's an unbelievably flexible engine.'

There are now few clues to this DB2/4's rallying past. Outside, only the clips on the rear hatch and at the bottom of the front wings, together with the front spotlights, give the game away. Inside, it's the pen holder in the glovebox and the fuel gauge on the right of the dashboard.

The new gearlever is exactly the same height as the original and mounted just half-an-inch further back than with the standard transmission, and there's even a five-speed gate etched on the knob over the original's old four-ratio diagram. 'It's one item no-one would ever notice,' says Tim. 'From every angle you look at the car, under the bonnet and in the cabin, the transmission looks standard. Only when you start

to drive it do you realise it's a little bit special.'

In fact, the moment one selects first gear, two things are apparent: the ease with which the ratio is engaged and the lightness of the clutch. Move off and gone is the familiar whine of the David Brown four-speed 'box; purists might argue that the latter's inherently heavier engagement of ratios and its lack of synchromesh on first gear are part of the character of a car this old, and to a large extent I agree. But the sheer everyday practicality of the Dundrod Conversion and its invisible installation are hard to argue against.

Plenty of low-down torque is available from the 2.9-litre straight-six – it peaks at 175lb ft at 3500rpm, as against 144lb ft at 2400rpm originally – and the combination of good power and torque gives the motor its great flexibility, which perfectly complements the Trinity gearbox.

Another major benefit is reduced engine revs when cruising, further aided by a 3.54:1 axle ratio (an original option) instead of the normal 3.77:1. That means 60mph in top equates to 2200rpm, 70 to 2500, 80 to 3000 and 110 to 4000, whereas a standard gearbox-equipped DB2/4 in fourth gear at the same revs will pull 47, 54, 65 and 86mph respectively.

The worm-and-roller steering is comfortably weighted at speed but at low velocity it is a tad heavy, thanks to the Dunlop Taxi 175x16 radials fitted for rallying – crossplies would, of course, have been fitted in the 1950s – and one needs strongish arms to park. But that really is the only thing that dynamically gives away this Aston's age. There is some body roll when pushing on – spring rates for the coil spring/

1955 Aston Martin DB2/4 five-speed

SPECIFICATIONS

Engine
2922cc straight-six, dohc, twin sidedraught SU HV6 carburettors

Power
139bhp @ 5000rpm

Torque
175lb ft @ 3500rpm

Transmission
Five-speed gearbox, rear-wheel drive

Suspension
Front: independent via coil springs/torsion bar, lever-arm dampers. Rear: live axle with parallel trailing arms and Panhard rod, telescopic dampers

Brakes
Servo-assisted drums front and rear

Performance
0-60mph 11sec
Top speed 125mph

Value
£55,000-60,000

torsion bar front and leaf-sprung rear are Trinity's own, designed for fast road use without compromising ride quality too much – but it is still possible to corner with considerable vigour.

As with most cars of this vintage, particularly in road trim, one needs to wind on some lock in preparation for a corner just before it is reached rather than when it is entered. Despite those tyres, the rear grips well and any oversteer is limited to little more than a chirp from the rear rubber. The back will break free but it is just a case of keeping the throttle down and winding the lock on and off as one exits. The all-round drum brakes, fitted with rally-spec linings and assisted by a servo, are quite adequate for the performance available.

This Aston is a car one could really live with on a daily basis, though some might baulk at the heavy steering when manoeuvring – crossply tyres would certainly improve matters. But the good news is that Trinity is currently working on the design of a power-assisted steering rack. 'If we get two or three people who want it, we will do it,' says Tim.

'I think we achieved everything Simon wanted,' he adds. 'To be able to crawl around the M25 or drive into London in a car that's smoother, lighter to handle and more progressive. With fifth gear there's a fuel saving, too.'

Simon, too, is more than happy. 'Previously, jumping in the car and going to a restaurant in London was inconceivable; the difference between then and now is like night and day. I'm thrilled, absolutely thrilled.'

Trinity Engineering: +44 (0)1932 862040, www.trinityastonmartin.co.uk.

Aston Martin
DB3S

The DB3S was Aston Martin's first front-line racer for four seasons, starting in 35 major races and scoring 15 outright wins, 13 seconds and seven third places

Words: Chris Nixon Photography: Michel Zumbrunn

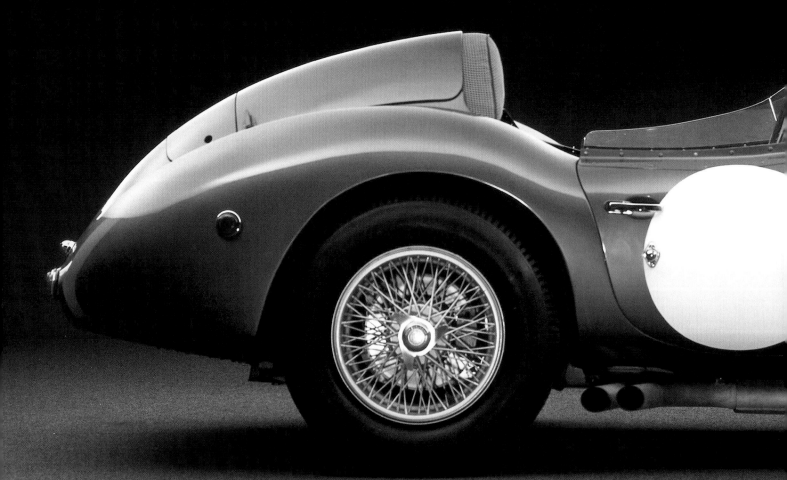

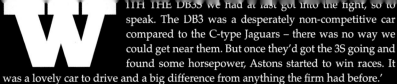

WITH THE DB3S we had at last got into the fight, so to speak. The DB3 was a desperately non-competitive car compared to the C-type Jaguars – there was no way we could get near them. But once they'd got the 3S going and found some horsepower, Astons started to win races. It was a lovely car to drive and a big difference from anything the firm had before.'

So said George Abecassis, who raced a DB3S on only one occasion, and that was its debut at the 1953 Le Mans 24 Hours race, where all three works Astons failed to finish. However, from that point on the 3S was a roaring success in 1953, entering five more races and winning them all. This was in marked contrast to the DB3, which could barely get out of its own way and had proved to be a huge disappointment to Aston Martin's patron, David Brown, and his team led by John Wyer.

Known to one and all as DB, Brown had bought Aston Martin in 1947. Shortly afterwards he bought Lagonda, impressed by its car's 2.6-litre, six-cylinder engine, which he put into his new Aston, the DB2. With Lagonda came stylist Frank Feeley, who produced a very handsome, all-enveloping fastback design. Although Brown had bought Aston Martin as a hobby, he decided to enter his cars in competition as a way of promoting his family business, the long-established David Brown Gear Co, in Huddersfield. To this end they became David Brown Aston Martins.

The DB2s were moderately successful, their finest hour being their third, fifth and ≫

seventh places at Le Mans in 1951. However, they were up against much more powerful Ferraris, Alfa Romeos, Jaguars and Cunninghams, so DB commissioned a proper racer, the DB3. He wanted three to be ready for Le Mans in July, but progress was very slow and the first car saw the light of day only in September. It made its debut in the Tourist Trophy at Dundrod, where it ran its bearings after 27 laps.

Throughout 1952 the DB3 failed to win a race until September, when Peter Collins and Pat Griffith won the Goodwood Nine Hours, but only after the leading C-type Jaguars had all fallen out. Clearly, the DB3 was too heavy and too slow – a new car was needed for 1953. It was Willie Watson (who had designed the Lagonda engine under the direction of WO Bentley) who came up with a solution.

His idea was to reduce the gauge of the DB3's main chassis tubes and crossmembers, to crank the sidemembers to seat the driver lower and to reduce the wheelbase and track from 93 to 87in and 51 to 49in respectively. The result was a much smaller and lighter car – the DB3S. Whereas the DB3 had weighed in at a hefty 2010lb, the 3S was a mere stripling at 1850lb. It was powered by the latest version of the Lagonda engine, now bored out to 2.9 litres and producing 182bhp.

Below
Inevitably, the 3S gained weight over the years. This 1956 version weighed 2061lb, an increase of 11.4% on the original. Power increased from 182 to 237bhp.

The revised chassis was covered in gorgeous new bodywork styled by Frank Feeley. The DB3 would never have won any beauty contest, but for the DB3S Feeley excelled himself, and where the DB3 had been all straight lines, the 3S was a riot of curves. He borrowed a characteristic from the V12 Lagonda he had styled before the war and built a Gothic Arch into the front and rear wings. This not only sharpened up the car's appearance, but added strength to the bodywork, as did the

fact that sports car regulations now required only a driver's door. But what really set the DB3S apart were its cutaway front wings which, as Feeley revealed, were no styling gimmick.

'We had a lot of cooling problems with the DB3, which is why the DB3S looked so different. We put a heatshield between the rad and engine to deflect hot air from the coolant out behind the wheels, via the cutaway sides. The result was beautiful, but those cutaway wings had nothing to do with styling – they were there for a purpose and they worked.'

So did the DB3S. Team Manager John Wyer decided to take DB3S/1 to Monza at the end of May 1953 (right after the Mille Miglia), in an attempt to put 1000 high-speed miles on it and confirm the specification for the three cars which were being built for Le Mans, just seven weeks away. Peter Collins did most of the driving and after he had covered just over 500 miles, a broken con-rod brought the Aston to a halt. As the Mille Miglia DB3s were on hand, Wyer had the engine taken out of one of them and fitted into the 3S. As luck would have it, this engine was the same one that Collins had used when testing a DB3 at Monza in December, so Wyer now had a unique frame of reference for the performance of the new car against the old. The result was most encouraging, for Peter's best time with the 3S was 2 mins 13.1 secs, as opposed to the 2 mins 17.4 secs he had achieved with the DB3.

The Le Mans cars were to be driven by Reg Parnell/Peter Collins, George Abecassis/Roy Salvadori and Dennis Poore/Eric Thompson. Things looked good after practice, for Abecassis' fastest time of 4 mins 39.0 secs was a full 20 secs quicker than that of the 2.6-litre DB3 the previous year.

Sadly, however, the 24 Hours was a disaster for the new »

'The engine was the same one that Collins had used when testing a DB3 at Monza, so Wyer had a unique frame of reference for the new car against the old. The result was encouraging'

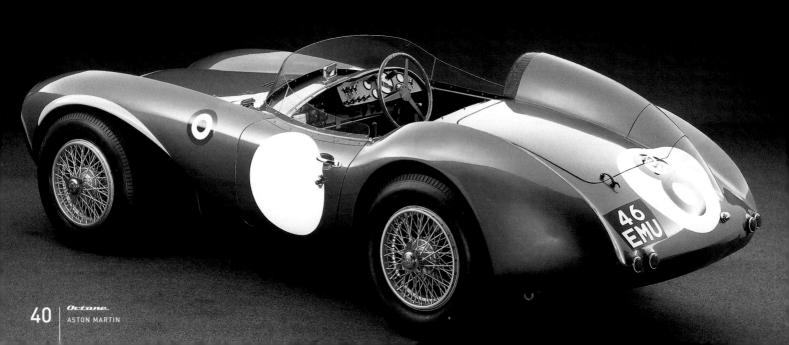

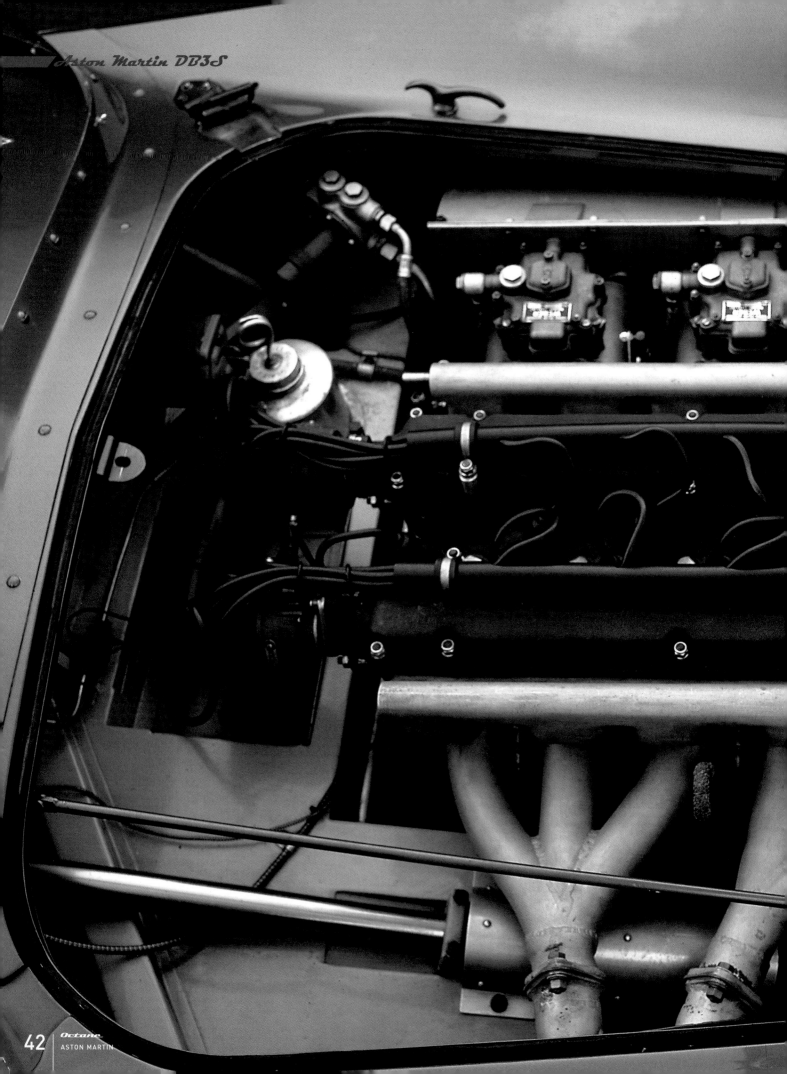

Left
For the DB3S
number nine,
Lagonda's engine
had been stretched
to 2.9 litres, gained
twin spark plugs
and managed an
impressive 237bhp.

Aston
Martin DB3S
SPECIFICATIONS

Engine
2992cc, 83x90mm
bore and stroke,
six cylinders in-line,
three Weber 45 DCO
carburettors

Power
237bhp @ 6000rpm

Suspension
Front: trailing arms
and torsion bars
Rear: trailing arms
and torsion bars with
de Dion tube

Brakes
Girling AM discs

Length
12ft 10in (3.91m)

Width
4ft 11in (1.50m)

Wheelbase
7ft 3in (2.21m)

Track
4ft 1in (1.25m)

Dry Weight
2061lb (935kg)

Abecassis was back in the pits with clutch slip after seven laps; Parnell crashed on lap 16 and two laps later Poore stopped to have a broken exhaust tappet changed, which took 41 minutes. None of the cars finished the race.

For the rest of the season, however, the DB3S was unbeatable. Furious with himself for his mistake at Le Mans, Reg Parnell made amends a week later by winning the British Empire Trophy race in the Isle of Man. He followed this up with victories at Silverstone, Charterhall and Goodwood, where he and Eric Thompson won the Nine Hours race. Peter Collins and Pat Griffith then rounded off Aston Martin's year in fine style with a superb victory in the Tourist Trophy at Dundrod.

Clearly, the winning ways of the DB3S should have continued throughout 1954 with proper development, but they did not. David Brown was well aware that its engine could not be made any bigger, so in order to compete with the larger-capacity Jaguars, Ferraris and Alfa Romeos he commissioned a 4.5-litre, V12 Lagonda sports-racer. When this finally appeared in 1954 it was seen to be an overweight 3S in appearance and the design of the V12 engine was seriously flawed. Nevertheless, DB insisted that the project

go ahead and so time and money which would have been better spent on developing the DB3S went into the Lagonda. As a result, Aston's 1954 season was an unmitigated disaster. In January three cars took part in the Buenos Aires 1000kms and only one finished, in third place. From there they went to Sebring for the 12 Hours race. All three retired. Two were entered for the Mille Miglia and both crashed.

The Lagonda finally made its debut at Silverstone in May, as did two new Astons, DB3S/6 and /7. These were what Wyer called saloons, the thinking being that closed cars might do better at Le Mans than open ones. Frank Feeley smoothed out the curves of his '53 model and produced two very good-looking coupés, but they had been built too hurriedly and, driven by Roy Salvadori and Graham Whitehead, they struggled home in seventh and 12th positions at Silverstone. Aston then did itself no favours by taking five cars to Le Mans: the two coupés (Peter Collins/Prince Bira and Graham Whitehead/Jimmy Stewart), a supercharged DB3S (Reg Parnell/Roy Salvadori) and a 1953 model (Carroll Shelby/Paul Frère). The Lagonda was entrusted to Eric Thompson and Dennis Poore.

As in 1953, the race was a disaster. The Lagonda and both

'Furious with himself for his mistake at Le Mans, Reg Parnell made amends a week later by winning the British Empire trophy race in the Isle of Man'

coupés clashed; the 1953 car broke a stub axle and the supercharged machine eventually expired with a blown gasket. The team's humiliation was so complete that John Wyer was all for withdrawing for the rest of the season, in order to regroup and prepare for 1955. However, David Brown insisted that they carry on, but there were so many crashed Astons littering the Competitions Department that he had to hand over his own road car, DB3S/5, to John Wyer. It was hardly worth the effort, for although Astons finished 1-2-3 in a minor race at Silverstone, they failed dismally in the Tourist Trophy.

Over the winter serious work at last went into the DB3S and two new cars were built for 1955 to replace the coupés, which were scrapped. These were open models with a single, wrap-around windscreen and even sleeker bodies, Frank Feeley having refined his design to perfection. Among several mechanical improvements were twin-plug heads (which helped the 2.9-litre engine produce 225bhp), Girling disc brakes all round and ZF differentials. To avoid paying purchase tax, these cars were given the chassis numbers of the coupés, 6 and 7, and registered for the road as 62 and 63 EMU.

They were an immediate success, Reg Parnell and Roy Salvadori demolishing the D-type Jaguar opposition in the One Hour sports car race at Silverstone. They then went to Le Mans, where they were joined by DB3S/8, which had started life as a production 3S (winning at Spa with Paul Frère), before being upgraded to works specification.

Although faster than before, the Astons were still way off the pace at the 1955 Le Mans compared with the Mercedes-Benz 300SLR, the D-type Jaguar and the Ferrari 121LM. Peter Collins and Paul Frère brought DB3S/6 home in second place, but it was a false result in that Mercedes had withdrawn after the tragedy that killed more than 80 spectators.

However, the 300SLR with its space-frame chassis was obviously the star of the show and made a big impression on DB and John Wyer. Immediately after the race they commissioned their designer, Ted Cutting, to produce a space-frame Aston, the DBR1, for 1956, when three cars were to be entered for Le Mans. And that should have been the end of the run for the DB3S, but such was the furore after the Le Mans disaster that the ACO took an age to issue its regulations for the '56 race. As a result, it was not possible to build three DBR1s in time, so Aston made two more 3Ss, DB3S/9 (the subject of our photos here) and DB3S/10. These were Frank Feeley's fourth variation on his original theme,

Below
DB3S was built for the 1956 Le Mans, when the regs demanded a proper sports car with two seats, two doors and a full-width windscreen.

»

Octane
ASTON MARTIN 45

with two doors, open cockpits and full-width windscreens to meet the new regs. The '55 3S had Feeley's definitive Aston Martin radiator intake (which the company uses as its template to this day), but during the season the cars acquired extra air intakes for the carburettors and cockpit. For 1956 Feeley combined them all into one oblong opening. He also put the headlamps under glass and fitted a headrest.

Both new cars were entered for Le Mans, but were given a shakedown at Rouen first, with 3S/6 and /7. Peter Collins drove 3S/9 and blew it up in a big way. He and Stirling Moss then drove the car to second place at Le Mans, unable to do anything about the Ecurie Ecosse D-type of Ron Flockhart and Ninian Sanderson. Moss then won the Daily Herald Trophy at Oulton Park and at Goodwood in September Roy Salvadori finished second behind Tony Brooks in 3S/7.

The DBR1s were ready for the 1957 season, but Astons retained DB3S/9 and /10. Tony Brooks drove 3S/9 to third place at Goodwood on Easter Monday and then both cars were taken to the Nürburgring as practice models for the 1000 Kms, which Brooks and Noel Cunningham-Reid famously won

in the DBR1. At the end of the year DB3S/9 was sold to Ampol Oil in Australia and raced with great success throughout 1958 by David McKay, who scored eight wins in nine starts. The next owner was Stan Jones, who soon sold it to Ray Barfield. He raced it a few times before storing it in a barn on his farm in Perth in 1961, where it stayed for the next 25 years!

Kerry Manolas eventually prized it away from him in 1988, recalling: 'It was like something out of a time machine. Luckily, Perth is a fairly dry part of the world so, although the Aston was tatty, it was free from rust and everything was there. And the engine and gearbox had been stored in a drum of oil.' Manolas had it completely rebuilt by Auto Restorations in New Zealand before sending it to England, where it failed to sell at auction in 1990. Eventually, Dudley and Sally Mason-Styrron bought it, keeping it for five years before selling it to Peter Livanos. He in turn sold it to Lukas Hüni in 1999, who sold it to Nicolaus Springer in 2001 only to buy it back a year later. Since 2003, it's been in a private Swiss collection.

All pictures used in this feature are copyright Lukas Hüni AG.

Below
After a superb rebuild by Auto Restorations in New Zealand, this Aston won the 1991 Best of Show at the Louis Vuitton Concours in London.

1959 DB4 GT

2009 DBS

Servicing Aston Martins for over 50 years...

The ASTON MARTIN
SERICE DEPARTMENT
— *Newport Pagnell* —

Exceptional cars deserve exceptional treatment and where better to find such treatment than here at Aston Martin Works Service, our unique factory-owned workshop, where real passion, unrivalled experience and a tangible sense of heritage govern everything we do.

In fact from the moment you book your Aston Martin or Lagonda in with us, you can be absolutely certain that our team of highly-qualified engineers and craftspeople will apply the ultimate in knowledge, skill and attention-to-detail to every aspect of your car's requirements.

From regular servicing and maintenance to mechanical and electrical upgrades, from re-trims and repaints to accident repair and award-winning restorations, no job is too big or too small - and, what's more, every single thing we do is documented and archived on-site, ensuring your car's provenance is fully preserved.

So treat your car to the very best, and treat its service book to a stamp like no other. You deserve it. And so does your Aston Martin. Ask about our competitive menu pricing for servicing, styling enhancements, engine and suspension upgrades across the model range.

ASTON MARTIN WORKS SERVICE LIMITED,
Tickford Street, Newport Pagnell, Buckinghamshire MK16 9AN England

Telephone +44 (0)1908 619264   Facsimile +44 (0)1908 216439
Email service2@astonmartin.com   www.astonmartin.com/worksservice

Aston Martin
DBR1

No other Aston Martin has achieved the motor sport success of the DBR1. No other Aston provokes the same appreciation from now legendary drivers. Here's how it feels when pushed hard, and why it feels that way Words: Mark Hales Photography: Ian Dawson

'The revs rise and you need a big dose of opposite lock, and for that you need a well-braced torso and strong arms'

STON MARTIN'S DBR1 and Jaguar's D-type were fellow countrymen locked in a titanic battle for Le Mans which would surely bring sales in the showrooms. And, at a glance, they even look similar. Long bonnet, oval air intake for the radiator and humps to clear the tall 16-inch wheels, vestigial doors that flex and bend as you pull them shut, then leave your shoulders feeling exposed. Like products of the time.

But look again, only more carefully this time. See that the Aston has a slightly more delicate appearance. The curves are longer and more gentle and the whole car looks smaller, seems to sit lower overall, which makes it look wider and more ready to hug the ground. The result is a body described as 'one of the most beautiful of all sports racing cars', made from wafer-thin 20-gauge aluminium, rather than the D-type's 16-gauge, as part of a quest for lightness and woe betide anyone who moves to lean or sit, or the photographer who makes ready to attach a camera sucker. Then as you look closer still, you begin to notice the engineering differences under that swooping skin, the design inspiration that could be the key to success on the track but which had to be built and tested to be proven.

You see that the DBR1 has a spaceframe chassis made of welded steel tubes rather than the D-type's aircraft-style monocoque tub. The tubes criss-cross the cockpit floor and

have to be spanned by a sheet of plywood to support the heels and, whereas you sat low down in the D-type, nicely trapped between transmission tunnel and sill, in the Aston you perch in a vestigial seat – borrowed in this particular case from a DBR4 Grand Prix car – and only because that was better than the yet flimsier original which still graces the passenger side. Then the transmission tunnel seems impossibly slim and surely not large enough to contain something like the Jaguar's tough four-speed gearbox, an impression confirmed when you can't find a gearlever sticking through a hole. Instead the lever sits level with your left knee, short and stubby like a single seater's, and when you lift off the boot lid you discover this is because it leads via a rod to a five-speed gearbox and differential which is mounted at the back, driving the rear wheels via a pair of double-jointed half shafts. It was then that I began to realise just how different the Aston was from its fellow Brit.

Whereas the D-type could claim all sorts of advanced engineering features, like a riveted monocoque, dry sump lubrication, all-synchromesh gearbox and aluminium disc wheels, the overall layout was simple and conventional. Big, tall iron block engine in the front, four-speed gearbox in the middle and a big beam axle at the back hung on five simple links with traditional double wishbones for the front suspension. Simple, proven technology, all of it built with the extra needed to guarantee stamina.

Above
Delicate curves of the DBR1 are matched by the equally delicate metal they are formed from.

»

The DBR1, though, has that magnesium-cased transaxle between the rear wheels, just like you'd find in the tail of a Maserati 250F or Birdcage or a BRM V16 Grand Prix car and, like those three, the Aston boasts five dog-engaged gears instead of the Jaguar's four. The aim is to equalise weight distribution in a front-engined car although the downside is that the propshaft always spins at engine speed.

There's de Dion rear suspension too – something that Jaguar apparently tried but rejected in favour of that big beam – with telescopic shock absorbers and a Watts linkage for lateral location, and links to operate the torsion bars, which run forward along the cockpit floor, the ends just visible to the sides of the seats.

Back in the cockpit, you see that the right-hand sill covers the exhausts, which jut out just below your elbow while the left is filled with the battery and two separate oil tanks, one to feed the gearbox and another for the dry sump engine, which holds no less than 20 litres. Obviously the designer didn't want oil starvation to be an issue in a long race but they wanted to reduce the effect of weight on the handling by putting it in the middle.

Now lift off the bonnet and, as you do, notice the rows of neat catches which remain flush until you poke a finger at them, whereupon they obediently rotate inwards and click open. Feltham, where the Aston was made, was close to the

centres of English aircraft production and many of the Aston workforce came from there so that's what they knew. Although it's detailing which takes more work than two bolts and a leather strap, the catches secure a panel against a passing airflow but open quickly and provide no opportunity to lose a clip. Exactly as they would on the aeroplane from which they were borrowed.

The engine that all this reveals was specially made for the car rather than derived from a production model like the Jaguar's and it is lighter thanks to an aluminium block instead of iron, but it is smaller in displacement (3 litres rather than 3.4). It looks physically smaller too, sits lower and the magnesium cam covers don't shine like the bare aluminium ones from Coventry so it doesn't quite dominate the underbonnet ambience in the same way. Two plugs per cylinder rather than one are fired by separate distributors driven from the back end of each camshaft and although you could argue that this would keep you going if you lost a plug or a rotor arm, it probably had more to do with flame travel in a hemispherical combustion chamber and the need to get the mixture burnt effectively.

The advantages of the Aston's front suspension layout are rather harder to determine, though, because where you might expect to find the accepted geometric ideal of double wishbones, instead there are large trailing links, the top ones

Below
At speed in the DBR1. Head in the airflow, wheels faithfully communicating every ridge and bump in the road.

operating a lever arm shock absorber rather than the much better telescopic type used at the back, which were adjustable even by 1959. Then you see that each bottom link operates a transverse torsion bar running across the car. Just like a Beetle...

Trailing links are an esoteric choice for front suspension which was favoured by the pre-war German manufacturers, so possibly this was a legacy carried over from Auto Union designer Professor Eberan-Eberhorst's original DB3 of 1951. It's all beautifully made, cast and forged, with roller bearings everywhere and neat offset bushes and splines for all the various adjustments, but it is undeniably complicated and it's hard to see why they did it like that other than because they could. Or maybe the Jaguar was only simpler because it was made on a line and built in volume for any comers with a cheque good enough for £3878. Seventy D-types sounds a lot compared with just five DBR1s, all but one of which were exclusively factory cars.

Our subject is DBR1, chassis no. 2, winner of five world championship events between 1957 and '58. Since 1993 it's been owned by the same arch enthusiast who drives it on track days but for the serious competition employs former Formula 3000 driver turned historic racer

Peter Hardman. Preparation is by Tim Samways' Bicester-based Sports and Historic Car Engineers and, inevitably, since the car is regularly used in competition, Tim and his team have been responsible for some development, which he says has been more in pursuit of reliability than outright performance. The last decade's continuous race programme would have made unreasonable demands on heads and blocks made nearly 40 years before and the exclusivity of the engine meant that replicas had to be cast and machined. Thanks to some logical extra fettling and some new camshafts, the result is about 285bhp – or 25 more than they ran in the shorter races, 40 more than the lower-stressed Le Mans-spec and about the same improvement as modern-day tuners have wrought from the Jaguars.

The Aston's engine, though, revs considerably higher. In the day the drivers used 7000rpm, close to Ferrari V12 territory and about 1500 more than allowed by Jaguar, and when you consider that the Aston weighs about 1900lb against the Jaguar's 2400 (and assuming that all the weights and measures are honest) the Aston's oft-quoted power disadvantage against the D-type doesn't sound so much – although Ferrari may have been a different matter. Samways has also improved »

'Thanks to some logical fettling and new camshafts, the result is about 285bhp - or 25 more than they ran in the shorter races and 40 more than the Le Mans-spec'

the gearbox with some different dog rings because although ideal in theory, he says the 'box was not thought very pleasant to handle at the time. The Maserati item which it resembles is a delight, with a shift so light and fast the lever might not be connected to anything. Samways says the Aston factory did fit one to the DBR1 as an experiment but then reverted back to the DB version when what they should have done is dismantled the Maserati 'box and found out what made it better.

The suspension is also a fair bit stiffer than it was with bigger torsion bars and a fair amount of work to the internals of the dampers. When Hardman first drove the car, he felt it was too soft and that didn't allow him to slide the car about and point it how he wanted, so the changes were made and the car is several seconds a lap quicker than it was. Some of that will be the tyres which although to original 16-inch width and pattern will have the benefit of more modern rubber compounds, and some will be the engine but I've never been able to understand why they didn't try stiffer set-ups at the time – or if they did, why it didn't work. But, enough of the technical stuff, and time to see where the car's advantage might be...

The replacement seat still has a back that is too vertical for me to be comfortable but it does boast another improvement in the shape of extra brackets to stop it flexing, because just as I have also discovered so many times, Hardman found he couldn't brace his body properly and ended up hanging on to

the wheel just when he shouldn't be. And yet again, I just don't know how they managed at the time, especially as they wouldn't have had the full harness on which Hardman, quite sensibly, also insisted. Flick the switches salvaged from an aviation parts bin and press the starter. Hear the musical wail overlaid with a searing crackle that only six cylinders arranged in line can make. Wait an age for the temperature in the vast quantity of oil to lift the needle on the gauge, then reach down for the stumpy lever, which falls straight into the palm. Lift the spring-loaded catch that guards first gear slot (the gate is modern-conventional with first left and forward and the catch is another Samways improvement which stops an enthusiastic shifter finding first instead of third...) and off you go.

Which turns out to be easy. The clutch (which is on the back of the engine) is smooth, and the gears – once the oil circulating from the tank has also warmed a little – are also easy. The gate is maybe not quite so well defined as the Maserati's but the lever's movement is minimal, maybe six inches in total, and the faster you throw it, the less effort it takes and the smoother the shift. It is definitely a fingertip rather than a clenched fist activity and so much faster than the Jaguar's change, which makes you wait for the synchros to catch up. The engine, meanwhile, is smooth and revvy and needs to be kept between five and six-eight for it to work best whereas the Jaguar's pulled from about four, but then it needs to because it has a four-speed

Right
Interior is set up for racing, not beauty. The driver's seat is not original but borrowed from an Aston DBR4 Grand Prix car.

'Feltham was close to the centres of aircraft production, and many more of the Aston workforce came from there'

'Now lift off the bonnet and, as you do, notice the rows of neat catches which remain flush until you poke a finger at them'

'box. One would be the recipe for an ultimate quick lap when you were sharp, but the other would get you out of trouble when you were tired... Decisions, decisions.

But what of the handling about which the drivers of the day were united in their approval? You can hear the creaking and groaning from the suspension as you ease out of the pit area, even above the rasp of the engine and the whistling whine of the transaxle that rises behind you, and the car now feels very stiff indeed, following each ridge and rut with faithful accuracy but as you up the speed it begins to flow. You can tell a lot about cars – particularly historic ones – from the first response to the wheel; does it roll as a whole or does it sit or sag at one end or the other? Is there lost motion when you straighten up, the kind that will add a bit to any input you make? And the brakes, the essential that compromised so many of these cars? The DBR1 has Girling discs all round with dual circuits which were standard at the time and, with the benefit of modern fluids and friction materials, are firm and powerful.

The Aston turns out to be an unusual mixture of ancient and modern, and not just because of the brakes and more modern spring rates but because the response to the wheel is instant and the car rolls as a whole – like the C-type I raced last year, only sharper. But then almost immediately the Aston takes a set without your asking, yaws its tail about five or ten degrees to the side. It's another familiar characteristic but, once again, the DBR1 seems to do it more quickly and there's no wait for the inertia to build. Then you have to hold that yaw with a dose of power, tickling it more and more through the corner

until you are flat by the exit. Too little and the car will lose its yaw and start to push at the front. Too much and it begins to slither wide.

When it does, you hear the inside rear tyre give up the struggle and start to spin. The revs rise and you need a big dose of opposite lock, and for that you need a well braced torso and strong arms. Hardman had Samways speed up the steering so he could catch the car, but it ups the effort and I'd be interested to know how heavy it was for Brooks and Moss. As it is, if you have to summon that effort, your momentum is gone anyway and it's a fine line you have to tread.

But the difference between this and, say, the D-type, is the speed of response. The D makes you wait, slides further but makes it easy to sort out. Lets you play like the feline it is, but doesn't have the claws if you overstep the mark. And the difference between others – like the GTO – which need to be drifted to keep up the momentum, is the balance. You have to lift the GTO and put it where you want it, manage the mass to get it going. The Aston does that for you and it does seem that the lower overall weight, the light engine and gearbox in the back for 50/50 weight distribution, are a major factor.

In a sprint race there would be no question, but driving it like that for 24 hours... You would of course, because that would be your job and you wouldn't think about it any more than they did. Or would you rather sit low in the calmer cockpit of the D-type and use the engine's low down punch to close the gaps between four gears? Tricky. I could let you know at about 3am.

Above left
Rear bodywork lifts off to reveal the transaxle, a defining characteristic of the DBR1's design.

Time with...
ROY SALVADORI &
CARROLL SHELBY

**Two legendary drivers who gave Aston Martin its
famous outright win at Le Mans in 1959 were recently
reunited.** Paul Chudecki **eavesdropped on the resulting
conversation between Salvadori and Shelby**

Archive pictures: Paul Chudecki Colour portrait: Steve Havelock

FIFTY YEARS AGO LAST JUNE, Aston Martin achieved its finest racing victory, vanquishing the might of Ferrari in the 1959 Le Mans 24 Hours. For David Brown and his team of DBR1s, meticulously overseen by the legendary John Wyer, it finally provided the icing on a well-baked cake, the recipe of which had until then tantalisingly produced only a trio of second places in the great French classic. And after 10 years of attempting to wrest the mightiest of endurance crowns, not only did Aston Martin achieve its aim, it also went on to clinch the World Sports Car Championship – the first time a British marque had done so.

Three DBR1 models were entered at la Sarthe that year, driven by Stirling Moss/Jack Fairman, Roy Salvadori/Carroll Shelby and Paul Frère/Maurice Trintignant. The Moss/Fairman car was to act as the hare to the Ferrari greyhounds, its purpose to push the 250 Testa Rossas beyond their limits; if it failed in the process, with luck by then the damage would have been done and the remaining Astons could pick up the pieces.

The strategy, of course, worked superbly, and just after 4pm on the Sunday, the DBR1 of Salvadori/Shelby took the chequered flag, followed home by the Frère/Trintignant car in second place.

Not long ago I had the opportunity to reminisce with the winning duo about their memories of that historic 1959 race, and the following is an account of that conversation and the fascinating insights it provided. The debonair Briton Salvadori and the laid-back Texan Shelby made a perfect pairing: both were excellent racers with similar driving styles; both were 6ft 2½in tall and of similar build – a major time-saver during driver changes; and, just as importantly, they were great pals on and off the track.

For Carroll it was to be only his second Le Mans, his DB3S having retired in 1954 after 98 laps, while Roy had suffered six retirements since his first try, also in a DB3S, in 1953. It was three years later that the Anglo/American pairing first shared a car, appropriately an Aston.

'Sebring 1956 in a DB3S was when we drove together for the first time,' recalls Roy. 'I think we finished fourth and won the class with two gears left.' Carroll pauses for a moment, then agrees: 'I find myself trying to remember things and I get corrected all the time!' he admits, though the memories soon come flooding back. 'Then another time we drove together there the gearlever fell off! I think it was '58; I remember the shifter broke off and it was a very poor weld, not like Aston at all. We had a wonderful group of guys putting it back together.'

'The team gave you a lot of confidence,' adds Roy, 'and I felt very confident about driving with Carroll, and very confident about John Wyer. He would get what he could get from you and could tell where you were losing time or gaining.' Carroll interjects: 'That's why I turned down a drive with Ferrari three times; you'd got to learn what the team's abilities were and I felt more confident driving for John Wyer – I guess I should say David Brown.'

'We were the ideal partnership,' explains Roy. 'Carroll and I were chosen together because we were the same height, and we could both put our left foot between the brake and clutch pedals – and if you were not quick enough you could jam your foot. And the reverse [gate] 'box was a bastard, it let us down time and again; the only time it behaved was at Le Mans. Sometimes it would simply lock in gear, you just couldn't get it out.'

'It didn't shift like any other gearbox I'd used in my life,' concurs Carroll. 'I've driven with a lot of special transmissions but I don't know why that one was so difficult. At Le Mans I double declutched and even then it would crash the gears, but it was much safer.'

'We were comfortable together and John Wyer

Below from left
Salvadori muses as David Brown is shown papers by Tim Parnell; Shelby takes over from Salvadori, sitting on the pit wall, late in the race.

'I FELT VERY CONFIDENT ABOUT DRIVING WITH CARROLL, AND VERY CONFIDENT ABOUT JOHN WYER' – *ROY SALVADORI*

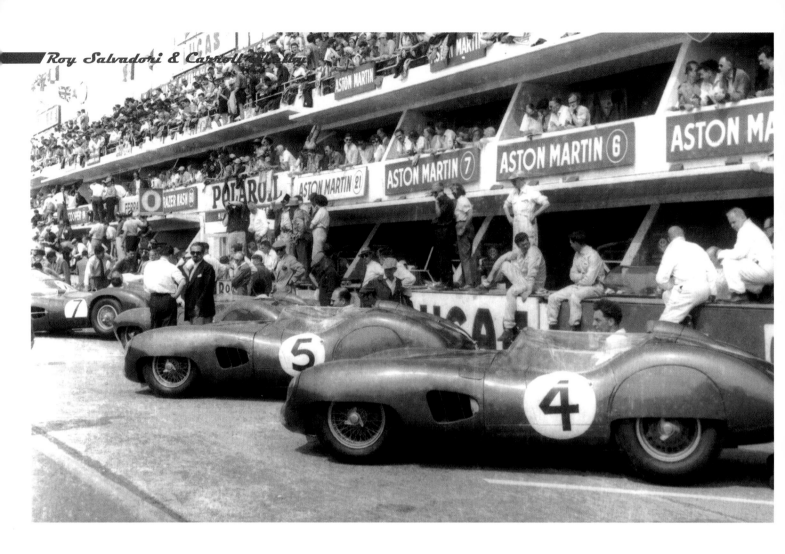

Above
Four Aston Martin DBR1s
line up before the start:
to the fore is the 'hare',
the Moss/Fairman car,
no. 4; then Shelby/
Salvadori's no. 5.

thought it a good partnership.' continues Roy. 'At Le Mans, apart from Carroll and I playing gin rummy, we did only one day of practice; John checked this and we'd done a mere seven laps each. On the last day he stopped at La Chartre [the team's base outside Le Mans] and we just said the car was OK.'

'And once you learn a circuit like Le Mans,' adds Carroll, 'you know everything that you want.'

The pair had clearly been happy with the car, and quite confident that they could comfortably achieve their target lap times in the race – in practice Salvadori had posted a 4min 12sec lap to Shelby's 4min 21sec and Moss's 4min 11sec, while for the race their lap time had been set at 4min 20sec (against 4min 22sec for Trintignant/Frère). 'There's no point in trying to go faster than necessary when you've got to last the race,' says Roy. 'We knew Stirling Moss was the hare, he had the four-bearing engine and the torque, and obviously it was a weaker engine; we had the seven-bearing crankshafts and were asked to keep the revs down.'

Salvadori and Shelby agreed to put all their effort into late braking and fast cornering, rather than overstressing the engine and transaxle; they also decided to make gearchanges at 5400-5500rpm rather than the usual 5700-5800rpm, as well as using second gear on a light throttle for the slow and tight Mulsanne and Arnage corners instead of the normally selected first gear. Only along Mulsanne would the higher rev limit be used in fifth when, says Roy, 'one could have a breather down the straight'.

The trio of factory Ferrari Testa Rossas, meanwhile – with 300bhp V12 engines against the DBR1s' 240bhp straight-sixes, while the Moss/Fairman car had 260bhp – had been marginally faster but, by virtue of a starting grid decreed by exact engine

capacity (all ran in the 3-litre prototype class), they would start behind, respectively, the Astons of Moss/Fairman, Salvadori/Shelby and Trintignant/Frère, while ahead were a Tojeiro-Jaguar, two Lister-Jaguars and a D-type Jaguar, all with around 250bhp.

Despite the set lap time of 4min 20sec, however, Salvadori, who started the race, was soon lapping comfortably some four to five seconds quicker, still maintaining the lower rev limit, and by the end of the second hour lay in fifth place. Shelby continued the pace (despite suffering from a debilitating stomach upset caused by a bad salad the night before), and by lap 50 the DBR1 was 3min 26sec ahead of the team schedule. The first works Ferrari to succumb to Moss's pace was the Cliff Allison/Hermano da Silva Ramos example after some three hours, its engine chronically overheating.

It was on lap 94, shortly before 11pm, that Roy took the lead from the Jean Behra/Dan Gurney Ferrari, the latter also suffering from overheating and a lack of oil pressure as a result of trying to keep up with Moss. The maestro's Aston, always considered semi-expendable, had retired from the lead on lap 71 with a broken inlet valve, its job hopefully done. Gurney eventually retired the Testa Rossa – the fastest of the three – from fourth place at 1.29am, after 130 laps, when Shelby was comfortably in the lead; the Trintignant/Frère Aston held third, but behind lay the ever-present threat of the still-healthy Oliver Gendebien/Phil Hill Ferrari. And when Salvadori took over from Shelby at 2.05am it inevitably allowed Hill to muscle in on the lead; within 10 laps the American held an almost four-minute advantage.

All, though, appeared to be running sweetly for the David Brown team, with the Salvadori/Shelby DBR1 redressing the balance when the Testa Rossa made a routine stop, and thereafter holding the lead for some four hours – until Roy experienced a severe vibration from the rear of the Aston on lap 161. By the time he had completed the seven remaining laps of his 30-lap stint, at a very slow pace of almost 6min per tour, had a wheel changed after thrown pieces of tyre tread was found to be the culprit, and Carroll was out again – having lost some 12 minutes in the pits Gendebien/ Hill had an almost unassailable lead with only half the 24 hours left to run. As Moss states in his book *Le Mans '59*: 'Seldom in a motor race have I seen so many faces so sad as there were in the Aston Martin pit at 4.30am that Sunday morning.'

Half-an-hour later, Gendebien led Shelby by four laps. Then, just before 6.30am, Trintignant in the third Aston, two laps behind, could no longer bear the increasing pain from his burnt right foot (caused by a blisteringly-hot throttle pedal, due to the re-routed exhaust, and for which he had already received medical aid). Nonetheless, the Frenchman stoically decided to continue, feeling that reserve driver Henry Taylor should not drive a maiden stint when there was an oil spillage on the circuit.

By 8am Salvadori/Shelby were just two laps behind Gendebien/ Hill, the latter having lost time during a pit stop, while Roy had found he could reduce his lap times by one to four seconds through even later braking and still conserve the car – 'very late braking points', adds Roy, 'that I wouldn't have thought possible'. Still, however, the deficit looked impossibly large to close in the time remaining. Then at 11am the lead Ferrari, now just over a lap ahead, suddenly slowed, pitting on lap 263 and again on lap 270, and then retired the following lap, chronically overheating as with its sister machines; unfortunately for Ferrari, its lower running

temperature during the cool of the night had been but a false dawn prior to the heat of the day. There were just four hours to go and the Salvadori/Shelby Aston led the race 20 laps clear of any threat from a rival marque, the nearest of which was a private Ferrari 250GT at some 25 laps down.

'The story of the race is that really we were in the lead for many, many hours,' says Roy. 'It wasn't planned and John Wyer had hoped we'd come into it well into the end of the race. Wyer normally set the lap time. We took the lead from Gendebien and Hill and I think we led for several hours. And then the whole car started to vibrate and I immediately thought it was the gearbox, so I called in and told Reg [Parnell, team manager]; he looked the car over and couldn't find anything wrong, and told me to go out for four laps and drive slowly. I thought it was going to explode, it was wandering all over the road, and then I came in for a refuelling stop. They still couldn't find anything wrong and then a mechanic found a piece of metal stripped from the tyre; then we lost almost 15 minutes and had to drive much harder.'

'Then I took over,' continues Carroll. 'We were going faster and braked later. The plan normally was to let up a bit just to give a five to ten percent margin for error; but brake a little later and you could end up half-a-second faster. The DBR1 was a very good-handling car but at Le Mans it was inferior to the D-type Jaguar – I remember Innes Ireland could pull 10mph more down the straight; it was also slower down the straight than the Ferrari but always superior to that machine in its handling, and superior to the D-type in the really kinky bits of the course. And you always felt safe in the car – you always wanted to drive the Aston. The first time I drove a DBR1 was in 1958, probably at Sebring.'

'THE DBR1 WAS A VERY GOOD-HANDLING CAR BUT AT LE MANS WAS INFERIOR TO THE D-TYPE' – *CARROLL SHELBY*

Clockwise from right
Drivers sprint to their cars at the start; Reg Parnell barks orders during the winning car's final pit stop; Salvadori on the way to Aston Martin victory.

Right
Shelby takes the chequered flag for Aston Martin's maiden victory at Le Mans. Behind is the class-winning Lotus of Lumsden/Riley.

'AT THE END I COULDN'T BELIEVE WE'D DONE IT, I'D DREAMED OF IT FOR SO LONG' – *CARROLL SHELBY*

Roy, too, had no doubts about the Aston's ability: 'I thought it was a super car. And going from one to the other, the Ferrari to the Aston, the Ferrari's engine and 'box were the best, but, oh boy, the Aston is the best car to drive!' 'I never heard a driver criticise it,' Carroll adds. 'Roy did have his feet burnt terribly after they rerouted the exhaust and he still has the scars from that Le Mans, and poor old Trintignant almost couldn't cope.' 'It was a terrible heat,' agrees Roy. 'I've never known anything like it; my toenails went green – and they still don't grow properly!'

'Actually, everything worked out very well,' Carroll continues, 'especially after the Ferrari cylinder blocks started losing water. I've often thought that if both Aston and Ferrari had stressed their cars, Ferrari wouldn't have been any faster; we could make it up in the tight bits and run all over them at White House – from Indianapolis through Dunlop and on back to the straight, we did well. Then they'd make it up on the straight – I went with Gendebien for 15 laps, so then I'd let him ahead; I could have stayed ahead but I felt it would be pushing the car too much.

'I chased to 10 o'clock on Sunday and I remember they [the Ferraris] were starting to have to come in at quicker intervals, and that's when I knew something was wrong with them. And we never once considered our car expendable, remember that; Ferrari's problem was a hole in the casting, and it blew out under pressure.'

Indeed, the Aston performed faultlessly. 'All we had to do,' adds Roy, 'was make sure things didn't let up and keep the Ferraris going – I think we were never more than one lap behind and the idea was to keep the pressure on; our other car could then pick up the pieces. Apart from the tyre problem, I can't remember a single thing that went wrong with it – it was just how you'd expect it to be after a couple of races in England. When they eventually took it apart there were only a couple of valve springs broken – but it would be the same on all the cars.'

He continues: 'And before the tyre trouble we were well ahead of the Hill car and I don't think it ever would have caught us. I personally think they were undergeared and weren't lifting, that's my feeling. One thing we could rely on was the brake pads, they were expendable, and we knew we had better roadholding – you don't catch up passing someone on the straight. In fact, it's reasonably safe to say that while we couldn't match Ferrari's times, they were struggling and had to push the cars to keep up with our speeds.'

'Early in the morning,' adds Carroll, 'Gendebien was driving very inconsistently: he made 200 yards on the straight and I was staying fairly close and then the next lap he would pull away – doing some speed. But Roy and I were both nice to the brakes, we both knew we had to be kinder. And we were confident.'

'We weren't!' interrupts Roy, with a laugh. 'We were relying on the Ferrari in front breaking – and fortunately it did!'

After the retirement of that last Ferrari, the pair was able to dramatically reduce the pace and hope that the DBR1's reliability continued. 'And then John [Wyer] slowed Trintignant and Frère so that we could cruise,' explains Carroll, referring to the sister Aston that was in danger of catching the lead DBR1 towards the end of the race – Salvadori and Shelby's advantage being so great that they could afford to lap at up to a leisurely 4min 50sec!

'But if it's too slow, you can lose concentration,' points out Roy. Carroll agrees: 'I think that's when you lose it, driving 90%; you slow down and that can be dangerous. Go slow and you won't give it 100% concentration. And we could have wrecked the car if someone had dropped a bit of oil. At the end I couldn't believe that we'd done it, because I'd dreamed of it for so long; at last to win Le Mans was the epitome. Aston Martin was like my family and I was very happy for the team – and John Wyer held them together and chose a good group of mechanics and drivers who worked well together.'

'WE WERE THE IDEAL PARTNERSHIP; WE WERE COMFORTABLE TOGETHER' – *ROY SALVADORI*

Notably, and not surprisingly, Stirling Moss had set the Astons' fastest race lap at 4min 3sec, but Salvadori's best – despite burnt feet – had been 4min 5sec, and Shelby's – despite the stomach bug that afflicted him for the last 18 hours – 4min 11 sec, against Behra's 4min 0.9sec when pursuing Moss.

'At the end of Le Mans I was terribly tired, in fact *so* bloody tired,' recalls Roy. 'I was a little upset with Reg: he said I should have known what had happened, and was very critical. But when you've got a gearbox problem, always a weak point of the DBR1, you don't know; I suppose I should have thought of something else but we had never had any trouble with the Avon tyres. Reg started shouting and I said a few things back. But with Reg there was no point in picking a fight, you wait 'til it's all over. John came and sorted that out.'

'There were many, many instances that year,' remembers Carroll, 'when John had to work things out with other members of the team. Reg made decisions John wouldn't have made.'

'But you can't expect Reg to have fitted John Wyer's shoes,' adds Roy in Parnell's defence. 'He'd put you in your place and tell you what to do, but he was never discouraging.'

'And John would never blame you for an accident,' Carroll continues. 'Whatever you did he would never criticise you. I've never known him speak unkindly to a mechanic, no matter what kind of mistake they made. I remember one time something broke on the engine and [mechanic] Jack Sopp went to John Wyer and said "I'm not sure if it was my fault"; John said, "Don't worry about it Jack, it's too late now." I never had a cross word with him.

'And there was never anyone better to drive for than David Brown – I never knew him to interfere with John Wyer or team tactics. The only time I ever saw him really pissed was after Le Mans; there was

Clockwise from right
Moss exits Mulsanne, luring on Ferraris; Frère about to finish second; Reg Parnell, Shelby and Salvadori receive *The Motor* Challenge Trophy.

always oil inside the car and it got on his cashmere coat!

'Now, if you look at Ferrari, if anything happened in the Ferrari team, there was a lot of trouble; Old man Ferrari caused that and that's why I never drove for him. Even the Jaguar boys had issues, and there were always problems at Maserati and always at Porsche; I drove for Porsche a couple of times and it was all intrigue.'

Roy, too, remembers a similar lack of harmony in other teams: 'It was difficult for us. In 1957 Carroll and I did Sebring with the Maserati team and we were separated from them. We'd arrive, wouldn't know what was being done, what car we were going to drive, and there were no instructions; then in the race they brought Carroll in after 19 laps and it should have been 20 and we were disqualified – that's how good they were!'

'Aston Martin really was very exceptional,' concludes Roy. As, indeed, was the 1959 Le Mans 24 Hours. △

Time with...
IN ASSOCIATION WITH

Chopard

Four PLAY

Aston Martin's DB4 is one of the great GTs of the early '60s. But which one would Sir prefer
– standard Series II, short-wheelbase GT, road-racer Zagato or Bertone 'Jet' showcar?

Words: Mark Dixon **Photography:** Michael Bailie

434 JNY

SEAN CONNERY HAS A LOT TO ANSWER FOR. It's said that half the world's population has seen a Bond film, and Connery's charisma is the reason why silver DB5s fetch such ludicrous prices today. On Her Majesty's Secret Service may be far superior to Goldfinger as a movie – and I'll fight the man who says otherwise – but few people have a burning desire to emulate George Lazenby by buying a DBS.

No other Aston Martin has achieved such celebrity before or since, but a close runner-up in the cool stakes is the DB4 Volante driven by Michael Caine in The Italian Job. As he pulls up outside the concrete facade of London's Royal Lancaster Hotel, early on in the film – and you get bonus points if you spot the mustard-yellow Alfa Giulia in the background – he's the epitome of 1960s success: young, handsome and classless, his sideburns as sharp as his silk tie and lightweight grey suit.

Until the DB4 came along in 1958, Aston Martin's road cars had been fine but rather dowdy-looking creations. It was the DB4 that moved the firm into the motorway age, rebranding it as the maker of international grand tourers that were as ➤

'The combination of light weight, short wheelbase and ample power makes the Zagato more agile than any other classic Aston of the last 40 years'

attractive to new-moneyed arrivistes as they were to aristocratic blue-bloods. David Brown, the owner of Aston Martin, fitted the profile perfectly – a no-nonsense Yorkshire industrialist turned South of France playboy, who married a 28-year-old former model when he was 76.

Touring of Milan won the contract to inject some Italian brio into this most English of marques after impressing general manager John Wyer with a couple of pretty dropheads built on DB2/4 MkII chassis. Touring introduced the superleggera (superlight) principle to Aston, by which alloy outer panels were wrapped around a framework of small-diameter tubes on a steel base unit. Aston's chief engineer Harold Beach would have liked to give the DB4 de Dion rear suspension – very much in vogue with 1950s race cars – but had to settle for a conventional live axle, allegedly because of NVH problems with the David Brown-sourced final drive. Front suspension was by coil-and-wishbone.

The engine was an all-new unit designed by Polish immigrant Tadek Marek. Originally intended to be of a 3-litre capacity, it had stretched to 3.7 litres by the time production began. Cast in aluminium, with twin overhead camshafts, it became Aston's mainstay of the DB series, in 4-litre form serving the 4, 5 and 6 models well and foregoing its well-earned retirement to do further duty in the DBS when Marek's new V8 was delayed.

Small companies are always the worst offenders when it comes to confusing posterity with the variety of models and sub-variants offered, and Aston Martin is no exception. The four very different DB4s we brought together at a test track near London are only a fraction of the variety produced over the 1958-63 run: no fewer than five distinct series, before you start talking about the more exotic GT spin-offs. A Volante like Caine's is the most significant example missing from our line-up, but since the rain was unrelenting for the duration of the photoshoot it wasn't greatly missed.

Representing the five series of standard cars is a solitary Series II, courtesy of Wiltshire classic specialist The Hairpin Company. Like the rest of Hairpin's stock, this sage-green example is truly exceptional, following a four-year restoration.

Moving up a notch in the DB4 hierarchy we have a very original dark-green GT, the short-wheelbase DB4 which has a more powerful engine and the faired-in lights that were also fitted to Series V Vantage versions of the standard car (told you this could get confusing). Standard DB4s had twin SU carbs, the Vantage gained three but the GT boasted triple 45 Webers, as befitted a car with a dual road/race role. Only 100 GTs were built, including 19 Zagato-bodied cars, and a handful of them frightened the Ferrari 250GTs in events such as the Goodwood TT. This one has just been acquired by long-time Aston specialist RS Williams for a total makeover; it has the look, feel and smell of a well-used but cherished car.

The utterly perfect silver GT Zagato is also courtesy of Richard Stewart Williams, who maintains it for owner William Taylor. It's a genuine Zagato, in that it was bodied by Zagato on an original DB4 GT chassis, but it received the Italian coachwork only four years ago... Supplied new to Sir Max Aitken, son of the famous press baron Lord Beaverbrook, it enjoyed a spell of notoriety as the recipient of a unique body, built in the late-1960s by the Aston factory at the whim of its then owner, which married a DB5-style front end with a DB6 rear. Journalist and racer Tony Dron inspected the car 30 years later and commented 'they got away with a pretty

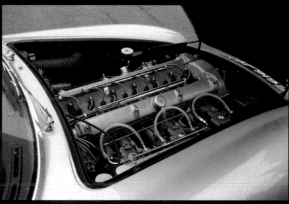

Aston Martin DB4 GT Zagato

SPECIFICATIONS

Engine
3749cc all-alloy straight-six, twin overhead cams, three Weber 45DCOE4 carburettors

Power
314bhp @ 6000rpm

Torque
278lb ft @ 5400rpm

Transmission
Four-speed manual, rear-wheel drive

Suspension
Front: independent, coil and wishbone, anti-roll bar, telescopic dampers. Rear: live axle, coil and trailing links with Watt linkage, lever-arm dampers

Brakes
Discs all round, no servo assistance

Weight
1209kg (2665lb) dry

Performance
0-60mph 6.1sec
Top speed 152mph

Value
Cost new £5470
Value now
£1,000,000-1,800,000

Left and above
Obsessive weight saving resulted in Zagato's pumped-up, bumperless look, and extended even to minimalist door pulls.

Aston Martin DB4 GT

SPECIFICATIONS

Engine
3670cc all-alloy
straight-six, twin
overhead cams, three
Weber 45DCOE4
carburettors

Power
302bhp @ 6000rpm

Torque
278lb ft @ 5400rpm

Transmission
Four-speed manual,
rear-wheel drive

Suspension
Front: independent,
coil and wishbone,
anti-roll bar, telescopic
dampers. Rear: live
axle, coils and trailing
links with Watt linkage,
lever-arm dampers

Brakes
Discs all round,
no servo assistance

Weight
1277kg (2816lb) dry

Performance
0-60mph 6.8sec
Top speed 152mph

Value
Cost new £4169
Value now
£350,000-550,000

Right and above
Short-wheelbase GT
is equally at home on
road or track, though
broad seats are built
for comfort rather
than lateral support.

poor job back in 1968', so it's not surprising its new owner commissioned a Zagato body through Richard Stewart Williams, who had already masterminded the creation of four 'new' Zagatos in the early 1990s. Unlike those cars, which were all-new machines taking previously unissued chassis numbers, Taylor's Zagato is an original GT and hence FIA eligible – though you'd have to be insane or simply insanely rich to risk its eggshell-thin alloy panels in the cut-and-thrust of historic racing.

While the Zagato is still recognisably an Aston, without prior knowledge you'd never guess our fourth and final DB4 started life in England. It's the one-off Jet car built by Bertone for the 1961 Geneva Show, and might have had more impact on public and industry alike if Jaguar hadn't unveiled its E-type on the same occasion... Owned since 1986 by Swiss enthusiast Hans-Peter Weidmann, at the time of our shoot the Jet was making one of its periodic visits to the Aston factory before an appointment at the New York Concours in October.

It's customary to begin with the earliest car and work forwards from there, but I'm going to start with the Zagato for the very good reason that I was lucky enough to drive it a considerable distance on public roads – and in the dry, too.

No one could deny that it's a gorgeous-looking thing. It's clearly an Aston yet, with its pumped-up rear arches and over-arching roofline, it's also unmistakably the work of Zagato. Practicalities such as bumpers have been discarded in the ceaseless quest to save weight; the outer door handles are nothing more than tiny loops of steel rod. The outer panels are formed of much thinner alloy than standard – 'If you've got bad breath, you'll dent them' as the owner puts it – all of which helps shave nearly 70kg off a standard GT's weight.

Inside, it's pure road-racer. Two bucket seats, two over-the-shoulders harnesses and a plain black dash. No glovebox, and no sun-visors either: just a subtle sunstrip incorporated in the windscreen's upper edge. It creates an irritating bi-focal effect for tall drivers like me, and the high driving position exacerbates irregularities in the moulding of the Perspex rear screen (only the front windows are glass), leading to much anxiety about whether the car behind you is 'civilian' or 'official'.

Three prods on the accelerator to prime a cold engine, then twist the key. There's a moment's hesitation while the Aston deliberately seems to be winding you up further and then it explodes into life, 3.7 litres of twin-cam straight-six snorting super-unleaded through three uncompromising 45DCOE4 Webers. For the first couple of minutes it's rough and slightly ragged sounding, until some vestiges of heat soak into the oil and coolant; then you blip the throttle a few times to clear its throat and it settles to a more regular rhythm. The noise isn't as ballistic as you'd expect – deep-chested and authoritative, but more road- than race-orientated.

There's a certain knack to making a smooth take-off, since the high first gear won't allow you to trickle away on minimal revs; equally, you don't want to fry the clutch or come across as a show-off by giving the engine too much right foot. Actually, the big motor pulls pretty cleanly from low down, with just the occasional fluffiness to remind you that it's really much happier when spinning above 3000rpm. The four-speed David Brown gearbox is stirred by the usual dainty little lever, the shifts clean though not especially light. No overdrive, just four ratios to take you up to 150mph.

With the engine good and hot, find a clear stretch of road, »

'This car makes a fabulous noise. It's not uncivilised, or even particularly loud: just completely evocative of what a GT car should represent'

drop down a gear, take a deep breath and press firmly on the throttle pedal. The response is vivid and immediate: the exhaust blares and the car gathers pace quickly and relentlessly, whether you're doing 50, 70 or even 90mph.

In contrast to the thin, plastic-topped gear lever, the steering wheel is thick-rimmed in wood and it operates in a beautifully damped fashion: heavy, of course, at parking speeds but light and accurate on the open road, which is where you want to be – not least because there's less chance of that paper-thin bodywork picking up a ding, when you're far from the madding crowd. Although the car never actually shrinks around you, the combination of light weight, short wheelbase and ample power makes it more agile than any other classic Aston produced in the last 40-odd years; barrel into a corner and the steering doesn't weight up alarmingly or the front end try to push wide, but the car obediently settles into a neutral stance and holds its line, the Avon Turbospeed radials gripping strongly.

On a wet surface, oversteer is available on demand but the steering is sharp-witted enough for drivers of average skill to experiment safely. Given room, the same could be said about the car's behaviour on dry tarmac, but you'd have to be exceptionally confident to practise your opposite-locking techniques in such a special motor. Then again, since the fuel

tank holds a huge 30 gallons and occupies most of the boot, when it's fully gassed up you might have little alternative.

If there's one dynamic shortfall, it's the brakes. True to spec they're unservoed, so high pedal pressure is required; and running for long periods on lightly trafficked fast roads means no heat gets into the linings, so they feel about as effective as blocks of wood. Not a problem in the constant fast/slow cycle of racing, but slightly worrying in long-distance touring. It's rather embarrassing to have overtaken, say, a new BMW coupé on a dual-carriageway, only to be undertaken at the next roundabout because you've been forced to go down through the gears as if you were sitting a 1950s driving test.

Clicking shut the Zagato's door and opening the GT's reveals a world that's similar, but different. The dash is broadly the same, except that you get a glovebox; while the rear parcel shelf is thoughtfully provided with straps so your Dunhill travel bag doesn't decapitate you under heavy braking. And the broad and comfortable seats are regular DB items.

Richard Stewart Williams had warned us that this unsorted car would be a bit of a dog to drive. Well, maybe it is to an expert of Williams' standing, but on first acquaintance there doesn't seem an awful lot wrong with it. The engine feels and sounds lusty, firing immediately and with a more rorty and, frankly, stirring growl than the Zagato's. All the GTs, both »

Right and below
DB wheel is only familiar fitting in Jet's unique interior; it's steel bodied, but mechanically it's pure Aston Martin.

'A massive fuel tank gives the Jet continent-shrinking range – Weidmann reckons he could do Lands End to John O'Groats on a single fill-up'

'The more you put in, the greater the rewards:
keep the power on and the revs up, and the
balance shifts from front to rear'

Aston Martin
DB4 Series II
SPECIFICATIONS

Engine
3670cc all-alloy straight
six, twin overhead
cams, two SU HD8
carburettors

Power
240bhp @ 5500rpm

Torque
240lb ft @ 4250rpm

Transmission
Four-speed manual,
optional overdrive,
rear-wheel drive

Suspension
Front: independent,
coil and wishbone,
anti-roll bar, telescopic
dampers. Rear: live
axle, coils and trailing
links with Watt linkage,
lever-arm dampers

Weight
1354kg (2984lb) dry

Performance
0-60mph 8.5sec
Top speed 140mph

Value
Cost new £3989

Value now
£80,000-200,000

standard and Zagato-bodied, had a twin-plug version of the regular DB4's straight-six, with compression increased from 9.0 to 9.7:1 and, of course, three socking great Weber 45s instead of the twin SUs of the cooking model.

This car makes a fabulous noise. It's not uncivilised, or even particularly loud: just completely evocative of what a 1960s GT car should represent. Open the floodgates on those triple Webers and the Aston lunges forward with a menacing snarl, which evolves into a thoroughbred howl as the rev-counter needle sweeps around that chrome-rimmed Smiths dial. It's solid and smooth, as befits a big 'six', but with an earthy English weightiness that sets it apart from the complex, higher-pitched wail of a contemporary V12 Ferrari. On paper, the GT's greater weight means it can never match the Zagato's performance, but in the real world you'd be unlikely to notice those extra fractions of a second when your foot's to the floor.

But you might spot the difference in corners, where the GT rolls a little more as it fights the centrifugal effect of another 70kg. This car is running period-spec Avon Turbospeed crossplies, whereas the other three are shod with Turbosteel radials; allowing for the fact that it's not in the prime of condition – and we were driving on streaming wet surfaces – it seemed as sure-footed and user-friendly as the rest. But it was also appreciably lighter at the wheel than our remaining pair, the Bertone Jet and the standard Series II.

We'll try the Jet first, because it's the last of our GT-spec trio. It's also the very last DB4 GT chassis built, no. 0201. Designed by 22-year-old Giorgetto Giugiaro, its early history is vague but it's known to have spent time in Beirut before a longer stay in America. Current owner Hans-Peter Weidmann had it totally restored in the late-1980s and then did the rounds of the concours circuit for a few years, picking up prestigious titles such as 'Car of the Show' at Villa d'Este and 'Best Italian coachwork' at Pebble Beach.

Fortunately, Weidmann – who has nursed a life-long love of Astons since he saw Goldfinger in 1964 – soon realised the error of his ways and decided to start actually driving the car. He's now done 35,000 miles in it, including a memorable 15-hour, 950-mile stint from San Francisco to Vancouver in one night. 'It was intended to be a grand tourer and that's just what I use it for,' says Weidmann, a cheerful soul who was not in the least perturbed to watch his multiple-concours winner getting thoroughly drenched by the English summer rain.

The Jet is one of those cars that looks better in the metal than it does in pictures. In photos the long, shallow rear deck makes it seem a little unbalanced, but that's not so apparent when you set eyes on the real thing – possibly because you'll be punch-drunk taking in the detailing of a model that looks much more like a Ferrari-Maserati cross than an Aston. Giugiaro did a fine job of disguising the body height dictated by the straight-six, and the result is a machine that has supercar presence yet also manages to look sleek and modern.

Inside it's just as different, with a unique facia that picks up on the Italo-American theme. It seems lighter than in the other Astons, because there's less metal in the D-posts. Only the bootful of fuel tank compromises its practicality as a tourer, although this massive tank does give the Jet continent-shrinking range – Weidmann reckons he could just about do Lands End to John O'Groats on a single fill-up. You won't be surprised to hear that one of these days he intends to try.

On the track, the Jet feels significantly heavier than the other two GTs because it's bodied in steel rather than light alloy. There's more understeer in corners and the steering

'The Series II is a proper driving machine, and its comparatively sober looks only emphasise that seriousness of purpose'

Above and right
All four cars show different versions of Aston's stepped grille – though Jet's is very subtle indeed.

demands a lot more of your upper arms and shoulders. But the upside is that the Jet rides more smoothly, in keeping with its sophisticated Continental image. If straight-line performance has been blunted by the extra weight, it's not an issue: this car is about relaxed high-speed cruising, not sprinting between corners on a race circuit. Like all the Astons here, its biggest failing is wind noise at high speed – a surprisingly important characteristic that manufacturers didn't really get to grips with until the 1980s.

After such a heady cocktail, you might expect the straight-out-of-the-box DB4 Series II to have all the glamour of a pint of bitter. But it's the standard car's understatement that is also its strength. In pale metallic green – subtle but refreshingly different in an age when every other car is painted silver – it looks simply exquisite. The detail is just perfect, from the vertical slivers of chrome and coloured glass that constitute the rear lights to the... well, that's it. The DB4 has no unnecessary flourishes. Wing and bonnet vents aside, it's as pure as a GT car gets.

This freshly-restored Aston is crying out for some serious use. The gearchange has yet to loosen up, the seats need a few thousand miles of pummelling by human backsides. It feels just like a new DB4 would have done in 1961. Like the dark-green GT, it has a glorious exhaust note, which means you don't really care that its acceleration can't match that of the triple-carb, short-wheelbase cars – it's fast enough, and it sounds better than anything that'll overtake you. The handling is also involving in the way that only old cars can be. Like the

Jet, it takes a little more effort to push it through a tight corner, and at a modest pace it understeers more than the lighter GTs. But the more you put in, the greater the reward: keep the revs up and the power on, and the balance shifts from front to back, allowing a degree of rear-wheel steer that diminishes the heft needed at the helm. It's a real driving machine, and its comparatively sober looks only emphasise that seriousness of purpose.

The slightly depressing reality is that fewer and fewer people are going to have the chance to find that out for themselves, since DB prices have gone stratospheric. At time of writing, Hairpin was asking £159,000 for the Series II, which sounds a lot until you discover that RSW's unrestored dark-green GT – about to undergo plenty of expensive work – was valued at £360,000. RSW had recently sold a particularly fine Zagato for £1.8 million and the one offered by RM Auctions at Monterey that August failed to sell at $2,450,00 (£1,325,000).

And that's a terrible shame, because very valuable cars tend to get used less, and the DB4 – any DB4 – should not be about three-mile trips to the pub on a Sunday afternoon. It's a car built for blasting along autobahns or storming the Alps, en route from one five-star hotel to the next. Jet owner Weidmann has the right idea; if only more Aston keepers were so adventurous. ◬

Thanks to William Taylor and Richard Stewart Williams, +44 (0)1932 868377, www.rswilliams.co.uk; The Hairpin Company, +44 (0)1249 760686, www.thehairpincompany.co.uk; and Hans-Peter Weidmann.

THUNDER THROUGH THE WOODS

HERITAGE

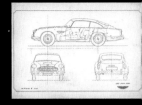

DB5 Technical Drawing
signed by Harold Beach
Chief Engineer Aston Martin
Limited Edition of 50

An evocative photo of the start of the 1959
Le Mans 24 Hours by Brian Joscelyne
Limited edition of 50

Original factory publicity image of
the glorious DB5
Limited edition of 75

A CELEBRATION OF OUR HERITAGE

AN EXCLUSIVE RANGE OF STRICTLY
LIMITED EDITION PRINTS FROM
ARCHIVE ORIGINALS OF SOME
OF OUR MOST ICONIC MODELS

1961 Factory Advertisement DB4
Limited Edition of 75

1964 Factory Advertisement DB5
Limited Edition of 75

1959 Factory Advertisement DBR
Limited Edition of 50

Photographs and signed Technical Drawings
(59 x 84cm) £196.50 each, Adverts (29 x 42cm)
£97.50 each. Prices exclude VAT and local taxes
where applicable

Available online at
WWW.ASTONMARTIN.COM/HERITAGE
amb@astonmartin.com | +44 (0)1908 305530

Instant Underdog

ASTON MARTIN DB4GT ZAGATO '1 VEV'

Truth be told, the DB4GT Zagato was never really competitive in period against the all-conquering 250GTOs – but it's a fabulous driver's car, finds Tony Dron

Photography: Matthew Howell

ABOUT 40 YEARS AGO somebody put a radio into 1 VEV. Today such vandalism seems mad, but perhaps it made sense then. During the model's recent restoration at RS Williams, staff found the evidence. It had been covered up in later years but there, deep inside, were the holes that had been cut to take a 1960s radio and its speaker.

Whoever was responsible didn't quite have the gall to desecrate the handmade Zagato body by drilling an aerial hole through it but, as Richard Williams told me: 'Concealed aerials were available then. Perhaps the car had one.'

The pair of Aston Martin DB4GT Zagatos, registered 1 VEV and 2 VEV on May 19, 1961, and campaigned by John Ogier's Essex Racing Stable, have long been a legendary part of Aston history. Heroically, they went into battle against the dominant Ferraris after the Works ceased racing officially. First they faced the 250GT SWB but then along came the fabulous 250GTO, which of course turned out to be one of the greatest GT racing cars ever made.

As the Astons were about 12% heavier than a 250GT

Below
Boot is almost entirely filled with spare wheel and massive long-distance fuel tank.

Above
Racing supremo Dron found 1 VEV remarkably satisfying on the circuit, even in 'soft' road trim.

SWB, they became instant underdogs. The DB4GT Zagatos were magnificent thoroughbreds but they just weren't quick enough. When the GTO appeared in 1962, it got worse: the Astons were then 18% heavier than the opposition. To be brutally honest, their position became steadily more hopeless.

Nevertheless, Ogier gave it his best shot. He ran a superb team, he hired the best drivers and 1 VEV and 2 VEV came out fighting. Unfortunately the account opened very badly when the brand new pair retired early in the 1961 Le Mans 24 Hours. Both suffered head gasket failure because the heads had not been properly tightened down. But that simple cock-up made no real difference to the race result. One hour in, Ferrari held the first four places and the new Astons were fading away without ever being near the top ten. A couple of outdated DBR1s were lying seventh and eighth early on, but not one Aston Martin finished the race – a sorry tale after the Works team's glorious outright one-two with the DBR1s in 1959.

Ogier's team got a great boost in their next race, the GT event supporting the British GP at Aintree. In damp conditions, Australian driver Lex Davison, in 2 VEV, gambled on the right tyres and seized the lead from Jack Sears on the very last lap to win by just 1.2 seconds. Jack should have been driving a Ferrari 250GT but an unfortunate mechanic had smashed it up, driving to Aintree on the road. Different days indeed! Jack raced an

E-type instead, a near-standard car with its soft-top raised, and very nearly won. The famous Lightweight E-types, which certainly were a match for the 250GTOs, were yet to come.

In fact, there was no Ferrari opposition in that 1961 Aintree race, the other 250GT also having been crashed before the start. One of our most respected magazines then made a blunder by reporting: 'Whitmore brought the other Essex Aston Martin Zagato home third.' John Whitmore did finish third, but he drove the Essex team's standard DB4GT, not a Zagato, and he was on dry tyres. It had looked like the smart choice but he was out of luck.

As things turned out, 1 VEV was never beaten by its team mate, 2 VEV. Back then, the chief mechanic in the Essex Racing Stable was Ian Moss. Now 70, and still extremely active – he's a keen badminton player – Ian recalls the 1961 and 1962 seasons clearly: '1 VEV was the car we used for most of the work. When testing, it was 1 VEV that we normally took. Those cars were perhaps half a hundredweight lighter than standard as they had no bumpers, lightweight racing seats and some interior panels had been left out in the build. The Ferraris were much lighter, had better traction and a much stiffer chassis. The way I saw it, Ferrari made a racing car and adapted it for the road while Aston took a road machine and converted it for racing.'

Half a hundredweight equates to 25.4kg: in other words, not a lot. A DB4GT Zagato was lighter than a standard DB4 but, as »

'It is set up for the road so the damping is a bit soft, calling for care in the fastest bends, but it likes a bit of sideways style'

Above
Zagato's bodywork
was lighter than a
standard car's, but
the Astons were still
heavy for racers.

we have seen, it was always an overweight racer. There was also plenty of bullshit over horsepower. Ian says: 'Despite official claims, 1 VEV never had more than 270bhp in those days. Horsepower figures sell cars, but torque wins races!' Aston Martin tweaked its 3670cc straight-six up to a compression ratio of 9.7:1 for the Zagato and claimed 314bhp, but nobody today denies the true figure was well short of that. Ian says they did see 310bhp from one engine much later on but it was a 3.9-litre, which went into the second 2 VEV after the original was wrecked at Spa in 1962.

Perhaps 1 VEV's finest moment came in its second race, the 1961 RAC Tourist Trophy at Goodwood. Roy Salvadori gave chase to the Ferraris and after 108 laps he finished a mere three seconds behind Mike Parkes' 250GT. It was a glorious result, even though he was 'only' a close third because Stirling Moss, in another Ferrari 250GT, finished a lap ahead of the entire field. That sort of performance was rather expected of Stirling then.

Recalling it, Roy says: 'Compared to a GTO or an E-type, the Aston Zagatos were much heavier to drive. You had to really thrash them to get the times down, but it was a wonderful team to be part of. We worked hard at our pit stops but somehow we always seemed to be stationary a little longer than the opposition, and that car was really hard on rubber.' He wasn't kidding: I looked it up and found that Roy had 14 new tyres fitted during that Goodwood race, and no punctures! Behind him, and another

lap down we should note, were Jim Clark in 2 VEV and Innes Ireland in a normal DB4GT.

But stop a moment, this is known history. What are we really talking about when we consider such famous, well-documented cars today? What is there new to say? Nearly 20 years ago, when I was on another magazine, we published the definitive history of 1 VEV and 2 VEV. It was a superb piece of work by Doug Nye. Writing about it now we can give a progress report on 1 VEV and, surprisingly enough, there's plenty of new information, not the least of it being our driving impressions after pushing it hard round Castle Combe circuit.

If this car looks great, it goes even better. Fresh from its absolutely perfect, wonderfully sympathetic rebuild, it's as good as new, if not better. We'll get to that but, first, let's take to the track. The car is waiting, in sunshine in the paddock, all ready to go, and the new owner, Adrian Beecroft, has invited us to take him round as fast as we like. Call him mad if you like, but we go back a few years and he trusts me for some reason.

There are no belts but the old bucket seats are comfortable, the engine starts instantly with a fabulous, deep, eager roar and we trickle away in first towards the circuit. Apart from the steering, which is heavy, it's as easy to potter around as a Morris Minor. Even the clutch is fairly effortless to manage and there's nothing harsh about 1 VEV. Out on the circuit, however, the performance is utterly stunning. On our second lap we come up behind a gorgeous new Aston Martin; it is being driven well so I can't imagine what that bloke thinks when we appear alongside, coming out of the tight righthander at Quarry, and release 1 VEV with full throttle in second gear. It takes off with a trace of opposite lock and wheelspin. There is just no contest. We have gone. On the longer straights, it fairly leaps ahead and the acceleration above 120mph is still very strong.

It's set up for the road at present, so the damping is a bit soft, calling for care in the fastest bends. It could get out of hand quite easily at speed but, aimed accurately, it is very stable, it likes a bit of sideways style and I am surprised at how well the Vredestein tyres hold on. The brakes are suffering from mild pad knock-off, needing an occasional bit of left-foot encouragement on the straights, but that's normal enough with new brakes and it's easily corrected. Even if the 250GTOs did beat this beautiful Aston on the circuits, I think 1 VEV would win hands down for road-driving pleasure. As Ian Moss said, this Aston Martin was basically a road car.

Back in 1962, *Autocar* magazine was allowed to road test a new DB4GT Zagato, an extraordinary privilege when you think that only 19 were made and the price new was £5470. Admittedly, an equivalent Ferrari cost even more then, but the price of a contemporary Jaguar E-type – just over two grand –

puts it into perspective. Several final drive ratios were available, that test car being fitted with a middle-of-the-range 3.31:1 cwp giving a rev-limited top speed of 153mph at 6050rpm on Dunlop R5 tyres – they gave 25.3mph per 1000rpm in top. The *Autocar* testers, renowned for their accuracy, recorded 0-60mph in 6.1 seconds and went on to a remarkable 0-140mph in 32.2 seconds.

Today 1 VEV is quicker than that. Its power is well above 1961's claimed 314bhp and the torque figure is now 348lb ft. With its Vredestein tyres and 3.06:1 final drive it does 27.3mph / 1000rpm and that equates to 165mph at the same 6050rpm. It would pull that easily. Richard says with the right back axle it'd do 180mph and I'm sure he's right. Match it against modern machinery and only the most outrageous supercars would see it off.

If this story serves to remind us of anything, it is this: owners of such fantastic cars usually tend to treat them appropriately. But in the late 1960s 1 VEV was nothing more than a used motor with very little value. As a former race machine, apparently of no great distinction then, it surely made an unusual road car with exceptional looks and performance, but no doubt it threatened to drop further in value while costing a small fortune to run.

For those who could afford it, 1 VEV provided entertaining motoring for a series of owners, one using it as a roadgoing hack for years. Perhaps the radio was fitted around that time. All of

Below
No belts – and no radio: 1 VEV has been restored to authentic period 1961 condition.

'Even if GTOs did beat this Aston on the circuits, I think 1 VEV would win hands down on the road for sheer driving pleasure'

**1961
Aston Martin
DB4GT
Zagato
'1 VEV'**

SPECIFICATIONS

Engine
3670cc straight-six, twin overhead cams, dual ignition, three twin-choke horizontal Weber 45 DCOE4 carbs, 9.7:1 CR

Power
314bhp @ 6000rpm claimed originally; 270bhp more realistic then (see text)

Torque
278lb ft @ 5400rpm claimed originally (see text)

Transmission
Four-speed manual all-synchro box; hypoid bevel final drive with 3.06:1 cwp (see text); Powr-lok lsd

Suspension
Front: independent by wishbones, coil springs, Armstrong telescopic dampers, anti-roll bar. Rear: live axle, parallel trailing links, Watt's linkage, coils, Armstrong tele dampers (in race spec, teles replaced standard lever-arms)

Brakes
Girling discs all round, separate master cylinders, no servo

Performance
0-60mph 6.1sec (1962 *Autocar* test) Top speed c180mph (see text)

Weight
1229kg (2709lb)

its owners appreciated what it represented, all the way down the line, but it wasn't taken as seriously as it is today.

Nobody guessed then that it might appreciate in value. Roy Salvadori told me that during the 1960s he had an Aston Martin DBR1 which he advertised in the right magazines for a year before anybody was prepared to buy it. He was relieved to get £1100 for it in the end. Today, 40 years on, if the whispers we hear are true, a DBR1 is worth about 9000 times that much – and 1 VEV is coming up fast.

Back in 1990, 1 VEV had just been restored and William Loughran paid £1.54m for it at auction. He soon sold it on for a small profit. A few months later, as the market collapsed all round the world, 2 VEV was auctioned in Monaco but was withdrawn when the bidding failed to reach £850,000. A year or two later, Loughran bought 1 VEV back and he owned it for 15 years before selling it to Adrian earlier this year.

'They're beautiful,' says Loughran. 'I've had five or six, and a few years ago I had one that had been rebuilt by RS Williams. When the weather was nice after work, I used to take 1 VEV home, just for the pleasure of driving it. It'd seemed great until I drove the car restored by RS Williams and realised that by comparison 1 VEV drove like a bag of spanners. I joined the queue and in due course it went to RS Williams for the works.'

Although 1 VEV had been restored previously, that was 17 years ago and time had taken its toll. Also, restoration standards were then not as high as they are today. A strong point in the car's favour was that it still had all its principal original parts, including the engine, gearbox and back axle.

Once Richard Williams had taken the car in and stripped it down, however, it was clearly in need of a full cosmetic and mechanical rebuild. The latter work was straightforward, but the body was rather more tricky. Not only had it been poorly repaired in the past, meaning that there was a great amount of filler under the paint, but somewhere way back in time it had also lost the correct shape of its rear wings.

It took some time to get that right. Ian Moss was called in as a consultant and William Loughran also inspected the car at crucial stages of the body builder's work. With the aid of photos, plus Zagato's original drawings and dimensions, this aspect of the resto was given the most painstaking attention. As all the DB4GT Zagatos were handbuilt every one is a little different, but finally 1 VEV's correct original shape was brought back into being to the satisfaction of all concerned.

The brief was to restore it as it was in 1961, not as a modern historic race car, even though some concessions were made to later engineering know-how. That's why it has the original low-backed racing buckets but no belts or rollcage. Although Adrian races other cars, the fact is that 1 VEV carries an unusual responsibility because is so stunningly original. What it's really worth now is a private matter, but there's no doubt that it amounts to several millions. More to the point, Adrian is acutely aware that it has never suffered anything approaching a serious shunt. Mainly for that reason, he aims to use 1 VEV only for more gentle events, such as the regularity class in the French Tour Auto. It should be ideal. ◬

Thanks to the St James's Place Wealth Management Group for inviting us to Castle Combe during its track day for existing and potential clients. Two senior partners of St James's Place were kind enough to allow us to test 1 VEV during the day.

ROOS
ENGINEERING LTD
Swiss Quality Workmanship
Since 1975

Roos Engineering Ltd
Murtenstrasse 103
CH-3202 Frauenkappelen
Switzerland

HERITAGE
Official Aston Martin Heritage Specialist

Phone: +41 (0)31 926 11 37
Fax: +41 (0)31 926 18 83
Email: rooseng@bluewin.ch
Web: www.roosengineering.ch

Red-hot Swede

It's the world's only Aston-engined Volvo and if circumstances had been only slightly different, it could have gone into production
Words: Malcolm McKay Photography: Matt Howell

THE MOST EXOTIC Aston Martins – 612bhp Vantage, DB3S, the first DB4GT – pass through Roos Engineering, outside Berne in Switzerland. But which car makes proprietor Beat Roos' eyes gleam with enthusiasm, which one does he choose to drive home at the end of the day?

The answer may surprise you because it's a humble Volvo P1800.

But this is no ordinary P1800. Under the bonnet lurks no cast-iron 1.8-litre Volvo four-cylinder: as the subtle badging explains, this Volvo is powered by Aston Martin. But how?

We've all heard of the Aston Martin Design Project cars – racers Project 212, 214, 215, or the first DB4GT, DP199. Well, lurking in the engine bay of this Volvo P1800 is DP208: a DB4 engine with two fewer cylinders; a 2.5-litre, twin-cam, all-aluminium four-cylinder with twin Weber carburettors that was designed in 1961.

Aston Martin officially retired from sports racing in 1959 and Formula One in 1960, so it had a surfeit of engineers. Sales of DB4s were going steadily, but David Brown and John Wyer

could see that greater turnover was needed to underpin the business – racing emptied the coffers in no time. There was little hope of increasing sales of exclusive, hand-built motor cars and to produce a smaller Aston Martin would cost almost as much, due to the way it was constructed. Selling the six-cylinder engine would be counter-productive, as it would enable other manufacturers to build a DB4 rival, but a 2.5-litre four-cylinder engine, sharing many components such as pistons, rods, valves etc, might appeal to volume producers as a way of adding cachet to their top sporting models. It wouldn't compete with the DB4 yet it would reduce its production costs.

That seems to have been the thinking behind DP208, which was sanctioned with a now-laughable budget of just £3000, on March 9, 1961: 'the design and construction of three two-litre four-cylinder engines to be made as far as possible from the pattern equipment and using as many parts as possible of the existing 3.7-litre six-cylinder engine.'

The original six-cylinder wooden engine

patterns were simply sawn off and shaped to make the casting tools for the four-cylinder. Precious little record remains of the project, but that the engines were made is in no doubt: 'I was in Production at the time,' recalls Arthur Wilson, who became chief engineer for the V8 engine series, 'whereas Experimental was still at Feltham. But I do remember seeing the blocks lined up outside the machine shop. I'm pretty sure there were four of them, though they may only have built up three as complete engines. I think a couple of them may have gone to Australia. The Volvo idea came along later, after the event, but I don't know what the thinking was behind making the engine in the first place. We did wonder if it was a stage towards making a V8; there was already talk of V8s back then.'

Colin Thew (who ended up managing Aston's overseas agents) recalls them too: 'I carted two of the engines back from Feltham when it closed in 1964. They sat in an outside parts store for years. I also spoke to the man who'd fitted the engine in the original Volvo, which he said was supplied new by the UK Volvo concessionaire; a year later the same man took the engine out again, so probably they put the Volvo engine back in the car before selling it. He left Aston Martin in 1963.'

Rumour has it that the engine was also tried in a Frogeye Sprite, but that's absurd – it was far too big; in fact a two-cylinder version would have been more appropriate to that car. AMOC Archivist Neil Murray has a better idea: 'I'm pretty sure it would have been a Big Healey, a 100/6 or a 3000. BMC was always casting around for another engine for that car and an Aston engine would've given it real cachet. Tadek Marek had come from Austin, where one of his last jobs was the design of the seven-bearing three-litre used in the 3000.'

No trace of a Big Healey with the Aston engine survives, though there is an enlarged Big Healey with a four-litre Rolls-Royce engine, which lends some support to Neil's theory. Nothing has surfaced in the Aston Martin archives to back up the Austin Healey installation either, but a supplement to the DP208 project sheet announces simply: 'Project to be increased in scope to cover installation in a Volvo P1800 Sports Car.'

Oddly, that sheet is dated July 29, 1965, but this has to be a typographical error: it has to be 1962 or even 1961. P1800 production got under way in spring 1961, with bodies produced by Pressed Steel at Linwood and assembly by Jensen in West Bromwich. It's possible that Volvo had expressed an interest in the engine – it would have added appeal to a car whose Frua-designed bodyshell already looked far more exotic than its badge suggested and it would have saved shipping engines over from Sweden.

'The Aston engine would have
added appeal to a car whose
Frua-designed bodyshell
already looked far more exotic
than its badge suggested'

Below
P1800's four-cylinder
Aston engine is a tight
squeeze, taller than the
Volvo unit. It's also
significantly heavier.

There is no doubt that such a car was built; after testing, the wife of engine designer Tadek Marek used the Volvo as her shopping car for a year. But the engine would have been very expensive to produce and added an unacceptable premium to the price of the Volvo. It was also a massive 30kg heavier than the cast-iron Volvo engine and was significantly taller, requiring too much re-engineering.

Eventually Aston Martin sold the engine to Aston specialist Richard Williams, who sold it to enthusiast Craig Dent. By 1974 Dent had sold it to Robin Hamilton and it subsequently passed to Jaguar specialist Guy Broad before going to ground.

Over in Switzerland, Beat Roos had long been fascinated by the story of this mystery engine and tried hard to find one, without success – until one day, around ten years ago, he received a phone call from a friend in Germany who had been asked by a man in Munich if Aston Martin ever made a four-cylinder engine. Beat immediately arranged a rendezvous and was delighted to find the very same engine that Robin Hamilton had owned in 1974, still with a spare crank and other parts.

'We stripped it down and the engine was near-enough new,' enthuses Beat. 'Both block and head are new castings, not cut-down six-cylinder ones. The bore size is the same as the DB4 and it shares the same liners, pistons, con rods and valves. The cams are new but have the same profile as a DB4. This was clearly the engine that had come out of the Volvo, as it still had a fabricated adaptor to mate up with the Volvo bellhousing: it bolts straight onto the Volvo gearbox.'

Beat's AM Heritage-approved workshops have turned out stunning station wagon conversions on Aston Martin and Lagonda and boast a state-of-the-art engine test bed. He wasn't going to be satisfied with the engine as a static exhibit, he wanted to drive it. Beat went to considerable trouble to find an early, Jensen-bodied, P1800: a lovely example that had been registered new in Switzerland.

Joining the engine to the gearbox wasn't a problem, but fitting the engine in the P1800 bodyshell still took a fair amount of experimental engineering work, as nothing was available from Aston Martin records to indicate how it had been done.

'We had to make a special radiator, mounted further forward,' explains Beat. 'The sump that came with the engine was cobbled together, so we made a new one – it's cut right back at the front to clear the front crossmember, yet the engine still needs a big bulge in the bonnet to clear the cam covers; it's very high. We added an oil cooler and put spacers in the front springs to counteract the extra weight, with Bilstein shock absorbers, though Eibach are now making new springs for us. Clearance for the steering was a »

'The P1800 is a comfortable high-speed cruiser and the Aston engine adds a frisson of excitement making it feel like a true sports car'

big problem, so we converted it to TR4 rack-and-pinion, which is much better than the original.

'The engine puts out 150bhp – at first we were told it had been fitted with a pair of 50DCOE Webers but they would be far too big, so we used 45s. With that power, the standard 4.55:1 rear axle ratio was much too low, so we fitted a 4.1:1; ideally I'd like to go to 3.78:1 to make it really nice. We also improved the braking by fitting a dual-circuit master cylinder from a later Volvo. We used many DB4 parts, as Aston might have done, including the air box and header tank.

'The car is nice on the road now. When I talked to Ted Cutting about it, he said the project was a failure because there was too much vibration at idle – but the cams were the same profile as the six-cylinder, so that was inevitable. He explained that the project originally used SU HD8 carburettors, but there wasn't enough room for them in the Volvo without modifying the inner wings.'

Now it's time for the moment I've been waiting for: to take the Aston-Volvo for a drive.

There's a wonderful, rorty sound as the engine fires up: it's clearly a four-cylinder on Webers, but it still has an Aston Martin quality about it. Beat Roos smiles as he hears the now-familiar growl: 'There's no choke,' he explains, 'but it warms up quickly so it's no problem.'

I scan the gauges nervously, conscious that whatever happens, I mustn't allow this now-unique engine to become damaged. The oil pressure gauge shows a healthy 75psi; so far so good.

With 185/70x15 tyres on Minilite wheels, steering is impossibly heavy when static, but with just a tiny amount of motion it lightens up considerably. The engine is really rather throaty – it's torquey but overfuels at low revs and has a flat spot around 2500rpm. It seems nothing that development of camshaft profiles

Volvo-Aston P1800
SPECIFICATIONS

Engine
2447cc four-cylinder, twin overhead cams, twin Weber 45 DCOE carburettors

Power
150bhp

Transmission
Four-speed manual gearbox with overdrive, rear-wheel drive

Suspension
Front: independent by coil-and-wishbone, telescopic dampers, anti-roll bar. Rear: live axle, coil springs, torque arms, Panhard rod, telescopic dampers

Brakes
Discs front, drums rear. Servo assistance

Performance
0-60mph c9sec
Top speed c120mph

and carburettor jets couldn't cure, though: above 2800rpm it really pulls and when it gets up to 5000 or 5500, it sings.

I stick to a 5500rpm rev limit in deference to the fact that this is a unique and largely untried engine, completely irreplaceable – but it's not rough and uncouth, as has been suggested; it's sporty and exciting. The clutch is on the heavy side but acceptable and the exhaust, which has cleverly been made to mate with the standard Volvo rear box, is quite loud but not unpleasantly so. The P1800 is a comfortable, competent, high-speed cruiser, especially with the optional overdrive as fitted to this car and the Aston engine adds a real frisson of excitement, making it feel like a true sports car.

Could it have succeeded as a top-of-the-range sporty Volvo? Perhaps, if the costs had been pared down, but with production problems dogging the P1800 (bodyshells getting damaged between Linwood and West Bromwich and assembly quality below required standards) Volvo had already decided to move production to Sweden as soon as possible. It was selling all it could make and there seemed little point in offering an alternative engine, which would become even more costly when exported to Sweden. Ironically, had UK P1800 production not been such a disaster, the Aston engine might have been just what Volvo needed to make the car fly, both on the road and out of the showroom. △

Dealing in Bonds

There were actually four James Bond Aston Martin DB5s – but only two of those appeared in the movies. Now, pay attention, 007...

Words: Mark Dixon

Tyre slasher
Extendible tyre slasher was one of the few gadgets that didn't actually work – the engineering would have been too complex.

Extremely low mileage
Living in a museum since 1971 means this Bond car has covered only 18,000 miles from new; it is said to drive very well indeed.

Bulletproof screen
In the original Effects Car, the 'bulletproof' screen was raised hydraulically, but the Show Cars used electric window motors.

Weapons tray
Sorbo-lined tray under the driver's seat wasn't seen in the films; it should house a Mauser automatic pistol, missing from this car.

Facing page
Bond car's interior is broadly similar to a regular DB5's, except that radio is turned 90 degrees to make room for radar screen.

ACCORDING TO POP ARTIST ANDY WARHOL, everyone will be famous for 15 minutes, but even in this celebrity-obsessed age not many people are likely to make their quarter-hour endure for as long as a certain Silver Birch DB5. James Bond's Aston had a total of only 13 minutes of exposure in the films *Goldfinger* and *Thunderball*, yet that tiny sliver of time has now expanded to more than 40 years of stardom.

Its phenomenal impact on popular culture earned the Bond Aston the moniker 'the most famous car in the world' yet in reality the title has to be shared between four examples. Two models were used in the making of the Bond films and another two were constructed for promotional purposes shortly afterwards. None of them had been on the market for 20 years but then, in 2006, this one was auctioned for $2,090,000. Is it a 'real' James Bond Aston Martin? Well, sort of.

When it comes to unravelling the complex history of the four Bond Astons the only reliable source is the definitive book produced by Bond author Dave Worrall in the early 1990s. In 1964, as an 11-year-old schoolboy, Worrall saw the 'real' Bond Aston when it visited Birmingham on a publicity tour, and his interest was rekindled when he read a newspaper article about the sale of the car 20 years later.

The article suggested that perhaps six examples had been used in the filming of *Goldfinger* but said that 'the record is a little fuzzy'. Amazed that no-one seemed to know the truth behind such a screen icon, Worrall spent the next six years interviewing as many people associated with the cars as he could track down. It's thanks to him that we know the story of DB5 body no. DB5/2008/R, the model in our pictures, and the other three Bond Astons.

No. 2008 is one of a pair of Astons that were bought by the Bond film production company, Eon, soon after the making of *Thunderball*, when it became clear from the huge success of *Goldfinger* that it needed more cars to parade around the USA and capitalise on all the hype surrounding James Bond. The other model was DB5/2017/R. Neither of them ever appeared in a 007 movie, but they were kitted out with most of the famous extras, such as the rear-mounted bulletproof screen and the smoke dispenser, to resemble the film vehicles. Worrall refers to 2008 and 2017 as the Show Cars, to differentiate them from the other two DB5s (the Effects Car and the Road Car) used in the films.

Not surprisingly, none of the PR men involved in touting the Show Cars around America worried too much about their true provenance. If the public chose to believe that they were looking at a car touched by the hand of Sean Connery himself, then the marketing men weren't going to disillusion them. Department store Sears, which obtained one of the Show Cars for a three-month tour, transported the DB5 in a truck that was provocatively signwritten 'You're trailing an actual James Bond 007 Aston Martin automobile – see it at Sears!' The word 'actual' is used rather loosely in this context...

Given the way that the press was lapping up anything to do with Bond at the time, you can forgive Sears spokesman Bruce Chamberlain for pretending that the DB5 was originally fitted with a spigot for dispensing beer chilled by a refrigerated tank in the boot – he clearly wasn't aware that Englishmen prefer their beer served warm.

To be fair, the Show Cars were convincing replicas, and contemporary ones of that, of the brace of Astons used in the films. Sadly, the car with the best claim to be the 'real' Bondmobile, DP/216/1, has disappeared. It was reportedly stolen from a warehouse in Florida in the 1990s and never

'SADLY, THE CAR WITH THE BEST CLAIM TO BE THE "REAL" BONDMOBILE HAS DISAPPEARED WITHOUT TRACE'

'Light' machine guns
Mixture of acetylene and oxygen, ignited by a spark plug connected to a car distributor, makes the twin Brownings appear to fire.

Revolving plates
Show Cars had the famous revolving number plates; JB 007 is fictitious, YRE 186H may date from Bamford's 1969-71 ownership.

recovered, as a result of which its insurer – doubtless with considerable reluctance – paid out over $4,000,000.

The loss of DP/216/1 is a shame because this was the car originally fitted with all of 'Q's little extras for *Goldfinger*. Known by the film crew as the Effects Car, it was registered from new with the famous BMT 216A number that appears in the Bond films. What's more, it was the prototype DB5 (hence the DP chassis number) and had been road tested by *Autocar* in 1963, as well as appearing in Aston Martin's advertising of the time. It was originally painted Dubonnet Red and was resprayed Silver Birch only after Pinewood's craftsmen had added all the Bond extras, which, of course, involved cutting open the roof to install the ejector seat hatch.

So what exactly was the 'special equipment' not available to an ordinary Newport Pagnell punter? The feature that everyone remembers is the ejecting passenger seat. Operated by a button concealed in the top of the gearknob, it flings out a hapless Chinese guard as Bond is being escorted into Auric Goldfinger's Swiss factory complex in the eponymous film. In reality, the guard was a mannequin, the seat was a lightweight shell ejected by compressed air and the Swiss factory was the exterior of the sound stages at Pinewood.

Oddly, considering that most of the DB5's screen time in *Goldfinger* is set in Switzerland, Bond never uses one of the gadgets demonstrated to him by 'Q' earlier in the film: the revolving numberplates that give a choice of British, French or Swiss registrations. In fact, quite a number of features built into the car never appear on film. They include a weapons tray under the driver's seat, containing a folding Armalite rifle, Mauser pistol with silencer, hand grenade and throwing knife (beat that, you Jag owners with your little tool trays); extending over-riders front and rear that could be used as battering

'THE CAR ORIGINALLY FITTED WITH ALL OF Q'S LITTLE EXTRAS WAS THE PROTOTYPE DB5'

rams; and a pipe concealed behind the offside rear light cluster that dispensed four-pronged nails called caltrops. Apparently it was decided the idea of strewing nails over a road might be just too tempting for urchins who had seen the film...

Other desirable extras that never made it into the final cut were a radar scanner contained within the offside wing mirror and a radio telephone built into the driver's door card.

Even so, the list of additions that do appear in *Goldfinger* is a long one. At the front end, twin machine-guns emerge from behind the sidelight lenses. At the back, Bond uses an oil-spray dispensed from behind the rear nearside light cluster in an (ultimately doomed) attempt to throw off Goldfinger's goons, along with a smokescreen that is projected from under the back of the car. The bootlid houses a contoured bulletproof shield that can be raised to protect the rear 'screen and the offside back wheel spinner doubles as a tyre slasher. Unashamedly lifted as a concept from the film Ben Hur, this rotating tin-opener is the undoing of Tilly Masterson's Ford Mustang convertible in *Goldfinger*, as both cars race along the approach to Switzerland's Furka Pass.

In reality 'Q's gadgets were the products of some brilliant Heath Robinson-esque invention on the part of the special-effects men. The revolving numberplates, for example, relied on a spring-loaded mechanism operated by Bowden cables from the centre console (on the Show Cars they were electrically operated). The oil spray was actually mixed from water and vegetable dye, and propelled by compressed nitrogen released by an electromagnetic valve. The bulletproof screen was made from duralumin for lightness, and raised by a hydraulic system hidden in the boot. Only the ejector seat and the extendible tyre slasher were not permanent, fully functional fittings, for reasons of safety and, of course, budget.

Below right
Anthony Bamford bought not one but two genuine Bond Astons in 1969, the pair of Show Cars nos. 2008 and 2017.

Centre console
Chromed switch is for bulletproof screen; three-position knob for 'plates; toggle for guns; push buttons for rams and dispensers.

Oil dispenser
Nearside rear light (lens removed for photo) conceals tube for spraying oil; on the film cars the whole cluster pivots as one.

DB5 badge
First of the Bond Astons, the Effects Car, was a prototype DB5; all
subsequent Bond cars started life as regular production models.

Chassis plate
Chassis plate – more accurately, body number plate – displays
identity DB5/2008/R; the other Show Car was DB5/2017/R.

The cost of devising and making all these gizmos for
BMT 216A was estimated to have been £25,000 – more than five
times the price of a new DB5 – but when filming was over,
Aston Martin stripped them all out and rebuilt the car as a
standard DB5. It was perfectly entitled to do this, since the
model had only been loaned to the film makers, but the
decision seems incredibly short-sighted given the amount of
publicity the Bond films were generating. The rebuilt Effects
Car was sold to an unwitting customer, Gavin Keyzar, as a
regular DB5 with the registration 6633 PP in August 1968 –
Aston having transferred the famous BMT 216A number to
one of the Show Cars, no. 2017, in case it was needed again.

Aston Martin had always been slightly offhand about its
association with the Bond franchise, however. The connection
with the original Ian Fleming novels was tenuous, since
while Fleming had Bond borrow a battleship-grey Secret
Service 'pool car' DB MkIII in *Goldfinger*, Bond's own car
was a Bentley – supercharged 4-litre in the early books,
Continental Mk2 in the later ones. These big machines were
too cumbersome for the film makers to contemplate, but the
newly introduced DB5 was ideal for their interpretation of a
1960s Bond; the trouble was that Aston, going through one of
its perennial financial crises, was unwilling to provide a car
free of charge, and the bean-counters at the studio wouldn't
countenance actually buying one. Only after intensive
lobbying by special effects man John Stears did Aston relent
and agree to loan out BMT 216A which, after all, had already
been put through the mill as a development car.

By the late 1960s the value of the Bond DB5s to Aston
Martin's international image had been proven again and
again, yet Aston was still apparently oblivious to the mobile
goldmines it had stashed away in the works. In 1969 it sold

the brace of Show Cars, 2008 and 2017, for a mere £1500 to Anthony (now Sir Anthony) Bamford of JCB excavator fame. If that was a bargain, then Sir Anthony was doubly lucky when a Mr Kenneth Luscombe-Whyte offered to swap one for a Ferrari 250GTO! Realising that a GTO for £750 was quite a good deal, even in 1969, Sir Anthony accepted the offer and traded the Show Car 2017. He still has the GTO today.

Luscombe-Whyte kept 2017 for only a few months before selling it on, and after a long spell as a curiosity at a Canadian restaurant it ended up at its present resting place in the Dutch National Motor Museum. Luscombe-Whyte had some fun with the car during his short tenure, however: he'd occasionally park it in central London, wait until a traffic warden had made a note of the number, then operate the revolving number plates when the warden was out of sight and hide until the warden returned to find an apparently identical Aston Martin with a different registration in the same spot!

Sir Anthony Bamford held onto his other Bond car, 2008, for a couple more years before selling it in 1971 for £5000 to Bruce Atchley's Smoky Mountain Car Museum in Tennessee. And until its RM sale, it had been there ever since, ensuring its survival in a remarkable state of preservation. At the time of the auction (and of writing), the total mileage was still only 18,000 and the car wore its original paint, albeit with a few minor scars and blisters. Most of the 'extras' such as the extending over-riders and bulletproof screen were in working order, although the oil sprayer and smokescreen layer had not been tried out. The final price was an indisputable reflection of what must simply be the ultimate 'big boy's toy'!

And what of the fourth Bond car? It still exists and has been in the care of one American owner, Jerry Lee, since 1969. This DB5, no. 1486, was driven by Sean Connery in both *Goldfinger* and *Thunderball*, but originally had none of the

Radar tracker
In a pre-GPS age, the special effects crew couldn't make the radar work, and a paper map was pasted behind a ground-glass screen.

Bamford's brace
Show Car 2008 is on left of this c1970 photo, taken on the Bamford estate; note the dented rear bumper, still evident today.

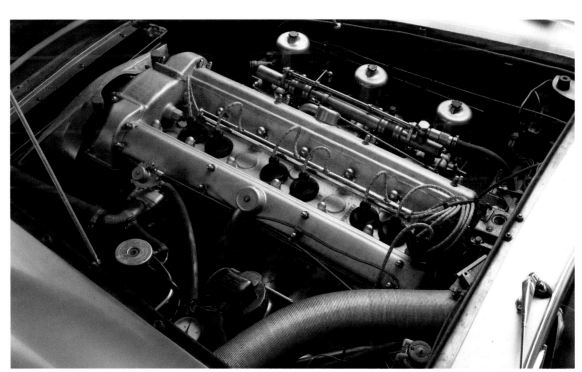

Wing mirror radar
Another gadget that didn't make it onto film, the radar scanner
built into the offside mirror rotated courtesy of an electric motor.

Mobile telephone
No miniaturisation here: Bond's car 'phone has full-size receiver
– if necessary, he could doubtless have used it to cudgel a villain.

gadgets fitted to its sister car. It was intended as a stand-in for
scenes considered too risky to use the Effects Car and was
referred to as the Road Car, since it was the first choice for
action shots. The Road Car was registered as FMP 7B but, of
course, dummied-up as BMT 216A for filming.

Generally, the Effects Car was brought in for close-ups or
shots where the gadgets were being deployed – but the Road
Car gets its own moment in the spotlight in the pre-title
sequence of *Thunderball*, where Bond escapes from a French
château by means of personal jet-pack (of course) and has to
stow it quickly in the boot of his DB5. If he'd been using the
Effects Car, he would have had a slight problem trying to
stuff his jet-pack into the space occupied by a large,
retractable, bulletproof screen...

Shortly after this, the Road Car was equipped with the same
extras fitted to the Effects Car, which was retired from film
use and moved onto the promotional circuit. Now that the
Effects Car is missing, presumably dumped or scrapped, Jerry
Lee's DB5 is undoubtedly the World's Most Valuable Bond Car.

As for the other mechanical co-stars from *Goldfinger*, the
1937 Rolls-Royce Phantom III driven by Oddjob was auctioned
along with the DB5 Effects Car by Sothebys in 1986. But does
anyone know what happened to the white Mustang driven
by Tilly Masterson (actress Tania Mallet)? It was brought into
the UK for a publicity shoot but was never seen again. Is it still
out there, another 'Bond car' waiting to be discovered?

Thanks to RM Auctions (+1 800 211 4371, www.rmauctions.
com) and Dave Worrall, whose book The Most Famous Car in the
World can be ordered from www.bondbooks.biz.

'BOND WOULD
HAVE HAD A
PROBLEM TRYING
TO STUFF HIS JET-
PACK INTO THE
SPACE OCCUPIED
BY A RETRACTABLE
BULLETPROOF
SCREEN'

Aston Martin are rare cars. We deal in the rare Aston Martins.....
Not available in all stores: Zagato Vanquish Roadster. Drive it home now.

ASTON MARTIN OF NEW ENGLAND

Aston Martin of New England / Lotus Motorsports, Inc. 85 Linden Street, Waltham, MA 02452 1-781-547-5959 astonmartin-lotus.com

RICHARD STEWART WILLIAMS LTD

SHOWROOM
Visitors are always welcome to our facilities in Cobham, just off the M25 and A3 where we have a selection of the very finest models presented in exquisite condition, all with our 12 month parts and labour guarantee.

PARTS DEPARTMENT
With over one million pounds worth of stock, our parts department holds massive quantities of Genuine Aston Martin Parts for cars built from 1959 to the present day.

WORKSHOPS
We have several workshops, each specialising in Aston Martin care including; servicing, mechanical rebuild & enhancements, restoration, electrical and race preparation.

MACHINE SHOP
We have a fully equipped machine shop offering state-of-the-art technology, engineering excellence and exceptional facilities including CNC machining and engine dynamometer.

Richard Stewart Williams Ltd
Protech House, Copse Road, Cobham, Surrey KT11 2TW
(M25 - Junction 10)
Tel: 01932 868377 **Fax:** 01932 865515
Parts Department Fax: 01932 866513
Email: astons@rswilliams.co.uk
Website: www.rswilliams.co.uk

R. S. Williams Ltd have long been established as The Aston Martin Specialists, not only for race preparation, engine development and restoration work, but our engineering excellence is widely acclaimed by owners of DB4, DB5, DB6 DBS, V8, Virage, Vantage, and many more Aston Martin models.

HERITAGE

Octane | 99
ASTON MARTIN

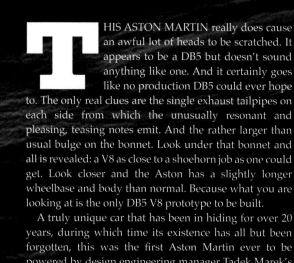

THIS ASTON MARTIN really does cause an awful lot of heads to be scratched. It appears to be a DB5 but doesn't sound anything like one. And it certainly goes like no production DB5 could ever hope to. The only real clues are the single exhaust tailpipes on each side from which the unusually resonant and pleasing, teasing notes emit. And the rather larger than usual bulge on the bonnet. Look under that bonnet and all is revealed: a V8 as close to a shoehorn job as one could get. Look closer and the Aston has a slightly longer wheelbase and body than normal. Because what you are looking at is the only DB5 V8 prototype to be built.

A truly unique car that has been in hiding for over 20 years, during which time its existence has all but been forgotten, this was the first Aston Martin ever to be powered by design engineering manager Tadek Marek's excellent V8 engine.

Chassis 001/D/P, registered NPP 7D, was used as a mobile test bed to develop the all-alloy, four-camshaft motor for almost four years, together with the de Dion ≫

Aston Martin's first V8

**Hidden for over 20 years, Aston's unique
V8 development car, based around a DB5,
has now finally been completed**
Words: Paul Chudecki Photography: Paul Harmer

rear axle which would first see service in the DBS and then DBS V8, covering thousands of miles in Britain and Europe.

Marek's V8 was to play a major role in continuing the success of Aston Martin under David Brown's tenure in the post-war years. Although plans to produce the engine went back to the late 1950s it was 1963 before he began work on the V8. The brief was to produce a low-stress, high-performance engine for Aston models well into the future and some of the development work would take place on the race track.

John Surtees, who two years before had become the only man to win the world championship on four as well as two wheels, struck a deal in 1966 to run the engine in works Lola T70s in the following year's World Sportscar Championship.

The first V8 had run on the test-bench on July 29 1965, and eight months later it was producing 329bhp at 6200rpm from 4806cc. The time had come to put it on the road and the mysterious Experimental/R&D Department at Aston Martin, was charged with creating a mule.

By then, early in 1966, the DB5 had been superseded by the DB6, its 33in longer chassis designed to make the car a proper four seater. This allowed room to fit the de Dion rear axle planned for the DBS, and so a DB6 chassis was chosen as the basis for the V8 mule. Bill Bannard was one of the original staff in Experimental. 'NPP 7D was built specifically to put the V8 in and to go and run it,' recalls 66-year-old Bill.

'We took a standard frame and dickered around with it and took out what we felt would be in the way for getting the V8 in. It was a hell of a lot to get on with and they wanted it yesterday.

There was quite a bit done at the rear because the first de Dion went into that car and it was always on telescopic dampers at the rear. The frame was quite different: if you put two side by side you wouldn't shout about it, but the shock absorber mountings are behind the axle and not in front. We didn't know how the car would be, we were doing it from scratch. And we didn't want it attracting any attention.

'The body was a standard DB5 adapted. It was off the shelf metal with whatever was standard, and what was not was fabricated. The front end was certainly DB5 and the rear wings and boot, but it was longer behind the doors.' And being a development mule, the car's cosmetic appearance wasn't a priority: 'It was dark blue but it never got a second customer coating,' continues Bill. 'It wasn't finessed, it was definitely a little bit rough. It had black leather inside. I don't think it had carpets but wherever a standard bit would fit, it was fitted. It had a fibreglass gearbox cover and was never soundproofed.

'The dashboard was standard DB5 but I'm fairly certain it didn't have a proper heater. It had a heated front screen and the element worked both sides, a super bit of kit, though it was replaced because it cracked. We probably got the screen because we knew we might need the heater space. The flap [below the windscreen and later welded shut] was just a scoop to get air in. It ran well. I have a feeling we didn't use the bonnet bulge to feed air, we took that from the back of the engine bay.'

Although the purpose of this Aston hybrid was to develop the V8, work started with just the basics. 'We started with any engine castings that were not any good, using these bits and

Right
Interior was rough in prototype days; now beautifully trimmed in Connolly hide, with sat-nav screen too.

'The brief was to provide a low-stress, high-performance engine for Aston Martin models well into the future'

'The biggest headache proved to be controlling the under-bonnet temperatures, something not encountered in the much lighter traffic conditions of the 1960s'

pieces to mock it up,' says Bill. 'We were always going to have an engine tomorrow. They were having terrible problems with the rods, which were breaking. The first engine was a 4.8, then it went up to 5.4 because it had to be attractive to Americans and we wanted it as big as it could be. The decision was taken that it would go on and into the DBS. It was quite a compact engine and it went in the car and ran without any problems.

'The running gear was all DB6. I think there were one or two extra rows on the radiator and oil coolers, which we were opening up and trying to get better flow. The scoop started off as standard but we did a lot of development. It was a nightmare making up the exhaust manifolds, it was completely cut and shut. The wishbones were one of the real challenges, and the upper ends may have been one-offs. We just had to get the manifolds where we could bloody well get them!

'I remember cutting 3/8th of an inch off the steering box just so we could get the exhaust ports lower. The idea was to get it to run and run reasonably reliably and it more or less did that. It had painted wire wheels, not chrome, because they snap spokes more easily, Dunlop 15in and I suppose 6J width. It was producing somewhere in the low 300s, probably about 340bhp, but in the car with those manifolds I should think about 300.'

One of the jobs Bill had to do was help clock up as many test miles in the car as possible: 'I was doing some of the running: George Evans, the engine man, then Tadek and then me, and as near as possible we did 400 miles a day just blasting around the countryside. I did force the odd grin. It got away very well on those skinny tyres and ran out of puff in the 140s, because

we never really developed the intake system.

'It was exciting but it wasn't very stable with air getting under the front and you didn't feel in total control. It was a typical torquey motor, you didn't have to banshee it. I think a very good six would have stayed with it but the eight did it in a nice, easy manner. We did change the IDAs with 45 DCOEs with crossover manifolds and for the final running phases we went onto Brico fuel injection; it was ten years in front of Bosch and worked. It got the bonnet bulge just to get the IDAs in and was cobbled up as required, and it got Bosch injection in February 1968.

'We used a standard five-speed ZF 'box and the hypoid axle came from a dump truck. And we used great big, plunger type driveshafts and the de Dion tube all welded up, but it broke on more than one occasion. I think the first time was when Tadek went for his haircut at Woburn Sands. He got over-excited over a level crossing and ended up with the wheels in the wheelarches! The de Dion was a pig to get in and out and when we were having it checked, in went a live axle; Tadek had one made so it would slot into the car. Christ, it was exciting to drive like that! In the end the welded structure went away and we used a tube; you could put that under a 10 ton lorry and it would be fine.'

After almost four years and 66,636 recorded miles of hard use, NPP 7D was officially 'scrapped' on January 29 1969 and its V8 engine and de Dion axle removed. It had served its purpose which, together with development of the 5-litre version in the Lola-Astons, resulted in a bulletproof V8 for production. Subsequently, fitted with a six-cylinder engine and live rear axle, the car found its way to the late Vic Bass, a London Aston specialist, who was probably the prototype's first owner after the factory.

Vic then sold the car to a man in Plymouth who apparently never used it before selling it to dentist and well-known Aston racing exponent David Preece. 'I was talking to this bloke and said I'd like to build a DB4 or DB5 with a V8 engine,' recalls David, 'and he said he'd got the prototype that had the V8 engine. About three years later, about 1978/'79, he rang me and I paid about £6000. It was bolted together well enough. I knew Bill Bannard, and he gave me much-appreciated advice.'

Preece found and fitted the original de Dion axle and installed a 5.3-litre V8 with later, dogleg first, rather than the original dogleg fifth, five speed ZF 'box. 'I had an original 5-litre prototype engine,' he explains, 'but I understood it was not reliable and had a 5.3 anyway.' He also removed the wire wheels, the spokes of which were prone to breaking: 'Because of the performance and power I decided to stick it on V8 ventilated discs and alloy wheels. It went like holy shit. The fastest I ever did was about 145mph. It was incredible, really. I did the Birkett 6 Hours at Silverstone in it and it was certainly keeping up with the racing DB4s, then the servos stuck on; we had never sorted it, it was on road tyres, it wasn't stiffened or anything, it was totally as it would be on the road! I used it for 20 years off and on and only did 2000 miles maximum. I wish I hadn't sold it now.'

It was from Preece that renowned Aston specialist Richard Williams bought NPP 7D in 1999 and, once a buyer had been

Aston Martin DB5 V8

SPECIFICATIONS

Engine
All alloy V8, 5340cc, four overhead camshafts, two valves per cylinder, four downdraught twin-choke Weber 42 DCNF carbs

Power
352bhp @ 5000rpm
402lb ft @ 3500rpm

Transmission
5-speed ZF gearbox, limited-slip differential

Suspension
All independent via double wishbones at front with anti-roll bar, de Dion axle at rear with Watt linkage and radius arms. Coil springs, telescopic dampers all round

Brakes
Girling solid discs all round, twin servo

Weight
1800lb (817kg)

Performance
0-60mph 5.0sec (est); top speed 175+mph (est) Quarter mile: 14.3 secs.

Value
Around £500,000

found, a full restoration ensued over the next three years. The biggest headache, however, proved to be controlling under-bonnet temperatures, something not encountered in the much lighter traffic conditions of the 1960s.

'The owner said he must be able to use it daily,' explains Richard, 'to be able to sit in London traffic and go out to dinner.' And it was extremely difficult controlling the oil and water temperatures, you have all that heat and the only escape route is the two side vents. We fabricated in-house as a big a radiator as we could get in and had it replicated in aluminium, and then worked on getting cold air rather than red hot air under the bonnet. And obviously we put the problem to bed, which is wonderful. Early road tests also revealed unacceptably high gearbox temperatures and now the 'box has ducting.'

The confined under-bonnet space also created major problems optimising engine performance: 'We balanced and rebuilt the engine as normal, and it was desperately disappointing in its performance because it couldn't breathe. Then we started taking emission samples to see what was going on and found the engine couldn't suck air in and struggled to get it out. The exhaust is a straightforward copy of what came with it but you can see where you run out of room, and the top of the carburettors – standard V8 42 DCNF Webers – almost touch the bonnet.

'We had the engine in and out and on the dyno three times. We altered the valve timing but it was still disappointing. Then, with more dyno work and optimising the heads there was a significant improvement to take it to where it's at now. The advance curve was altered to optimise

'Make no mistake, this Aston DB5V8 prototype really is a superb machine and a unique and important part of Aston Martin's history.
At the time, though, no-one perceived it as such'

the breathing but otherwise it's bog standard V8. Finally we got a huge and impressive torque curve with peak torque of 402lb ft at 3500rpm, and 352bhp at 5000rpm. There was a huge amount of pain to control the oil and water temperatures, a huge amount.' Now, in static London traffic, the water never rises above 68 degrees.

One of the great things about this Aston is its Q-car nature. In fact, as I drove past it on arrival at RS Williams, I didn't give it a second glance. And, like so many DB4s and 5s, it now runs without bumpers, enhancing the beauty of the Touring styling. Inside, there is little different to a normal DB5, bar the gearlever of the later ZF 'box. But the engine is what this car is all about.

It will pull cleanly from 1000rpm in fifth allied to effortless acceleration which, on paper at least, should carry on to a top speed of approaching 200mph at 6200rpm thanks to a 3.02:1 diff' ratio; around 1250rpm in fifth equals 40mph while at 140mph – when the Aston is very stable – the revs are a leisurely 4375. And that torque curve really is flat: at 2000rpm it produces 323lb ft, at 3000 372, at 4000 393 and at 5000 368, while at 5500 there's still a hefty 315lb ft available.

The ZF handles it all well, as does the clutch – developed for RSW's 7-litre conversion – although the second to third synchro can baulk when making fast changes. But such is the torque and power that fast changes are not really necessary. The standard DBS non-ventilated brakes, ducted front and rear and with uprated, larger servos, cope well with the performance.

The steering via 205/70 Pirelli P4000s – on 16in rather than 15in wire wheels, the extra inch chosen for the strength of the spokes – is comfortably weighted on the move with plenty of feedback, and turn-in is swift and accurate. It changes direction with greater alacrity than a DB6, though on undulating fast B-roads there is a tendency to track cambers and ridges.

On the track, rear end grip is very high and breaking the tail is not as easy as one might think given the skip-load of torque. Pushing the Aston to the limits of adhesion, it feeels a little skittish at the rear with lift-off oversteer almost instantaneous and you have to catch it quickly. But on the road the DB5 V8 handles and holds the road extremely well. RSW's attention to steering geometry and spring and damper rates has clearly paid off.

And all the while that V8 emits a fabulous roar urging you to constantly exploit the throttle and acceleration: a constant surge, supremely effortless in any gear and at any speed, that will match just about anything one is likely to come across. You just want to drive it. A guess would put the 0-100mph time at about 12 seconds. There is, though, a cost: I averaged just 8.17mpg over 300-odd miles, but that did include the test track. An acceptable 15mpg is the usual average.

Make no mistake, this Aston DB5 V8 prototype really is a superb machine and a unique and important part of Aston Martin's history. At the time, of course, no one perceived it as such. 'I don't think anybody ever did,' adds Bill Bannard. 'It was made to be anonymous, it was never required to do anything other than rack up the miles and provide product information. I liked it, but in R&D you don't look back, you only look forward.' △

Thanks to Bill Ballard, David Preece and RS Williams (01932 868377, www.rswilliams.co.uk).

THE ROAD CURVES SLIGHTLY UPHILL, and for once the planners have had the grace to put in an overtaking lane. It's only a short stretch but the driver of the DB6 doesn't hesitate. Indicator on, foot down, and the sparkling blue-and-chrome missile shoots out and past the slower cars before their drivers have realised where the roar of a twin-cam straight-six at 4000rpm is coming from.

The red DBS that's been following close behind picks up the cue. With a brassy snarl from its howitzer-sized back boxes, it squats closer to the tarmac and launches up the slope with equal gusto. The DB6 is racing up the hill but it's not getting away, and seconds later both cars have left the Euroboxes behind in a faint haze of spent hydrocarbons.

In theory that shouldn't have been possible. Popular wisdom says there's no way a lardy, overweight and underpowered DBS can keep up with the ultimate incarnation of the original DB series, the DB6 MkII. That's why, the bar-room pundits will tell you, a DBS is worth only half the price of a DB6. The DBS was always supposed to have a V8, so the carry-over straight-six with which it was »

ASTON MARTIN
PRIDE AND PREJUDICE

You'd pay twice as much for an Aston Martin DB6 as you would for a DBS – but why? It's time a few bar-room myths were laid to rest
Words: Mark Dixon Photography: Charlie Magee

Facing page
DBS's massive girth – it's six inches wider than a DB6 – emphasises its shark-like leer.

Below
DB6 is effectively a two-plus-two version of the DB5 but manages to disguise the fact well.

introduced was never up to the job. The DBS is not really a proper Aston.

I've never subscribed to this theory and now, it seems, other people are coming to the same conclusion about the DBS. For years it's languished at the bottom of the Aston Martin hierarchy, just about the only Aston that an ordinary working man (or a journalist) could actually aspire to buy. Even now, running cars – especially the universally derided automatics – can be picked up for £10,000 or less. That's changing, though, as more people have the courage to make their own minds up about what is and isn't a desirable Aston.

The decision is easier if you insist on having the triple-Weber DBS Vantage, which is more powerful than the SU-equipped DBS yet was a no-cost option when the cars were new. Both our cars are to Vantage spec, although their individual circumstances are rather different. The concours-standard DB6 is fresh from a make-over by The Aston Workshop, while the well-used DBS

belongs to one of its customers.

So why didn't we choose an equally pristine DBS to pit against the '6? Well, totally restored cars all too often don't drive as well as they look, yet this red DBS is its owner's only transport, so he has been willing to spend the money on keeping it in top mechanical condition. It's also true that there aren't many top-notch DBSs around, as they've never been worth enough to justify full restos. That's another reason why the DBS's reputation isn't a great one: many of the cars out there are simply dogs.

You can only take the DBS justification so far, though, because when all's said and done the DB6 is the car with the looks. It may not have the DB4's classical proportions – its wheelbase was stretched by four inches to provide more rear room – but, unlike the E-type 2+2, the DB6 hardly suffered as a result. You can argue the aesthetic merits of the raised-lip Kamm tail but, either way, it has little impact on the DB6's louche lines.

No, the DB6 will always have more

showroom appeal. It's just as sexy inside, too, though the painted-metal facia and tall, broad-shouldered instrument panel have a 1950s Italianate GT look that must have seemed anachronistic when this Mark 2 was built in 1970. The whole feel of the cabin is very '50s, in fact, from the big three-spoke steering wheel to the short, stubby gearlever that would look more at home in a 1500cc MGA.

Turn the key – no '50s-style push-button start, at least – and the 4-litre straight-six fires immediately, with a woofle that's surprisingly civilised for such a macho piece of kit. Into first, and within yards any misgivings that the '6 will be a brute to handle at low speeds have been dispelled: power-assisted steering and a wood-rim wheel that's warm to the first touch turn slow manoeuvring into a sensual pleasure.

Turn onto the road and there's an immediate reality check, as the ZF manual 'box reminds you that its oil is still cold and it has no great enthusiasm for shifts. If the DB6 has one perverse flaw, it's the ⟫

'Why didn't we choose a pristine DBS to pit against the DB6? Because this DBS is its owner's only transport, so he's been willing to spend the money on keeping it in top mechanical condition'

'This DB6 is one of 46 that were originally fitted with AE Brico fuel injection, but today's buyers like to see three socking great carbs when they open a DB bonnet, so the car has been converted to Vantage specification'

DB6 Mark 2 Vantage

SPECIFICATIONS

Engine
3995cc straight-six with twin overhead camshafts and triple Weber 45 carburettors

Power
275bhp (estimated) @ 5750rpm

Torque
290lb ft @ 4500rpm

Transmission
Five-speed ZF manual, rear-wheel drive

Suspension
Front: independent, coil and wishbone, telescopic dampers
Rear: live axle, trailing arms, Watt's linkage, lever-arm dampers

Brakes
Girling discs front /rear

Weight
3302lb (1498kg)

Performance
0-60mph 6.5sec
Top speed 148mph

puny dimensions of its gearstick. This delicate little device may be in keeping with the sports-racer nature of, say, a DB4, but in a grand tourer like the DB6 it seems bizarrely inappropriate.

Once you're sure you've selected the right ratio, however, you can make suitably impressive progress. It takes a while for the big motor to warm through (there's an oil temperature gauge on the right of the dash, so you've no excuse for jumping the gun), but the three 45mm Webers pull cleanly from low down in the rev range, so restraint is no hardship. In fact, this DB6 is one of 46 that were originally fitted with AE Brico fuel injection, an option on the MkII, but today's buyers like to see three socking great carbs when they open a DB bonnet, so the car was converted to Vantage spec during its restoration.

Even when hot, such a newly minted example of chief designer Tadek Marek's classic straight-six deserves more respect than to be thrashed, and fortunately there is no need. Thanks to the 4-litre motor's ample torque – in his previous job at Austin, Marek had worked on battle tank engines, among other projects – upshifts at 4500rpm are quite adequate,

by which point the exhaust note has evolved into a stirring if understated yowl, bulked out by the subtle white noise of transmission whine. It's an aristocratic noise but it's not intrusive, and the DB6's GT credentials are never in any danger of being compromised.

This GT character is emphasised by the car's sheer heft, which is impossible to forget on the winding B-roads that criss-cross the moors just 20 minutes from The Aston Workshop's premises in Beamish, County Durham. It's easy to nail the throttle on a long straight – just watch out for those sheep – but you need to be prepared for the sudden changes in course that invariably lurk just the other side of blind crests. There is, after all, a live axle doing all the work at the back of the car, and it has a tough job staying glued to the tarmac when 1500kg of Aston need pointing in another direction at short notice.

Power through a tight corner and you can feel that Kamm tail lurch briefly into roll oversteer before it settles back onto an even keel; given space, it might be quite entertaining to pretend you're Moss or Salvadori and have a go at a four-wheel drift, but the weekday tourists

pottering the other way round the corner are unlikely to share your enthusiasm.

Like many upmarket Brit cars of the era, the DB6 has Armstrong Selectaride dampers, whose stiffness is supposedly adjustable by turning a knob on the dash. I've yet to drive a car where altering the setting made any difference whatsover, and this Aston is no exception. The ride is comfortable at legal speeds, but when you really start to press on, the sheer weight of the front end crashes into dips, the steering wheel jumps in your hands and suddenly GT man isn't feeling quite so calm and collected as he was a few moments ago.

On smoother roads, such as you'd find in almost every European country other than Britain, the DB6 would still cut the mustard as a long-distance express. Its five-speed 'box has the legs for relaxed motorway cruising at 90 or 100mph, and only the keening of the wind around the front quarterlights would spoil the pleasure of a long stint at such speeds. That, and the prospect of maxing your credit card at every fuel stop.

Surprisingly, the DB6's aerodynamics are reputedly better than the DBS's, mainly because the '6 has a smaller

'The DB6's five-speed gearbox has the legs for relaxed cruising at 90 or 100mph, and only the keening of the wind around the front quarterlights would spoil the pleasure of a long stint at such speeds'

'William Towns' sleek shape is a styling masterpiece, the quad-light front end and full-width stainless grille so much more classy than the *arriviste* V8 style that superseded it'

'The switchgear is perfectly evocative of the 1960s high life, right down to flat-faced knobs for the wipers and adjustable dampers that, with their brushed stainless finish, are exactly like the ones you'd find on a period hi-fi'

frontal area. The DBS is a huge car by British standards, a full six inches wider than its predecessor, though it's also fractionally shorter and two inches lower. To these eyes William Towns' sleek shape is a styling masterpiece, the quad-light front end and full-width stainless grille so much more classy than the arriviste V8 style that superseded it. It's not perfect – the spoiler beneath the bumper looks like the afterthought it was, added to boost the prototype's disappointing 131mph top speed to 140mph – but it's every inch the glamorous trans-European express, as exotic as anything Italian.

You feel the benefit of the extra width inside, where there's room to sprawl in an appropriately debonair manner on generously-proportioned and superbly comfortable seats (Towns was initially recruited to Aston as a seat designer, so he can take the credit here, too). In fact, as a transitional model the DB6 Mark 2 supposedly has exactly the same ones, but the DBS's just feel more enveloping and relaxing – possibly because this car has developed the patina that comes with everyday use, and has worn in like a favourite leather jacket.

The dash layout feels more of a piece, too, with dials and gauges strung out in a much more linear manner than in the DB6, although first impressions are deceptive because much of the switchgear is awkwardly positioned here and there on the centre console or down the A-post. It's perfectly evocative of the 1960s high-life, however, right down to flat-faced knobs for the wipers and adjustable dampers that, with their brushed stainless steel finish, are exactly like the ones you'd find on a period hi-fi.

There's something very American about the DBS's fastback lines, maybe a touch of Chevy Camaro about that wide-hipped rear end, but despite this radical departure from the DB6's 1950s-derived elegance the two cars share almost identical running gear. Because Marek's new V8 would not be ready in time for the DBS's launch, the existing straight-six was carried over unchanged into the new bodyshell, with the same options of triple SU or Weber carbs. Aston claimed 325bhp for a Weber-fed DBS Vantage; 270bhp would be more likely.

There was a significant change to the rear suspension, however, which gained the de Dion tube originally championed,

unsuccessfully, for the DB4 by engineer Harold Beach. This, together with the DBS's wider track and lower centre of gravity, gave the 'S a degree of traction in corners that the DB6 couldn't match and went a long way to compensating for the newer car's 90kg of extra weight.

The DBS sounds fantastic, too. The engines may be similar but this particular car has a thrilling, deep-chested snarl that's absent from the more genteel-sounding DB6. You'd never tire of hearing that noise whenever you settled behind the deep-dished wheel and twisted the key; it is an old-fashioned, politically incorrect shout of defiance that turns every shopping trip into an adventure.

With that billiard table of a bonnet stretching away in all directions, you might expect the DBS to feel cumbersome, but it doesn't. If anything it's easier to drive than the '6 because it seems better planted on the road, and the five-speed gearbox – yes, with a proper-sized gear lever this time – is easier to manipulate. And, crucially, it doesn't feel in the least bit slow. Quite the contrary: press the accelerator hard and this massive car surges forward impressively, with not the remotest

DBS Vantage
SPECIFICATIONS

Engine
3995cc straight-six with twin overhead camshafts and triple Weber 45 carburettors

Power
275bhp (estimated) @ 5750rpm

Torque
290lb ft @ 4500rpm

Transmission
Five-speed ZF manual, rear-wheel drive

Suspension
Front: independent, coil and wishbone, telescopic dampers
Rear: de Dion axle, trailing links, lever-arm dampers

Brakes
Girling discs all round

Weight
3503kg (1589kg)

Performance
0-60mph 7.1sec
Top speed 140mph

»

sense that it's being held back by middle-age spread.

If you measured it with a stopwatch the acceleration might not seem that spectacular, but it's the way in which it's delivered that puts the grin on your face. As the revs build, the exhaust note is drawn out into the mellow blast of a French horn, a sophisticated sound that perfectly complements the DBS's cultured image of wire wheels with triple-eared spinners. There's less wind noise inside the cabin than in the DB6, too, although you can actually see the slender window frames being sucked away from the door apertures at high speeds.

The DBS is not one of those cars that seem to shrink around you the further you drive it: it's just too wide for that. But when your sightline around a corner is good, it's fun to hurl this big GT into the bend and wind the needle around the tachometer once more. In the DB6, part of your brain would be on constant alert, ready to catch that wayward tail should it step out of line, yet the DBS feels more surefooted. Now I know that the apparently mismatched pairing of DBS and Ferrari Dino in cult TV series The Persuaders – Roger Moore as Lord

Brett Sinclair choosing the Aston while Tony Curtis's Danny Wilde favoured the Ferrari – wasn't quite so unbalanced as it seemed at the time.

As you've probably gathered, I loved this DBS and I take my hat off to its owner, Major Rupert Shaw RN, MBE, who took a chance five years ago and bought the Aston instead of the modern TVR he'd been intending to get. It's his only car and, while it doesn't get used for long periods while he's away on service, he's still managed to rack up 38,000 miles without any trouble. The key to reliability, he says, is electronic ignition, which helps enormously with starting. He even gets 18-20mpg on a motorway run.

I'm convinced, but what does the Aston trade think? A quick straw-poll reveals that British dealers broadly agree that the DBS is finally coming into its own. Peter Stratford of Aston London argues that the model is currently undervalued: 'The problem is that cars in the £12-15,000 bracket are invariably rusty or poor mechanically, yet they cost just as much to restore as a DB5 or '6. You need to spend at least £20,000-plus to get something worthwhile.'

Richard Stewart Williams is finding a small but steady stream of customers for conversions from the unloved three-ratio auto to a later ZF four-speed, which he says transforms the car. 'A well-sorted DBS is a bloody good vehicle to drive,' he adds, 'and it's definitely a favourite in the looks department.'

Across the Atlantic, Steve Scerio of Aston Martin of New England is more sceptical, although he admits this could be because he has only ever seen one really good example of a DBS in the States. 'Until the boom of the 1980s, people were cutting them up to keep DB5s and '6s alive. So maybe everyone thought they were crap because the survivors were in a crap condition.'

The final word should go to The Aston Workshop's Bob Fountain. 'The DBS is definitely an up-and-coming Aston Martin. We get enquiries for them weekly and we've just sold a beautiful, low-mileage twin-headlight V8 for £40,000. They're difficult to find in that kind of condition and you have to be patient, but it's worth the effort.'

Thanks to The Aston Workshop (www.aston.co.uk); and Major Rupert Shaw for the loan of his DBS.

'The DBS is not one of those cars that seem to shrink around you. But when your sightline around a corner is good, it's fun to hurl this big GT into the bend and wind the needle around the tacho once more'

ASTON MARTIN SPECIALISTS

SALES | RESTORATION | PARTS | SERVICING

Photography by Tim Wallace www.ambientlife.co.uk

We are probably selling and restoring more Aston Martin's than any other Aston Martin specialist anywhere else in the world.

Why not register with our bespoke computerised database designed to obtain a new home for your vehicle or find you your dream Aston Martin at
www.aston.co.uk/crm_index/php/action/seller .

You can also subscribe to our NEW eNewsletter at http://www.aston.co.uk/mailinglist_index/php

www.aston.co.uk

Red Row Beamish Co.Durham DH9 0RW Telephone +44 (0) 1207 233525 Fax +44 (0) 1207 232202 Email: astonworkshop@aston.co.uk

LORDING IT

Commissioned by a Scottish laird to carry fishing tackle around his estate, this unique Aston Martin is rarely seen in public Words: Richard Dredge Photography: Mark Dixon

JOHN BILLINGTON is a very lucky man, because he owns a Hillman Hunter tailgate. You're probably not insanely jealous at such news, but this Hunter tailgate is unique because it has an Aston Martin DBS attached. Built in 1970, this DBS estate is known to a surprisingly small number of Aston aficionados and, despite the car's advancing years, John is only its second owner.

Aston Martin shooting brakes are nothing new. At least a couple of dozen different examples have been created since the 1960s, some of which have enjoyed more fame than others. Elsewhere in this publication we introduce you to the Lagonda estate created by Swiss specialist Beat Roos, while other recent conversions done elsewhere have included at least three Vantage-based load-luggers. Undoubtedly the best-known Aston estates are the DB5s and DB6s converted by Radford **»**

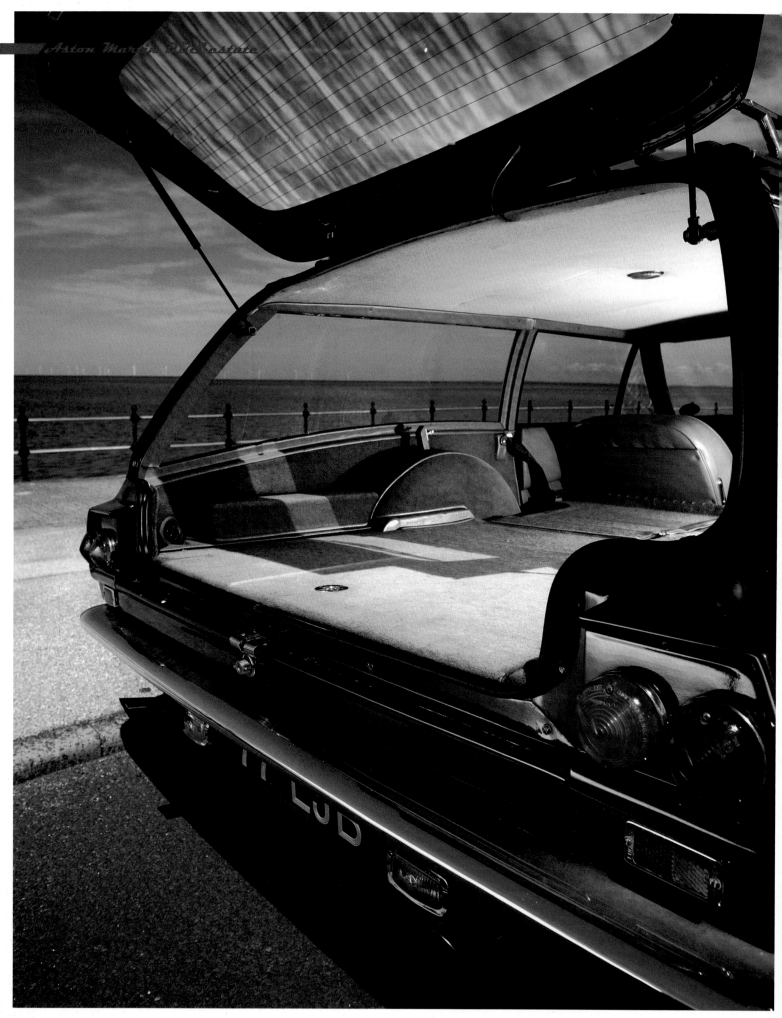

when they were new. Less familiar is the trio of DB6 shooting brake conversions carried out by FLM Panelcraft, which also modified just one DBS – the one you see here.

This car, chassis DBS/5730/R, was originally converted for a Scottish laird who had ordered it from London-based Aston dealer HR Owen. It's claimed that once the model had been built and word had got out, HR Owen was approached by several more prospective buyers. One can only assume they were interested up to the point where the subject of money cropped up, because the converted DBS is reputed to have cost as much as £10,000 – when the base car was listed at 'just' £5717.

Such a disproportionate price clearly wasn't an issue for the laird who ordered it: nobody knows who he was, but it seems he wanted something ultra-stylish and fast to carry his fishing tackle around his estate. Just in case he had a particularly good day emptying the streams and lakes, he commissioned a bespoke roof rack as part of the conversion. John isn't a fan of the rack, claiming it makes the car look like a hearse when fitted. With its chromed steel tubing and slatted wood there's no doubting it's as nicely made as the rest of the vehicle, but things get very noisy with it in place at speed. Besides, such extra carrying capacity is hardly needed when aft of the seats there's now so much useful space.

The conversion itself is very neat, with the back seat split in half, each section folding forward independently once its retaining bolt has been released. As the back rest flips forward, a panel slides down behind it to maintain a flat load bay: a very neat solution.

The clever interior is nothing compared with the exterior, however, which is superbly finished. The Coke-bottle curve over the rear wheelarch has been retained, dictating the side window line; while most Aston shooting brakes feature four pillars along each side, this one has just three and looks all the neater for it. And, whereas some other conversions address only the fresh metal aft of the doors, using a fill-in panel above the door glass, Panelcraft ditched the original plunging window line altogether, constructing a new door window frame instead. It's a much neater solution because the glasshouse appears seamless; it also apes the original chrome-trimmed glass of the

Left and above
Beautifully trimmed loadspace is unique to this particular car, but everything from front cabin forward is standard DBS.

original. However, such a move necessitated fresh windows being made, which led to problems later on.

John explains: 'The windows were made by Triplex of laminated glass, and one hot summer day when they had been left down the glass split due to unequal expansion rates. I had to spend a lot of money having new ones made; now I'm crossing my fingers that the replacements don't suffer the same fate. It's not just the front windows that are bespoke though, and already one of the rear side windows is looking the worse for wear; replicating it won't be cheap!'

While it's natural to assume the very '70s vinyl roof covering is there to hide a join, Panelcraft would probably have started from scratch with the roof, rather than extending what was already there, so it's unlikely there was any join to conceal. Less impressive are the parts bin tail lights, as found on various kits and specials of the time; it wouldn't have taken much imagination to retain the Aston units. Aside from the fresh tail lamps, all the DBS's bodywork changes are above the rear wing line, although a bespoke fuel tank also had to be made. It sits above the rear axle and has proved to be somewhat leak-prone, but John is hopeful that this problem has now been sorted.

When it first left Panelcraft the Aston was finished in a particularly vivid shade of metallic green, which was quickly changed to red. It was painted that colour when John bought it, but by this stage it had lost the leaping salmon perched on the bonnet – proof that good taste was optional in those heady days of the early '70s. John acquired the DBS from a Blackpool car dealer in 1975, and by 1980 its colour had changed once again to the discreet dark metallic blue shown here. It's a shade that suits the car well, showing up its subtle curves without looking flashy.

Aside from its various fresh coats of paint, the DBS has received very little attention over the years. That's perhaps no surprise as just 65,000 miles have passed beneath its wheels and it's always been looked after. Says John: 'It has never needed any work mechanically, but it wouldn't be a problem anyway because, as far as I can tell, the only changes made were to the bodywork and interior. Even the suspension seems to be the same as the coupé's, with no changes made for the possible extra weight over the rear axle. I guess when it's not loaded up, its overall mass

»

along with the weight distribution is the same as for the coupé – so it's no surprise that the car feels the same to drive.'

Surprisingly little is known about this model's very early history. The artisan responsible was Julia Trowell, who started at James Young in 1948 as an apprentice blacksmith, staying at the company until it was taken over by Jack Barclay in 1967. At this point he moved to FLM Panelcraft, which was staffed largely by ex-James Young employees. By the time Trowell joined FLM Panelcraft he was already an experienced and established panelbeater, capable of achieving amazing things with metal. He could work quite happily in steel as well as aluminium – or even copper, as requested by one Saudi prince when his stretched Volvo 760 was getting the full treatment in the 1980s.

Trowell rarely sketched anything in advance, preferring to work things out as he went along. He was the father-in-law of ex-Panelcraft trimmer Kevin O'Keeffe, who recalls: 'John ended up as a director of FLM Panelcraft and there's no doubt he was one of the firm's greatest assets, as his abilities were nothing short of remarkable. While Trowell was at James Young, one Frenchman wanted an all-steel body for his Silver Wraith and John just built one, indistinguishable from the alloy version. He even drilled holes in the structure to reduce the weight without compromising the structural integrity. Where John was concerned, anything was possible, so it's no surprise that he was given the responsibility of creating this one-off DBS estate.'

Panelcraft had started out by restoring pre-war Rolls-Royces and Bentleys, and towards the end of the 1960s it invested in a dozen very tired Phantom I hearses. The company set about rebodying them as boat-tailed roadsters, charging Trowell with rebuilding the engines and creating fresh bodies. With those rebuilt and

despatched, Panelcraft set about creating limited production runs of estate conversions, including the Rover P6 (for HR Owen), along with BMW and Mercedes versions for Crayford. At a time when factory-built luxury estates weren't available, the cars proved popular among those who could afford them, so it was no surprise that HR Owen turned to Panelcraft for the DBS model.

The conversion drives pretty much like a conventional DBS. With its automatic gearbox mated to a 3996cc straight-six, performance is brisk rather than startling, but it's the sound that's addictive: it's far more throaty than you'd expect.

Fire up the engine and it quickly settles to a burbly idle; accelerate through the gears and, such is the noise, it could easily be mistaken for a V8. When the DBS was new, buyers could choose between a Vantage specification, with three twin-choke Webers providing 325bhp, or the standard spec of three SUs and some 13% less power for the same money. This car wasn't built to Vantage spec so there are just 282 horses doing their bit; a kerb weight (in coupé form) of 1706kg translates to a power-to-weight ratio of 165bhp per tonne.

Performance isn't helped by the Borg-Warner three-speed automatic transmission, which not only saps power but also makes for jerky progress in stop/start traffic; although a five-speed manual ZF gearbox was a no-cost option, our Scottish laird clearly preferred his car to swap ratios for him.

So this is definitely a model for cruising rather than for enjoying twisty back roads. That's of no great concern to John, who loves it dearly but drives it only a few hundred miles each year. Nearly four decades after the car was made, it remains a recluse – which perhaps is all part of the mystique of this fascinating piece of Aston history. △

Below
Horizontal roofline – and that fabulous roof rack – are perhaps a little hearselike, but add to practicality.

'Trowell rarely sketched anything in advance, preferring to work things out as he went along'

3 of a kind

The seamless **union of our three companies** has allowed us to realise our mission of maintaining the legend, past and present

Whether you want to buy a fully re-engineered and refurbished Aston Martin, have your own shell completely restored, order parts for your cherished heirloom, or service your everyday Aston, we have the facilities , the knowledge, the experience and most importantly the passion.

Always priced competitively, we take real pride in our workmanship - nothing bar nothing leaves until we are 100% satisfied.

We are always looking for vehicles to add to our portfolio, so if you are looking to sell your Aston then give us a call. We can also track down and acquire specific Astons on your behalf, just tell us what is important to you and using our extensive contacts we can see if it's out there.

Desmond J. Smail

T 01234 713083
E sales@djsmail.co.uk
W djsmail.co.uk

ASTON SALES KENSINGTON

T 020 7985 0111
E sales@astonkensington.com
W astonkensington.com

ASTON SERVICE LONDON

T 020 7727 1944
E service@astonservicelondon.com
W astonservicelondon.com

NOBLE SAVAGE

Aston Martin's V8 Vantage looks like a brute of a '70s supercar
and has long been overshadowed by its older brethren. But it
has hidden depths, as **Robert Coucher** is surprised to find out

Photography: Stuart Collins

**Above
and right**
There's still a great
satisfaction in seeing
the 'built by...' plate
on an Aston engine;
hard, shiny plastics
of the switchgear are
rather less pleasing...

THE ASTON MARTIN V8 has serious presence. It looks a bit of a brute, typifying the British Bulldog breed in a well-cut suit. This 30-year-old V8 in Vantage spec, with its huge bonnet bulge, tarmac-scraping front spoiler and blanked-out intake grille, seems especially pugnacious. It sits on fat, old-tech tyres mounted on sturdy, seven-inch-wide GKN alloys, while the large Cibié spot lights (remember them?) that are frenched into the front grille command, 'Get out of my way!'

Open the surprisingly lightweight door – the bodywork is all aluminium – and slide into the ample seat. There is plenty of 'sprawl room', as designer William Towns called it. The seat is low and the dashtop high, with the large solid-looking gearshift sprouting from the central console. The steering wheel is quite small and thin-rimmed, but otherwise the interior is man-sized, including a properly large cigar ashtray.

Aston introduced the V8 in 1969, with the hotter Vantage following in 1977. This early 1978 Apple Green example is one of only 25 original-style Vantages made before the Osca India model arrived in 1979. Therefore it is a light, pre-wood veneer dashboard variant and features the back-to-the-future vinyl unit, which is only just now beginning to reappear... er, funky?

Once comfortable behind that low-set steering wheel, your view out of

'NO WEBER-CARBURETTORED FERRARI HAS EVER OFFERED SUCH AN OBEDIENT AND INSTANT THROTTLE RESPONSE'

»

the cockpit is panoramic. The windscreen is large and you can see both front corners of the car, which is most helpful as we are planning to drive the Vantage around London before going for a blast on the North Circular.

The fly-off handbrake nestles between your left thigh and the large central tunnel. The gearknob has the shift pattern picked out in white on its top and you notice that first is away on a dog-leg, with the remaining ratios in the normal plane.

Right, let's fire up the big 5.3 double-overhead cam V8. There is no dash-mounted starter button: the Vantage simply requires a turn of the key and a tickle of the throttle pedal. The starter engages and the engine fires instantly. No heavy metal churning required.

The engine immediately settles down to a rock-steady 900rpm idle. Allow your right foot to kiss the pedal and the revs rise with alacrity: a razor-sharp response that is surprising, as this rip-snorting Vantage has a row of four double-choke 48mm IDF Weber carbs lurking under that huge bonnet bulge. At standstill, the engine is already displaying good manners and breeding. No Weber-carb Ferrari has ever offered such an obedient and instant throttle response, in my experience.

Next, it's the he-man clutch that we all know is as heavy as hell in these meaty Astons. So, coiling the thigh... and the clutch goes lightly to the floor. Hang on, there's something wrong with this picture. This supposedly obstreperous brute, sometimes known as

Above
So much room! Long footwells and restrained, unintrusive dashboard mean occupants will never feel claustrophobic in the Aston V8. Decent air-con keeps them cool.

the rich man's Capri, is not behaving as expected...

The old Aston joke was always that the gearshift was the car's weak link (company owner David Brown manufactured gearboxes), but with the V8 the choice of cog-swapper is a ZF five-speed. Slot it back into first, engage the light clutch and off you trundle on the ample low-end torque, with no help from the throttle really required.

Many of us grew up watching the 1971 television series, *The Persuaders!*, where a rather camp Roger Moore played Lord Brett Sinclair, blasting around Monaco in his Aston Martin V8 (anorak fact: it was actually an earlier six-cylinder DBS dressed up to look like a V8 because the producers could not land the later model). The Aston, registration number BS 1, looked dashing and muscular, and Sinclair always seemed to get the girl.

But, grumbling through early-morning London, this fabulous Vantage is behaving perfectly. In the 1970s, Aston Martin was having a rocky financial ride and, with it being effectively a struggling cottage industry, you would rightly expect its cars to be badly thrown together. Not a bit of it. This '78 model feels refined and well considered.

The ride is smooth and free of modern-car jiggle at low speed. With Koni dampers at each corner mated to moderately firm springs, the Vantage has excellent damping characteristics. The gearshift is very much of the period but co-operative as soon as you learn to let the spring-loaded lever find its way around the long-throw gate. The

'THE MID-RANGE URGE IS ASTONISHING AND THE PRODIGIOUS POWER AND TORQUE THUNDER THE ASTON DOWN THE ROAD'

power-assisted steering is beautifully weighted and accurate. But the clutch? It's ridiculously pleasant to use.

I am enjoying the said 'sprawl room' offered by the capacious interior and am motoring with Graeme Hunt of Bramley of Kensington, who has brought this very original V8 Vantage out for our breakfast run.

'This is a one-owner car and has been very well cared for,' he says. 'The full maintenance history verifies its 157,000 miles, which might seem high for a V8, but it has been used and properly looked after, which is why it drives so well. Aston has rebuilt the engine and everything works as it should. The clutch is a later and improved component, hence much lighter than the original.'

Swinging onto the motorway, there is now room to stretch the Vantage's very long legs. The V8 engine picks up from no revs at all and surges through the gears. Until now there has not been room to explore the full length of the throttle pedal travel. Full depression is about a foot long and, when it's used,

the mid-range urge is astonishing. Although the Vantage weighs 1800kg (about the same as a current DB9), the prodigious power and torque thunder it down the open road. Aston was always coy about power outputs, but figures of 390bhp at 5800rpm and 390lb ft at 4000rpm had to be declared for the German market for the Vantage. Surprisingly in this hotter spec, which is reckoned to be about 100bhp over the fuel-injected models, it is the torque that really impresses, not just the top-end wham.

At normal road speed the Vantage is relatively refined. Obviously, when you're letting the engine off its leash the V8 does start to roar. But the sound is very different to an American V8's. The Vantage, with its two sets of double-overhead cams driven by chains and eight Weber carburettor venturi, has a distinctive European sound akin to a racing engine; which, of course, it is. The exhaust system does a good job of quelling unwanted boom but, as the revs crest five thou, the Aston shows its breeding. When road tested by magazines

Aston Martin V8 Vantage

SPECIFICATIONS

Engine
5340cc all-alloy dohc V8,
four Weber 48IDF carbs

Power
390bhp @ 5800rpm

Torque
390lb ft @ 4000rpm

Transmission
Five-speed ZF manual,
rear-wheel drive

Suspension
Front: independent via
coils and unequal
wishbones, Koni dampers,
anti-roll bar. Rear: de Dion
axle located by parallel
trailing arms and Watts
linkage, Koni dampers

Brakes
Ventilated discs all round

Weight
1800kg (3968lb)

Performance
0-60mph 5.7sec
Top speed 165mph

Cost new
£20,000

Value now
£55,000

---

in the mid-1970s, the Vantage managed the 0-60mph dash in 5.4 seconds, with a top speed timed at 165mph. This made it the fastest road car then tested.

And on uncrowded roads, it certainly feels like it. Throwing the Aston into roundabouts, the 255/65 tyres have their work cut out. The Vantage feels quite soft as you go in but it soon settles into a good balance, the de Dion suspension keeping things planted at the rear. As the ventilated disc brakes warm up so does their bite, and soon you find yourself hustling along at considerable speed, which belies this car's conservative good looks.

So, while the Aston Martin was at the forefront of the performance envelope at the time, it suffered from the vagaries of fashion. Here was a very traditional-looking car that in 1969 evolved out of the DB6 and DBS models that preceded it. Both of these were perceived as being heavy and underpowered. Come the mid-'70s, the auto industry began to offer some futuristic-looking engineering and design propositions, on paper at least. In the brave new world of the startling Lamborghini Countach LP400, cutting-edge Ferrari 365GT4 Berlinetta Boxer, technological Porsche 928 and smooth and refined V12 Jaguar XJ-S, let alone the mad turbocharged Porsche 930, the big old Aston Vantage appeared rather conservative.

But the Aston V8 appealed to a well-heeled and discerning clientele who bought it in sufficient numbers to keep the model in production until 1989, by which time

1600 had been built, of which just 320 were Vantages. The convertible Volante appeared in 1978 and appealed especially to the American market, and the early Bosch mechanical fuel injection was replaced with easier-to-maintain carburettors and thereafter electronic Weber-Marelli fuel injection in 1986.

So from the mid-1970s and throughout the '80s, while performance cars became mid-engined, turbocharged or four-wheel drive, Aston continued to refine and evolve its DBS design of the '60s, retrofitting carburettors in place of fuel-injection and adding wood veneer to the dashboard!

The upshot is that the venerable Aston Martin V8 remained faster than most of its competitors. It was (and still is) more practical to own, easier to live with and much more manageable to drive really quickly. It was built as a businessman's express to blow the doors off anything from BMW or Mercedes. Would you choose to drive across Europe with a passenger and all her luggage in an air-conditioned Aston V8, or in a Countach or Boxer? Exactly.

While earlier DB4, 5 and 6 values soared in the last decade, the later 1970s and '80s V8 languished. But the market's perception of these cars has now changed from out-of-fashion barges to drivable gentlemen's GTs. Consequently prices are on the move. Good examples that were £40,000 a couple of years ago are now worth over £80,000, which represents good value when you consider it will cost £100,000-plus to completely rebuild a V8. The Aston V8 is now rightly in

»

'WOULD YOU CHOOSE TO DRIVE ACROSS
EUROPE WITH A PASSENGER AND LUGGAGE
IN AN ASTON, OR A COUNTACH? EXACTLY'

Far left
Tadek Marek-designed V8 was also used in the Nimrod and AMR1 race cars – it's extremely tough, but it suffered teething troubles.

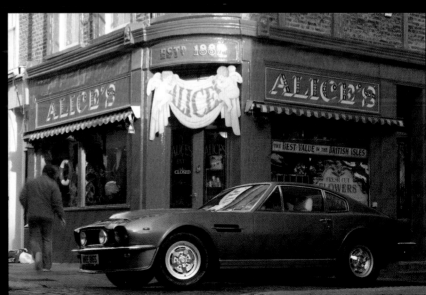

'THE V8 IS NOW RIGHTLY IN VOGUE AS A FAST, RELIABLE, ATTRACTIVE CLASSIC CAR THAT'S GREAT FUN TO DRIVE IN THE REAL WORLD'

vogue as a fast, reliable, attractive classic car that is great fun to drive in the real world. A good example is considerably less expensive than the ubiquitous DB, and is certainly a lot more usable.

Because the V8 was in production for two decades, there are distinct variations to choose from. Early examples are purer if less refined, Vantages are the slam-dunk powerhouses, Volantes offer comfortable open motoring for four, especially in automatic guise, and later-model V8 coupés can now be upgraded by specialists to give near-Vantage levels of performance with everyday practicality.

From an *Octane* point of view, an early Vantage like this example is a desirable machine. Rare, raw, exciting and still very fast, the sharp-edged Aston makes for an exciting sports car or an epic grand tourer, depending on how far you push that long-travel throttle pedal.

Thanks to Graeme Hunt of Bramley of Kensington, London, for this 1978 Aston Martin V8 Vantage: 18-23 Radley Mews, London W8 6JP, +44 (0) 207 937 8487, www.graemehunt.com.

RICHARD WILLIAMS
OF RS WILLIAMS

RS Williams
Cobham, Surrey
+44 (0)1932 868377
www.rswilliams.co.uk

RICHARD WILLIAMS was apprenticed to Aston Martin and started his business in 1968. He managed the Nimrod Team at Le Mans in the 1980s as well as the Ecurie Ecosse C2s, which were World C2 Sports Car Champions in 1986. RS Williams' Aston Martins are regarded as being some of the best.

'We are probably known for our work on Aston DBs: GTs, Zagatos, Project racers and that sort of thing. But I think that the V8 is the last affordable, proper classic Aston. They are terrific cars because they are tough, well made – the later ones particularly so – and can be vastly improved with a couple of mods.

'We do a handling pack, a brake pack and an engine upgrade to seven litres, which pushes the power over 500bhp and makes for a very fast Aston. Don't forget, this is the motor we used in the Nimrod and the AMR1. The initial problems Lola had with the engine at Le Mans in the 1960s were down to the plugs and a detached crankshaft vibration damper, but the bottom end of the unit was strengthened considerably and now they are

sturdy and reliable if properly maintained. Early engines did suffer noisy cams but, again, these were rectified. And from 1976 the core plugs for the oilways in the crank were redesigned.

'The early cars suffered fuel-injection problems. The Bosch mechanical injection mounted the metering units within the vee of the engine and they got very hot, so the seals went, with the result that the motor would run badly. They can be sorted out but the carburettors are easier to maintain and the later electronic injection after '86 is much improved. Vantages remained on Webers throughout.

'Although we have been dealing in and working on V8s for years, it does seem that they are now on the up. You need to ensure you buy a good one with a history of maintenance, as they are costly to repair or rebuild. A car that has benefited from improvements, like a later clutch and properly set-up suspension, is a joy to drive. I know because, apart from my DB4, I own two V8s: a Lagonda four-door and a Zagato.'

GRAEME HUNT
OF GRAEME HUNT LTD

18-23 Radley Mews
Kensington, London
+44 (0)207 937 8487
www.graemehunt.com

PREVIOUSLY MANAGING DIRECTOR of Jack Barclay, Graeme Hunt is now the proprietor of Graeme Hunt Ltd, dealing in fine Rolls-Royce, Bentley and Aston Martin cars. His workshop in Kensington, London, undertakes meticulous restoration of these handmade British marques.

'Today's customers are very discerning and they want their classic cars to be right. It's detail, detail, detail, and we pursue that to the nth degree. With the Vantage you featured here, we changed the tyres, fitted new belts throughout, serviced the engine and went through all the mechanicals. It is a very good example so it has not needed much but we have to ensure it is correct.

'Since it is such a lovely original car we have tried to save the headlining, but it is shot so will have to be replaced. The paintwork has a bit of road rash around

the grille but I think that's part of the car's charm. Of course it can be stripped to bare metal and repainted, but let's see what the customer wants to do first.

'I think that Aston Martin V8s of all configurations are undervalued but that will change soon: the next generation is becoming interested in these cars because they were the supercars they wanted as youngsters.

'At our works we restore and maintain Rolls-Royces, Bentleys and Astons because they are the cars we know best and because they are so beautifully made. Being largely built by hand means the vehicles can be deconstructed, detailed and then carefully put back together, which is the really time-consuming task. But working with stainless steel, aluminium, wood and leather is a pleasure, and bringing a lovely old car back up to first class is rewarding.'

ASTON MARTIN V8

From 1969 to 1972 the Aston Martin was known as the DBS V8. It retained the bodywork of the earlier six-cylinder DBS but was fitted with the Tadek Marek 5.3-litre V8 and troublesome Bosch fuel injection. With the change of ownership of the company in 1972 the car was simply retitled the Aston Martin V8 and remained so until production ended in 1989. The V8's frontal treatment was changed to single headlamps and alloys replaced the wire wheels. Power output was circa 280bhp.

ASTON MARTIN V8 VANTAGE

From 1977 the Vantage nomenclature returned with the 390bhp Weber-carburettored V8, featuring larger inlet valves, and revised cams and manifolds. After 1979 it was known as the Oscar India model, with detail changes including wood-veneer dashboard. Only 320 were built and it's the choice of the gentleman driver.

ASTON MARTIN ZAGATO

Announced in 1985, this hard-core supercar is short on looks but big on driver involvement. The 432bhp Vantage could top 187mph with its lightweight coachwork, which reduced the weight by around 10%. It was also available as a Volante convertible. Only 50 coupés and 37 Volantes were built, so these limited-edition Aston Zagatos are the ones to buy now. Prices start at around £100,000.

NICK MEE
OF NICHOLAS MEE

Nicholas Mee and Company,
Wellesley Avenue, London
+44 (0)208 741 8822
www.nicholasmee.co.uk

AFTER SPENDING 16 years as part of Aston Martin Lagonda (including a spell on its management team), Nick Mee established Nicholas Mee and Company in 1991. His team has a collective experience with Astons of over 50 years, and can supply and maintain classic examples of the highest quality.

'With most quality marques, the very earliest and very last models in a range are the most desirable, and this is true of the Aston Martin V8. We find that the later cars are very popular because they are extremely well sorted, mechanically tough and reliable if properly maintained, fabulous to drive and underpriced. Many of our customers are owners of modern sports cars who are sick of haemorrhaging vast sums of money on depreciation. They want an exciting machine to drive but one that will at least retain its value.

'Vantages are rare beasts. With just 320 built, not all of which are right-hand drive, there are very few examples to be had. Travelling around the country we see that many V8s are now being restored. This is expensive, so good cars are no longer around £50,000: they are more like £90,000. The preferred model is the coupé but the Volante is a super open four-seater which, every time you drop the roof, makes you feel like you are on holiday.

'For today's world a late-model, fuel-injected V8 with the automatic gearbox tweaked for sportier shifting, plus a sports exhaust and suspension packs fitted, makes a superb road car that is almost as quick as a Vantage at half the price.

'For the really smart investor the rare Zagato is currently undervalued. Sure, it is a more hard-core machine and the looks are functional rather than beautiful, but there were only ever 50 Zagato Vantages and 37 Volantes made. Super-rare cars for around £100,000 – at the moment...'

TOM
PAPADOPOULOS
OF AUTOSPORT
DESIGNS

Autosport Designs, Inc
Huntingdon Station,
New York, USA
+1 631 425 1555

AUTOSPORT DESIGNS in New York is one of America's leading Aston Martin dealers, where Tom Papadopoulos has been selling, servicing and restoring Astons since 1989. The Volantes are the most popular with his clientele but he likes the 'proper' coupé.

'I own and enjoy a 1985 V8 Vantage. The best way I can sum it up is a quote from Paul Frère, who wrote many years ago that "it is a civilised Ferrari Daytona". I also own a Daytona and I wholeheartedly agree!

'Rust in the sill areas can be common but it is rare to have very bad rust in structural areas. The paint on original examples can crack – 23 coats of hand-rubbed lacquer is not ideal on a large, heavy, aluminium-bodied automobile. Engines are tough if they have been maintained properly from new.

'While the Vantage models are great cars I have found many people prefer the authentic, original look of the standard V8 body without the air dam, blanked-off grille, spoilers etc. These days the power of the Vantage is not always usable and many owners seem to prefer the usability of a standard-spec V8 coupé or Volante in automatic form. As such, there is immediate torque and mid-range power – the Volante is by far the most popular option here in the States.

'The US-spec V8 had restrictive exhausts and catalytic converters, which really cut the horsepower. These days we can restore most of the power by installing European downpipes: hey presto, a proper Aston. This is now legal in the USA because any automobile that is 25 years or older is exempt from emissions testing. The post-1986 cars with Weber-Marelli injection can also be uprated to European-specification exhausts and they can be immediately enjoyed the way the factory intended.

'The Aston Martin V8 offers power, reliability and cost-effective ownership if, and only if, it is a proper and well-maintained example from the start.'

ASTON MARTIN LAGONDA

Only seven four-door Lagondas were built between 1974 and 1976 – and they were all constructed for David Brown and his friends, including the man who owned Tetley's Tea! They have a strange-looking grille and all boast automatic transmission; Richard Williams owns one and, as you'd expect, if an example comes on the market prices are rather high!

ASTON MARTIN V8 VOLANTE

The choice of the American market, although rather detuned there (see Tom Papadopoulos's comments, left), the Volante arrived in 1978. A spacious open tourer with room for four, the Volante was viewed in the USA as a sporty alternative to a Bentley Continental convertible or a Rolls-Royce Corniche.

ASTON MARTIN V8 VANTAGE VOLANTE

The open-top Volante was given extra appeal when it was offered in higher-power Vantage specification from 1986. Unfortunately it also gained spoilers and flared wheelarches, although a dozen late Volantes were built to Prince of Wales spec without spoilers or flares, which rendered them slightly more tasteful.

Octane tries a unique Lagonda shooting brake, crafted many miles from Newport Pagnell but as sharp and uncompromising as the William Towns' original
Words: Malcolm McKay Photography: Matt Howell

Estate of grace

S WITZERLAND: where Teutonic efficiency meets French chic and adds a touch of Alpine beauty. Home of the world's best watches, wealthiest banks, superb chocolates and unique Aston Martin conversions

It's true. In the fertile fields west of Berne lies Roos Engineering, the Swiss capital's principal agent for Aston Martin Lagonda, a specialist with a flourishing new-car business and astonishing repair and restoration workshops. Proprietor Beat Roos, a quiet, slight but insightful genius who is never happier than when wearing his workshop coat and figuring out an engineering problem, grew up in South Africa but has

'ITS UNCOMPROMISED STYLING, CARRYING THROUGH THE
LONG, LOW LINES, DOES A TERRIFIC JOB OF LOOKING AS
THOUGH WILLIAM TOWNS HIMSELF HAD PENNED IT'

spent his working life in Switzerland. There he has developed a reputation that sees Astons arriving from all over Europe – one customer even flies his car over from the West Indies for servicing.

The Roos shooting brakes have been built for special customers, and are demonstrations of the skills and ingenuity that Beat Roos has nutured in his workforce: 'We have made only three,' he explains. 'Each one is unique and it would not be fair on the customer to build another, although we have certainly been approached to do more.

'The Lagonda was the first and, in some ways, the most difficult; it was a project for a Hong Kong customer. My idea with all the shooting brakes is that the basic model must still be clearly the Aston Martin or Lagonda: it would be easy to make a complete new car on the chassis, but it's much more difficult to make the conversion entirely cohesive with the original design. The body was two years' work: I like to have one panelbeater on one project, so it's "his child" – the quality is always better that way.

'There's a long tradition of Lagonda shooting brakes – the books always start with the DB5 but in fact Aston Martin had two 2.6-litre Lagondas bodied as shooting brakes by Tickford to use as support cars for the DB3S on the Mille Miglia in the early 1950s. The William Towns' design was particularly difficult to adapt to a shooting brake body but the key was to replace the entire roof from the screen back. The original roof tapers in, but now it's straight. The car is just 1.3 metres high.

Above and right
Love it or hate it, that's an astonishing silhouette; TV helps pacify cramped rear passengers.

'The chassis and wheelbase are untouched and the doors are the originals, but the top of the rear wing is completely reworked. The sealing of the back hatch was a particular problem and the rear side windows are divided to accommodate pillars, giving stiffness needed for the tailgate. We don't have the problems that the Virage shooting brakes built elsewhere have had – they're quite floppy and once you've shut the tailgate 20 or 30 times you have to start the job again. We've built a Vantage shooting brake [see picture on p130] that has 612bhp, so the bodyshell has to be stiff! Another thing you have to think about is a decent-size fuel tank – our Vantage has a 100-litre tank, whereas the new Bertone Jet has only 40 litres, which doesn't give much of a range on a €750,000 car.'

'On the Long Wheelbase Virage shooting brake [p132] we've made the rear seats fold flat; that wasn't the plan on the Lagonda, where we wanted to put an extra air-conditioning unit in the rear seat back. The Long Wheelbase took four years and over 10,000 hours – we started with a convertible, of which only 63 were made. Now we have a project on the new Rapide four-door...'

After William Towns' success with the muscular and massive DBS body, Aston Martin gave him an even freer rein to design the next Lagonda, with the brief that it must have four doors and look stunningly modern and fast. Announced on October 12, 1976, it was a dream car made real, boasting monster performance from the 280bhp/360lb ft V8 combined with car-of-the-future electronic digital dashboard, touch-

sensitive switches, self-levelling rear suspension and a dramatic wedge body that was 5m long and 1.3m high. Aston Martin relied on the highly-regarded Cranfield Institute of Technology to develop the car's computer system but this move delayed production and the system itself earnt a reputation for unreliability – although the computer's dependability did steadily improve during production. By 1984, the set-up had acquired a synthesised voice in English, French, German and, as you might expect, Arabic.

Fuel injection replaced the Webers in 1986, before the styling was softened in 1987 to suit current tastes (although, without the central swage line, it did end up looking a bit slab-sided). Pop-up headlights and touch-sensitive switchgear were also abandoned. Production finally ended in 1990 after a total of just 637 cars (plus six prototypes) had been built over 14 years.

It's a delight to see a Lagonda in such stunning condition – so many around today disappoint with tired, dirty trim and signs of neglect. This car is better than new.

You climb into a leather armchair, the height of luxury, and are surrounded by switches: so many it's reminiscent of a light aircraft cockpit. Everything is electrically operated and the seats move in every direction. There are electric releases for the two fuel-filler flaps, soft/loud horns, no fewer than five light switches and even an electrically-operated bonnet release. Then, of course, there are the trip computer, air conditioning and electric mirrors.

Leather wraps every tiny panel on the console, the

Aston Martin Lagonda Shooting Brake

SPECIFICATIONS

Engine
5340cc V8, two overhead cams, Weber-Marelli fuel injection

Power
300bhp @ 5000rpm

Torque
320lb ft @ 3000rpm

Transmission
Chrysler Torqueflite three-speed automatic, rear-wheel drive

Suspension
Front: twin wishbones, coil spring/dampers, anti-roll bar. Rear: De Dion, twin radius arms, Watt linkage, coil springs, lever-arm dampers

Brakes
Vented discs all round

Performance
0-60mph 8.9sec
Top speed 145mph

armrests, the steering wheel and the doors, as well as the seats. The rooflining is suede, with aircraft-style air vents and map/reading lights in front and rear. Between the front seats is the first non-standard part of this car, a beautifully-integrated console for the extra switchgear to open and close the two rearmost windows and operate the back wash/wipe.

Insert the key and turn, and the digital dashboard springs to life. A particularly nice touch is that first, for a few seconds, the Lagonda emblem is lit up across the screen before it settles to the total and trip mileage display. Fire up the big V8 and you discover that the dashboard scribes graceful arcs for the revs on the left and speed in the centre, with fuel and temperature stick-type gauges on the right: all are supremely clear and easy to read, cleverly using the flexibility of a digital display to emphasise what you need to know rather than just mimicking conventional gauges.

But we've been sitting here too long, wondering at all the complexity: it's time to drive the beast and I'm not sure I'm looking forward to it. The last Aston I drove, a bulbous 1980s V8, disappointed; it was impossible to sling around English country lanes because I was constantly reversing to wider parts for oncoming traffic. The Lagonda appears huge from the outside and, on the inside looking over my shoulder, the back of the car seems the length of a football pitch away – and I have to start by reversing out of a car park.

Manoeuvring goes better than expected. Automatic reversing sensors are a useful aid; however, they are not essential as you can see the rear pillars from the driving seat

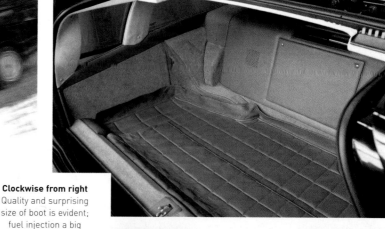

Clockwise from right
Quality and surprising size of boot is evident; fuel injection a big improvement on earlier carbs; interior is as angular as bodywork.

From far left
Other examples of Roos' estates include Vantage and long-wheelbase Virage.

'THE LAGONDA APPEARS HUGE FROM OUTSIDE AND, LOOKING OVER MY SHOULDER, THE BACK OF THE CAR SEEMS THE LENGTH OF A FOOTBALL PITCH AWAY'

and, though the very front is not visible, you can see most of the bonnet. If in doubt, putting the headlights up is helpful. Out onto the road and floor the throttle: the Lagonda sits down and surges forward with impressive verve. Its weight means it isn't stunningly accelerative, especially uphill, but it's quick enough and, when the road opens out, speed just continues to build inexorably and seemingly ever more quickly until you chicken out and lift your right foot.

Through twisty roads the car springs its biggest surprise: it's remarkably nimble and doesn't feel as big as it looks from the outside. You expect a great wallowing whale and it does roll a bit, but not too much as the weight is low and between the wheels. Through narrow spaces the car is far better than expected – its low overall height makes it seem immensely stretched – and the wheelbase is relatively short, with overhangs that, though long, taper gently at both ends so they are not an embarrassment when manoeuvring.

In the back seats, space is a bit limited – photographer Matt comments that it feels a bit like sitting in Economy in an aircraft with First Class up ahead. Presumably because of the multiple electric motors under the front seats, there's no room for rear passengers' feet to tuck into, which would improve comfort dramatically. The TV in the centre offers some compensation, though. Tickford did offer long-wheelbase Lagondas in

1984 but the price was prohibitive and only three were made.

But what of the boot? Is this shooting brake just an expensive gimmick or is it a practical estate car? Here the care and thought that has gone into the Roos conversion really shines through. Its uncompromised styling, carrying through the dramatic long, low lines, does a terrific job of looking as though Towns himself had penned it this way. That means, of course, that the roof tapers down very gently towards the tail and the height is very low there – but since the tailgate is cut well back into the roof and lifts high, access is very good to the large, sloping-floored rear compartment. The hatch, of course, is electrically closed: lower it, press gently and you can hear the electric latch slide into place.

First registered in March 1987, this Lagonda was one of the last of the original shape. As such, it boasts the final and most reliable version of the digital dashboard along with the fuel-injected engine and the initial, uncompromised styling. Its conversion to shooting brake form was carried out in 1998–'99 and the car hit the road on January 1, 2000, with a new engine, running gear, interior and electrics as well as the body modification. Roos now maintains the car for its owner and it turns heads wherever it goes: exclusivity made unique. △

Thanks to Roos Engineering, +41 (0)31 926 11 37/38, www.roosengineering.ch.

RML RACE TEAM CHIEF Ray Mallock squared the circle when he took third in the Group C GTP class in the 2004 Le Mans Legends race in the Aston Martin Nimrod. He had last raced the car at Le Mans in 1984 and run as high as fifth until forced out by accident. Involved almost from the outset of the Nimrod project until its final Le Mans appearance, his input was huge and he was a fundamental part of the group that kept the Newport Pagnell marque in the forefront of sports car racing.

Le Mans and Aston Martin have long been synonymous, despite the famous British marque historically achieving just one outright victory, in 1959 with Carroll Shelby and Roy Salvadori's DBR1 success. Even when the company's fortunes dictated otherwise, there was never a shortage of enthusiasm for Le Mans. Today, the famous badge is seen again at La Sarthe – but if the dream of any current endurance team is to »

Mighty hunter

All British eyes are on Aston Martin in today's Le Mans 24 Hours races – but back in the early 1980s, it was this privateer Nimrod that came so close to beating the all-conquering Porsches in France

Words: Andrew Roberts Photography: Ian Dawson

topple the seemingly unstoppable diesels, back in the 1970s and early 1980s Porsche was the target. The 936 and 935 had delivered a quartet of victories over a six-year period when in 1981 the first intimations of interest from the Aston Martin camp were heard. Aston enthusiast Robin Hamilton, who twice campaigned a prototype V8, including finishing the 24 Hours in 1977, believed that there was the potential for a long-distance sports car powered by the same engine. He was encouraged by the new Group C Regulations, introduced on January 1, 1982. Key points were a stipulated minimum dry weight of 800kg, the banning of skirts – although ground-effect venturi were permitted – and a maximum fuel capacity of 100 litres (22 imperial gallons). This had the effect of limiting competitors to five refuelling stops over a 1000km distance, equal to 25 stops at Le Mans. The engine choice was free, providing the manufacturer had any cars homologated within Groups A or B.

Hamilton set about designing a car around the IMSA regulations for competition in the US, but the technical requirements were to prove very different to Group C. He brought in Eric Broadley of Lola cars to design the chassis, which drew on that of the Lola T70. When there was a further change in the control of Aston Martin, with American Peter

Sprague and debonair Englishman Alan Curtis calling it a day, Hamilton judged that the time was now ripe to approach the company. Arch enthusiast Victor Gauntlett had just become the new chairman of Aston Martin Lagonda and also retained the same position at Pace Petroleum, the independent fuel company. Hamilton had tapped into a kindred spirit and the outcome was the founding of Nimrod Racing Automobiles.

'I contacted Michael Bowler at the factory at the end of 1981,' says Mallock, 'when I heard that Aston was planning a comeback into sports car racing. I was invited to one of the tests in early 1982 and, subsequently, to drive the Richard Williams-managed and Viscount Downe-owned chassis.

'Lord Downe was very much a Le Mans enthusiast and entrant, with Richard Williams managing his teams. My involvement started as a driver and one of the test drivers for the team. I had worked with Williams when he was team manager for the Fisons Lola I first drove at Le Mans.

'When I drove the Nimrod it was apparent that both the aerodynamics and the suspension required work so we quickly got stuck into a development programme, which involved modifications to the front splitter and the rear wing area and various ducting details around the original Robin

Below
One of the two Le Mans Nimrods was destroyed in an accident but this car survived and is now driven in Group C historic racing.

'Ray Mallock was a fundamental part of the group that kept the Newport Pagnell marque in the forefront of sports car racing'

'It was obvious that with the car weighing some 200kg more than the rival Porsches, changes would have to be made for 1983'

Above and right
Distinctive livery on restored car is down to original sponsor Bovis, the house-builder/developer.

Hamilton body shape. For the suspension, my father Arthur [creator of the Mallock U2 cars] carried out the initial analysis on his computer programme. This showed that the roll-centres and camber curves weren't as they should be for the tyres. We instigated suspension geometry modifications and spring and roll-bar changes and those resulted in a more user-friendly car that handled much more consistently. We were regularly able to outpace the works car. We didn't have a spare engine and we were using only around 6500 revs. We were able to out-qualify them and finish all our races that year.'

Le Mans 1982 was a triumph for the Viscount Downe car. Entered jointly under his and the Pace Petroleum banner, no. 32 was driven by Ray Mallock, Mike Salmon and Simon Phillips. Running as high as third in a race ultimately dominated by the Porsche 956s of Jacky Ickx/Derek Bell, Jochen Mass/Vern Schuppan and Al Holbert/Hurley Haywood/Jurgen Barth, the Nimrod covered its 2684.93 miles at an average speed of 111.87mph to finish seventh overall. 'The car ran beautifully until 7am, when we suffered a burnt valve and spent quite a lot of time trying to analyse the problem,' says Mallock. 'We were lying third behind the 956s during the night and were running a competitive fourth/ fifth place, which was quite an incredible performance.'

Despite a season that had seen the Aston Martin Nimrod finishing third in the World Sportscar Championship, courtesy of Mallock and Salmon taking another seventh at Spa, it was obvious that with the car weighing some 200kg more than the rival Porsches, changes would have to be made if it was to become competitive for 1983. Hamilton decided to take his Nimrod to the US and the Viscount Downe car became, to all intents and purposes, the works entry. Additional sponsorship came from housebuilder/developer Bovis.

'I talked to Lord Downe and Victor Gauntlett about the need to improve the body design and we agreed a budget for producing a wind-tunnel model going to MIRA,' says Mallock. 'We developed a complete new shape to give more downforce and less drag. The 1982 cars had an extension to the windscreen, which we called the taxi sign, to meet the minimum height requirement. This incurred a huge drag penalty.

'We embarked on a programme through the winter months to improve the aerodynamics and reduce the weight of the car. We were a lot more successful on the aerodynamics than the weight because it was very difficult to do much with the fundamental chassis, suspension, the engine itself and the Hewland VG gearbox. The wind-tunnel work paid dividends: we reduced the drag by about 10% and increased the downforce by a factor of three. The net result was that at Le Mans, using the same chassis, suspension and tyres, the

Aston Martin Nimrod

SPECIFICATIONS

Engine
5340cc V8, twin ohc per bank

Power
560bhp @ 6800rpm

Transmission
Hewland VG five-speed

Suspension
Front: wishbone and rocker. Rear: radius rods, parallel lower links, single top link, Koni dampers

Performance
Top speed 220mph

Weight
1000kg (2205lb)

»

'The two Bovis-
liveried Nimrods
ran strongly until
a deflated tyre saw
John Sheldon crash
heavily on the
Mulsanne Straight.
He was lucky to
escape with his life'

Above
Aston V8 was designed
by Tadek Marek, who
was against it being
used for racing as far
back as '67 in Lola T70s.

Nimrod was 11 seconds a lap faster between '82 and '83.'

The 1983 Le Mans was dominated by the 956, taking nine of the top ten places. Despite the Nimrod's aerodynamic improvements and weight saving, it was well off the Porsche qualifying pace. But Le Mans is about being there at 4pm on Sunday afternoon. The Nimrod trio of Mallock/Salmon and American Steve Earle looked set for a strong finish until, after 17 hours 13 minutes of racing, the normally reliable Aston V8 threw a rod and the garage shut for the last time.

For 1984 the Nimrod was to return to the 24 Hours, this time as a two-car team. In the US, the Hamilton outfit was acquired by British amateur sports car racer John Cooper. His Daytona 24 Hours entry, where he drove with Bob Evans and Paul Smith, made seventh. Unfortunately a change of plans saw the end of his involvement and the car came to Europe. Such was the pace of the Porsche 956 opposition that Tickford turbocharged the V8, to produce a reputed 710bhp. One ran at the pre-Le Mans Silverstone race but lost its oil.

Despite this, and with the cars reverting to normally aspirated form, Le Mans was approached with optimism. The works Porsches were not participating, although the 956 teams of Joest Racing, Brun Motorsport and Porsche Kremer Racing

were there. In the event, the two Bovis-liveried Nimrods ran strongly until a deflated tyre saw John Sheldon crash heavily on the Mulsanne Straight. He was lucky to escape with his life after suffering severe burns. Tragically, a marshal was killed in the incident. The other Nimrod, driven by Drake Olson sharing with Mallock, then lying in fifth, was eliminated as a result of this accident. Olson was unsighted by a Porsche and crashed into the Armco while trying to avoid the blazing wreckage.

It was a dreadful end. But a minuscule budget had brought the Aston Martin name back into the endurance arena.

Happily, the Mallock/Olson car was restored to its original race condition in the ownership of Roger Bennington (of the Stratton Motor Company) and has regularly been seen in historic Group C events over the last few years.

Mallock had been preparing the car for some time. 'I jumped at the chance. It is such a driver-friendly car and it's great to get back behind the wheel again – and it has also given me the opportunity to drive with my son Michael,' said the RML MD.

Thanks to Roger Bennington, Ray Mallock, Michael Mallock and Donington Park for their help in preparing this feature.

Absolute power

Once a stock 5.3-litre Virage, this Aston Martin is now a 7-litre turbocharged supertourer with twice the horsepower and more than three times the torque. Could it be the fastest Aston in the world? Words: Paul Chudecki Photography: Paul Harmer

M3 AMV

A S Q CARS GO, they don't come much more extreme than this. True, an Aston Martin is expected to be very fast – but we're talking here about well over double the standard horsepower and close to three-and-a-half times the torque. And in a Virage that outwardly looks pretty much like it did when it rolled off the Newport Pagnell production line more than a decade ago.

This appearance aspect of the car was at the very top of the list of priorities when the owner commissioned Lynx Motors International, better known for its Jaguar C- and D-type recreations and XJ-S Eventer estate, to re-engineer the Aston. Already the car, then with 35,000 miles on the clock, was one of the less-common Virages, being one of the nine Limited Edition examples that ended the model's production run in 1996.

These had dark metallic British Racing Green paintwork, Connolly saddle-brown leather seats, matching green and beige headlining and door trim, and burr elm rather than walnut dashboard finish. The dash also carried a brass plaque stamped with the chassis number, in this case 50413, and the owner's name. Externally, the differences were limited to flared wings similar to those of the twin-supercharged Vantage and a radiator grille with its mesh in a distinctive vee-formation.

This Limited Edition Coupé cost £137,000 new in 1994. Its second, current and extremely wealthy owner took it to leading Aston specialist RS Williams for the standard 5.3-litre V8 to be uprated to a 7-litre. Interestingly, the brief was for a torquey motor with not too high a power output in deference to the

automatic transmission, producing around 530bhp and 450lb ft in comparison with the original's 330bhp and 350lb ft.

Clearly, even this performance was soon deemed inadequate, leading to the owner's knock on Lynx's door. 'The brief was to turbocharge the engine and provide a high-performance grand touring car without altering the vehicle externally,' explains Lynx MD John Mayston-Taylor. 'He didn't want Vantage or Vantage Le Mans bodywork. It wasn't easy but that's why we get selected. The biggest problem was heat: there are now six or seven radiators under the bonnet and fans in the front wheelarches, because he didn't want louvres in the bonnet.'

So what motivated the owner to want such a car, given the difficulties and hurdles of the engineering involved? 'Just as a project, really,' says Mayston-Taylor. 'He liked the idea of owning the fastest Aston in the world. He wanted it understated, so that's what we tried to come up with: like a Bentley Turbo R with more grunt, but an Aston. It had never been done before.

'We worked with the Aston Martin factory on this; we came up with ideas and they said 'That's what we would have done if we'd developed the car.' But then Ford took over and there were product liability issues. It's companies like ourselves who can develop these things, and Aston Martin is happy to give unofficial assistance – although it would probably never admit this in public. Really, from the B-posts back it's a new car.'

The RSW 7-litre conversion includes a steel billet crankshaft and steel con-rods, so already the bottom end of the all-alloy V8 was plenty strong enough to take the extra power and torque. 'The starting point was where to put the turbocharger,' explains

'THE OWNER LIKED THE IDEA OF HAVING THE FASTEST ASTON IN THE WORLD. HE WANTED IT UNDERSTATED, LIKE A BENTLEY TURBO R WITH MORE GRUNT, BUT AN ASTON'

Clockwise from right
Car looks like a standard Virage; brakes are always up to the job; alloys were custom-made; vee-grille a factory fitting.

project manager Andrew Parkinson. 'Then we realised there was enough room in front of the engine. It's a big turbo, a hybrid built specially for the car. It's quite trick, having special ceramic bearings so it doesn't need to be water-cooled.'

On the subject of cooling, the twin exhaust manifolds, which sweep back from the turbo into one, are ceramic-coated inside and out, while everything susceptible to under-bonnet heat, including the wiring and air-con pipes which link to a heat exchanger that cools petrol returning to the racing-spec bag fuel tank – is shielded. A larger radiator, in front of which is an F1-sourced intercooler for the turbocharger, is supplemented by a smaller one behind where the nearside foglight lived, while the opposite side houses a duct for the air box. Several oil coolers help keep fluid temperatures down and hot air in the engine bay is extracted by fans in each wheelarch, thermostatically controlled like those for the gearbox and differential coolers.

The engine management system is of a type used on older F1 cars, programmed 90% on the dyno and ten on the road, with a resulting 720bhp at 4500rpm and a huge 1146lb ft at 3000. Also programmable are the shift points and shift speeds in the GM four-speed auto, which has normal and sport settings: 'It's basically a Bentley Turbo gearbox but the torque converter is completely hand-built with Kevlar parts,' adds Parkinson.

Where one can really see the substantial re-engineering done to the Aston is on the underside. To harness the massive torque loads to the chassis, the Virage's A-frame main location for the de Dion rear axle has been replaced by the Vantage's wider parallel trailing arm set-up, together with the supercharged Aston's co-axial spring/dampers. 'The complete underside is Vantage throughout but with uprated metalastic bushes,' adds Parkinson, 'and we made our own trailing arms so you can really set up the geometry, more so than on the Vantage. It meant totally cutting out the back of the car and putting in the whole rear chassis of the Vantage. And we massively upped the spring rates – 400lb at the back against the Vantage's 250.'

To prevent the torque ripping the differential out of the car there is a clever system of five mounts that work under compression: 'The more power, the more they wind up, and you don't get any axle tramp.' There are also two additional mounts high up on the engine and a heavy-duty gearbox support that's normally used on American dragsters.

Aston Martin wouldn't supply the Vantage V600's brakes so at the front are Alcon 14.8in discs with six-pot calipers, and at the rear 12.8in items with Vantage calipers plus the Aston's anti-lock system. Wheels are bespoke 18in Compomotives, wearing 255/45 ZR Pirelli P Zeros, heavily offset to the inside to allow them to fit within the standard wheelarches.

Another requirement was for the Virage to retain a standard cabin. Some minor gauges have been substituted with readouts showing boost and fuel pressure, intercooler exit temperature and battery voltage. There are also choices of Off, 12% or Maximum settings for traction control and either eight or 14psi for boost.

The immediate impression is of a ride harsher than that of the standard Virage, but only a little more so than the Vantage's, and of an appropriately informative chassis. First gear is a little

Above
Dark-green paint of Limited Edition Coupé is perfectly suited to this understated but extremely powerful modified Aston

'THE ONLY DOWNSIDE OF THIS ASTON IS THAT IT DRINKS FASTER THAN AN OVERWEIGHT DARTS PLAYER ON A WINNING STREAK'

Right and below
Detailing of turbocharged Virage is restrained, but twin ceramic exhaust headers from turbo dominate engine bay.

tall, so pick-up from rest is not quite as impressive as one might expect. Once rolling, however, that instantly changes, the big Aston surging forwards with the deceptive smoothness of the Starship Enterprise in full warp factor mode.

Such relentless acceleration doesn't ram you back in the seat, the smooth upchanges no doubt playing a part: it just remains very powerful in any gear and feels almost limitless until common sense dictates lifting off the throttle. Accompanying all the while is a pleasing double-bass exhaust note together with the turbo whoosh as each gear picks up.

And talk about torque. At 2500rpm, equivalent to 704lb ft, we're already well and truly flying, and from 3000 (1146lb ft and 577bhp) the pull is just tremendous. Pick up from 2000rpm, holding the J-gate in third, equivalent to 80mph, is fantastic, the Aston hitting 135 in little more than two blinks of the eye. Even at 5500rpm the motor is pushing out 643lb ft and 673bhp, although it won't quite pull this thanks to a rev limiter set just below these revs, limiting maximum velocity in top to around 175mph. Front-end lift could become excessive at speeds higher than that; otherwise 6000rpm would be equivalent to 200mph. The long-stroke engine's real playground is between 2500 and 4500rpm, and no more than this is needed.

The chassis is almost more impressive in the way it handles such prodigious torque and power outputs. The back end, even with traction control off and turbo boost at maximum, remains well planted: quite a feat given the car's 4850lb weight and the huge torque and power. Well-weighted steering with ample feedback and accurate turn-in encourages one to exploit the power through corners, yet even taking what seem like liberties never produces more than a touch of smoothly corrected oversteer. The

brakes, too, even when motoring at very considerable speed, remain reassuringly effective.

The only downside of this Aston is that it drinks faster than an overweight darts player on a winning streak; even a 35-gallon tank at 5-10mpg doesn't go far if you're really enjoying yourself. This may explain why the car has covered only some 2000 miles in three years (and 1000 of those were during development), the frequent refuelling perhaps making life just too tedious to travel any further than the nearest golf club.

Look at the car more as a high-octane fix, suitable only for dedicated petrolheads who appreciate and can afford a real touch of class, and this unique Virage makes more sense; while you may not use it very often, you know that when it is unleashed there's more chance of winning the National Lottery than coming across a car that the Aston can't comprehensively blow into the roadside weeds.

Educated guesses suggest all this cost in excess of £300,000 to develop over two years, yet at time of writing this hugely rapid Aston was for sale at Duncan Hamilton & Co for a mere £85,000. But why sell it after all the hard work and expense? 'I think the owner was more interested in the project than the car,' says Mayston-Taylor. 'And like most of us he's busy and he just doesn't use it. It doesn't do it any good sitting around, although we've had the car down here on a regular maintenance programme.'

Considering the sheer effort and cost that has gone into this very special Virage, it's a snip at the price. △

Thanks to Duncan Hamilton & Co, +44 (0)1256 765000, www.duncanhamilton.com, and Lynx Motors, +44 (0)1424 851277, www.lynxmotors.co.uk.

DB7 GT
vs
F355

Ferrari's F355 and the Aston Martin DB7GT are now comparatively affordable by supercar standards. But which is the better choice? Mark Hales **finds out**

Photography: Paul Harmer

'Neither the Aston nor the Ferrari is old enough to be called classic, but they are both out of a classic mould'

NK03 NGU

HE BRIEF FOR THIS ONE SOUNDED SIMPLE; take two established exotics that have recently dropped to more 'affordable' levels and see what you might get for your money. And if the idea that, right now, £50,000 is affordable could have some of us choking on our cornflakes, the notion grows more interesting when you delve into the detail. Neither the Ferrari 355 nor the Aston DB7GT are old enough to be called classics and yet they are both out of a classic mould that has changed little in years.

The one, mid-engined, Italian, inevitable in red, low-slung, with a short nose and sculptured flanks to feed multiple ducts with air for oil coolers and intakes for an engine smaller in displacement and revvier. It's like Ferraris have been since the Dino of the 1970s. A little fatter maybe, but the lineage is obvious. The other, with its longer nose to house a bigger, lazier engine up front and driving the rear wheels via an in-line gearbox just like almost everything once did, harks back to the DBs of the 1960s. The body looks taller, more curvy and feline than the Ferrari's, strikes less of a pose from 30 paces. This one is silver, but it could easily have been green...

And of course there are the names on the badges. Ferrari is a relatively common name in Italy – maybe a bit like 'Brown' as in David Brown, the DB in Aston – but just say 'Ferrari' to yourself in a quiet moment. So hard not to affect a cod-Italian accent as the word rolls round the English tongue with mythic significance. Then, I hear one of our number idly contemplating how he would probably have to buy an Aston sometime just so he could say he'd been an Aston Martin owner. For him, two names are better... But, well before driving either far enough to make any assessment, I have already been asked the question several times. 'So, which one would you buy then...'

Clearly, the name matters more to some than what lies beneath but consider this. The Ferrari 355 in the photos was made in 1997. The DB7GT rolled from the Bloxham factory in 2003. At time of writing, both are wearing a similar £47,950 tag. One is nearly twice the other's age and yet it's the same price. When you consider that an 11-year-old volume model is almost a scrapper these days, 50 grand is either a brilliant piece of residual value (half its original purchase price), or a lot of money for an old motor.

The Ferrari is provided by marque expert Nick Cartwright of Matlock in Derbyshire and, having only recently arrived from Ireland, has yet to go through the workshop for its pre-sale preparation. This is a detail that provides a handy insight into the joys of owning and operating a 355. There are a genuine 26,800 miles on the clock and from the other side of the road it is – to use the motor trade vernacular – a real eyeful.

Cartwright then takes us on a guided tour. Looking more closely, the interior is faded and frayed in places (the scuffed carbonfibre seats are a £3000 extra) and the engine bay and aluminium parts on the engine are corroded. 'They always are,' says Cartwright, 'and they also rust here.' He points to the seams on the tops of the rear wings where the water comes up from the wheels – 'and here', at the base of the windscreen – 'and here...' The last is apparently the worst and it's the panel behind the front wheelarch.

This car hasn't suffered too much in these areas but Cartwright will nevertheless expect to spend more than £5000 preparing it for sale. The engine will come out (the car goes on a lift and it drops out the bottom on its subframe, complete with gearbox and rear suspension) and all the tinware will be repainted, the cam covers will be refinished and all the rusty nuts and bolts will be replaced. Cambelts have to be changed every three years

– regardless of mileage (a £1500 job) – so the service history is very important, and that will reveal whether the car has had its annual checks (about £700), the big service at 12,500 miles (about £1200-1500), or maybe exhausts, which can cost £3000 per side if you need the catalyst as well. 'The real problem with these now,' says Cartwright, 'is that they are getting into the hands of people who can't really afford one, so they don't have the essential maintenance done. You can find one for £30,000, but it will be horrible if you look really closely, like most of them. Really good ones are increasingly hard to find.'

By comparison, the Aston already looks more like a volume model, but according to Quentin Parker of The Aston Workshop in Co Durham there are still things to look out for, even if the maintenance regime turns out to be much the same. The body is part-galvanized and tends not to corrode but that is not true of the bottom part of the bulkhead near the transmission tunnel, or the front spring top platforms. Repair would attract a large bill. Smaller items such as subframe mounts, damper bushes and driveshaft joints, Parker says, make a bigger difference to the way the car drives but are relatively cheap to replace.

The normal service intervals and costs are similar to the Ferrari's; a yearly one is essential and will set you back about £800, the next is at 7500 miles and costs about double, but the Aston's Big One is further down the road, at the 45,000-mile mark. This calls for changing the spark plugs, which involves removal of the induction system from both banks of the V12. Expect a bill for about £2000.

On the plus side, Parker says that the Aston's gotchas – apart from the obvious ones like rust and damage – are relatively few. There is the air-conditioner evaporator, which involves removal of the whole central dashboard to access, and the ignition coils, each requiring the same amount of work as replacement of the spark plugs. Whether any of this is needed is more a matter of luck than anything – and whether the car has been used rather than stored – but, thus far, the maintenance costs aren't horrendous for either car; nor the service burden which, like the parts prices, is generally about the same as for an upmarket volume saloon. The main mechanicals too are just as tough; the main problem is the potential penalty if the car isn't used or the maintenance isn't carried out. It all makes you realise how well sorted and hard-wearing the average family car has become, and what good value they are.

This 355 is a stock example of a model that changed little between 1994 and '99. The 3.5-litre V8 engine has five valves per cylinder, revs to 8500rpm and pushes out 375bhp. It also has a 180-degree crankshaft like the Cosworth DFV's (and, just for the record, pushes out nearly as much power as the first DFVs in 1967). A 'flat plane' crank is lighter but makes for a different firing order and is why the sound is more like two fours than the ragged rattle of a traditional Yankee V8, which has an offset shaft. The engine is a compact, lightweight package (total 168kg) and this, allied to things like an aluminium petrol tank, helps toward an all-up weight of less than 1360kg.

This Aston is the GT variant – of which only 69 were built – of the best-selling DB7, and features slightly more power (435bhp, up from 420), a twin-plate clutch (of which more later), a shorter final drive, slightly lower suspension with firmer bushing, and tougher brake pads, plus deeper bucket seats in the front. Outside there are five-spoke aluminium wheels and some aerodynamic changes, the most obvious being the lip on the bootlid and the mesh grille, part of a more widespread programme intended to reduce lift at three-figure speeds. The V12 engine under that long bonnet is big both physically and in displacement – six litres is nearly twice the

'**Each is capable of 180mph and will fill the road with smoke on their way to 60mph in less than five seconds**'

Below
They're both becoming cheaper to buy as they get older – but proper maintenance with both of these is the key to happy ownership.

Ferrari's total and it needs a beefy gearbox and differential. It also helps towards a hefty weight in excess of 1800kg.

Each of these cars is capable of 180mph and more, and will fill the road with smoke on their way to 60mph in less than five seconds, so the next piece of re-education – as if you needed it – is the state of the roads where you will be driving your purchase. The temptation to use the full performance anywhere outside a closed circuit these days comes down to how long you want to live, or how much you like prison food. Sadly, then, the mechanicals must now have more to do with how they make the car feel to the driver, and thankfully the pair's driving styles are very different.

Crouching down and swinging into the Ferrari is easier than you think, thanks to the large doors, but from there on it's an ergonomic nightmare and for no good reason. The pedals are offset well to the left to clear the front wheelarch and, although there's plenty of length for a six-footer's legs, my right knee hits the steering wheel just below the halfway mark. The wheel swings up and down but through a very small arc, so, if you push the seat right back, you still can't reach the rim and inevitably you accelerate and brake with the side of the foot. That's extremely tiring. If I owned the car, I'd change the wheel for one with an extended boss and forget the airbag.

One of our number simply can't fit in the car at all and it's a pity because it's hard to get past the discomfort. It spoils an otherwise

'The Aston is taller than the Ferrari, its curves more feline, with a longer nose to house the front engine'

seductive introduction which is understated in inverse proportion to the spectacular looks. The apparently vestigial carbon seat is comfortable and holds you in place perfectly, the engine hums contentedly behind you, giving no clue to its willingness to rev, the clutch is light and, once you get used to guiding the gearlever in the slotted gate, the shift is a thing of pleasure. The synchros become sweeter as the oil warms; then you learn that a swift but fluid hand movement without gripping the knob or being brutal gives a very quick and smooth change. Takes a while to coordinate so the revs don't drop and then pull up as you lift the clutch (or flare because you were too eager and gassed it before the clutch was home) but, like the click, clack and scrape of the lever against the gate, it's an essential part of a Ferrari's ambience.

Meanwhile, the front end bobs and patters gently over the bumps and ridges as only a mid-engined car can, moving its haunches a fraction of a second later and a bit more slowly. Another essential part of the Latin vibe. The steering is very light and low-geared, without a great deal of feel, and there's a tendency to take more than one bite at a bend, but at this pace it's pretty sharp and makes the whole car feel taut and precise. Maybe a bit more of a rattle and squeak from the cabin than you'd expect in a car that cost £100,000 but, given the general hubbub and the roar of the tyres, it hardly matters now. It all feels good at a sensible, legal pace, pulls gently and without a splutter or hiccup from as low as 1000rpm and is generally easy to drive – almost an anti-climax, given the way the

thing turns heads as you drive through town. Why, even the air-conditioning works…

The Aston offers a whole different experience. The dash is higher, thanks to the front-mounted engine, so even if the wheel adjusts in much the same way as the Ferrari's (up and down but not in and out) it's raised up and misses your legs. Then you sit much further back, higher up in a softer, squashier seat, looking out over a much longer bonnet. Still not sure about the speckled composite scattered about the dash, or the large dose of sombre black upholstery which makes the cabin look dark and old-fashioned and smaller than it really is – just check out the pair of rear seats. Meanwhile, the engine is already more intrusive than the Ferrari's, and dominates from very early on.

That's probably a good thing, mind, because the clutch needs muscles of Garth to depress and is tiring in city traffic. The gearshift is notchy too (the six-speeder has a shorter throw, which is usually a bad move) and needs care across the gate because the spring bias is a bit vague. Not that this really matters when you have an engine like the Aston's. The V12 is sensationally muscular, pulling from 1000 to 7000rpm in any gear you want. If you tire of the clutch, leave it in fourth and head for the horizon at a missile's pace. Maybe make that fifth, because the engine is loud too, thanks to valves that bypass the main silencers over 3500rpm.

The Aston is already more intimate, partly perhaps because of the beefy engine that responds massively to the slightest touch of the pedal, »

'It's like Ferraris have been since the Dino of the '70s. A little fatter maybe, but the lineage is obvious'

and partly because the steering has so much more feel. There's more weight over the front wheels so the initial reaction is inevitably swifter, and the car is more softly sprung so the overall response from the chassis is more noticeable, but there's also the E-type effect. Where you sit in the car makes a difference to the messages reaching your backside and, being aft of the mid-point, with that long bonnet pointing the way, there's a much more involving feel to the whole thing.

It's also ballistically fast – especially if you decide to use the gears. The rear tyres (265/35/18 Bridgestones, slightly skinnier than the Ferrari's 275/40/18 Michelins) begin to scrabble when you gas it over a less-than-smooth surface, while at the same time you begin to notice the weight of the components and the amount of energy involved in the drivetrain. The rubber in the mountings for engine, gearbox and subframes starts to move about and there's the odd graunch and bonk through the cabin, plus an occasional hint of tramp from the rear wheels. Same from the front when you mash the big Brembos and watch the car dart and skitter over the ridges, ABS twittering away. On the open road, though, and as you up the pace, the steering stays pointy without being fractious as the car starts to steer more from the rear – and, if there's a trace of float from the body over crests, the whole thing stays in check pretty well.

There's already a sense that the makers would probably have stiffened up the car a deal more if they thought more people were going to hoon it round B-roads with the rear tyres on fire, but then they'd have lost the ride quality, which is good given the available performance. They might also have lost some of the intimacy that is one of the car's great tactile strengths. Big engines in relatively small cars always were a recipe for hooliganism but at least this one doesn't completely fall apart when you go there.

It is time to revisit the Ferrari and prod the beast a little more because, when you do, this car completely changes character. The engine pokes out nearly as much power as the Aston's but a whole lot less torque because it's smaller, so you have to wind it round the dial beyond 8000rpm. The hum turns to a hoarse wail – at last sounding like the race »

Above
Ferrari's seats look welcoming, but are not good in practice. Its 3.5-litre V8 will happily wind to over 8000rpm.

'When you prod the beast a little more, it completely changes character. You'd need to go to a track to take advantage of it'

engine its layout so resembles – while the car relentlessly gathers pace. This wakes up the rest of the machine and sets it jiggling and rocking over cambers and changes of surface while the steering, which had previously felt quite sharp despite the low gearing, does the reverse and begins to feel a bit limp. It probably has to, because the engineers couldn't risk making it pointy when there's a greater proportion of the weight sitting behind you, but the mid-engined layout means there's also less weight on the front wheels. You'll never get quite the same response as with a front-engined car, but the bonus is that even in the face of 8250rpm and 375bhp the rears never remotely feel like breaking traction.

You'd need to go to a track to take advantage of this, though, where you know there's nothing coming the other way and you can load up the front wheels on the brakes, then use the weight on the rears to handle the power. Nothing you can possibly do on the public road, in other words.

Make no mistake, these cars really are very fast, but they achieve much the same performance in very different ways. The Aston is better at blasting between two points while keeping you intimately up to date with what's happening beneath the wheels. You drive it in classic fashion, slow in, fast out, reading the grip via the controls. The Ferrari stays more remote, gives you less information, requiring you to build a picture of what best makes it move. It needs more thought – and more care because, like any mid-engined car, when you do finally motivate the mass at your back, it wants to carry on swinging. Apply the correct technique, though, and it would be quicker round a lap.

So, given that you can't do this most of the time, it really is a matter of how these cars make you feel, and I grow to appreciate the character of each more as the day wears on. The look from the other side of the car park and the badge on your key ring will always be a matter for the individual but, even if neither is sufficiently time-served for classic status, they might just constitute a classic for someone who can't be bothered with classic operation and classic maintenance. Just remember: they are as different to drive, and as interesting, as they are to look at. △

Thanks to Nick Cartwright Specialist Cars of Tanley, Derbyshire, www.nickcartwright.com, for the F355; and The Aston Workshop of Beamish, Co Durham, www.aston.co.uk, for the DB7GT.

Above
Big in both dimensions and capacity, Aston's V12 pumps out a tarmac-shredding 435bhp with immediate response.

'The Aston is better at blasting between two points, keeping you intimately up to date with what's happening between the wheels'

H E ISN'T MUCH to look at in photographs. Bespectacled, with receding hair and a toothbrush moustache he comes across as a shy and diffident man. A town hall clerk, you might guess, or an accountant. But how wrong you would be, for Sir David Brown had a lifestyle that made him a kind of 'Bentley boy' of the post-war era.

Except that it was Aston Martins rather than Bentleys with which David Brown was intimately connected. He owned the company for 25 years, the era when it achieved its biggest racing successes and produced its most glamorous road cars. Even though he ceased to have control of it after 1972, his initials continue on today's DB9 and DBS.

Aston Martin has come a long way since the David Brown era. But, as chairman and Ford exec Walter Hayes said back in 1993, 'His influence remains so much a part of Aston Martin'. Over the following pages we hope to show how that influence has permeated the lineage of all the road cars – DB1 to new DBS. »

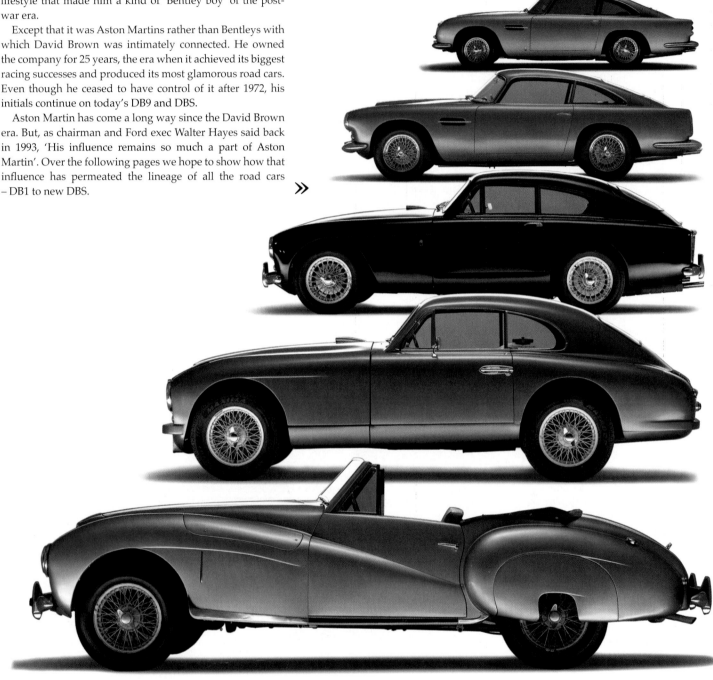

EVOLUTION

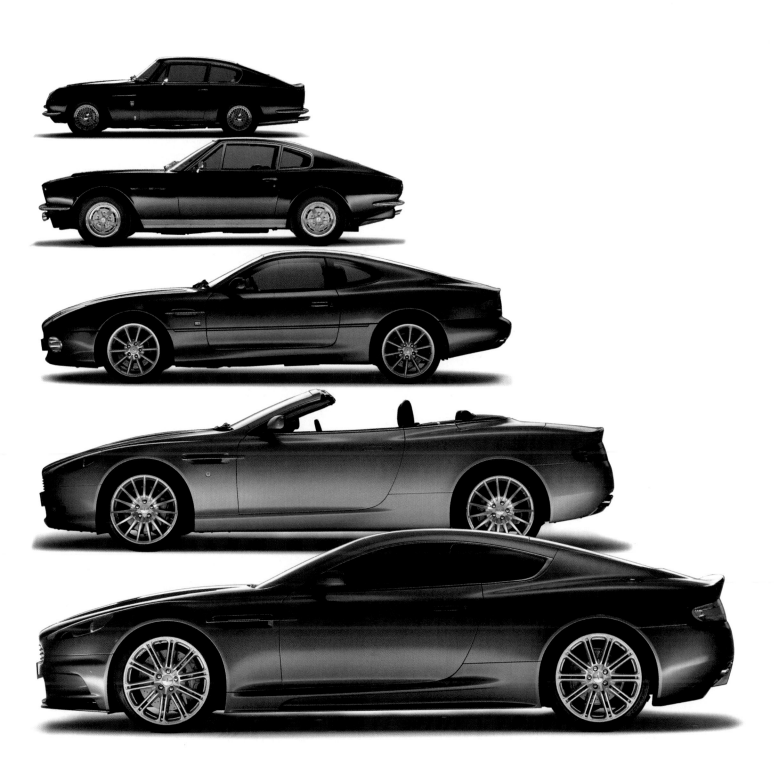

OF THE SPECIES

All the DB Aston Martins, from DB1 to new DBS - Octane explains the continuing life cycle of a legend
Words: Malcolm McKay Photography: Matt Howell

THE FIRST DBS was built in 1908 – and no, that's not a typographical error. The two-stroke DBS Valveless was an early venture into car manufacture by the David Brown Gear Company, which made about 700 of them. One is on display in the Tolson Museum in Huddersfield, heartland of the one-time David Brown empire.

But it was gears and transmissions that formed the backbone of the David Brown business. The company had been founded by the grandfather of 'our' David Brown, who was born in 1904 and schooled into the family business. He even spent time in the South African gold fields, helping to oversee the installation of David Brown gears in mine machinery when he was just 18 – a task he was obliged to take on because the director with whom he was travelling spent most of his time in an alcoholic haze.

David's appetite for adventure was clear from the start. He married his 'older woman' girlfriend Daisy against his parents' wishes, and ditched the sidecar from his motorcycle combination so that he could enter trials and speed events – at which he was so successful that Douglas motorcycles offered him a place as reserve rider on the Isle of Man TT. But his father Frank put a stop to that, as he did to the DOHC straight-eight engine that David had started to design and build in company time.

Unabashed, David made up a 'bitsa' car from a Meadows engine in a home-made chassis, which served well as daily transport. He also impressed Amherst Villiers enough to be offered a Villiers Vauxhall supercharged special at a knock-down price, with which he competed in various Lancashire sand races Then, in 1932, his father suffered a heart attack and within weeks David found himself in sole charge of the business.

Cars and motor sport had to take a back seat for a while. Instead, the David Brown Gear Co diversified into tractors; initially with Harry Ferguson and then, after Harry and David fell out, by going it alone. The outbreak of WW2 brought a big contract from the RAF for airfield bomb tractors – think back to your school days and you may remember the tiny 1:72 replica that came with the Airfix kit of the Short Stirling bomber.

It wasn't until 1946 that Aston Martin and David Brown crossed paths, when an advert appeared in *The Times* offering a 'High Class Motor Company' for sale. The company turned out to be Aston Martin, and David was sufficiently impressed by its Atom prototype to put in an offer. He bought it, as he freely admitted later, purely as a bit of fun.

But then Lagonda came on the market too, and with it a new WO Bentley-sponsored 2.6-litre, DOHC engine. David instantly saw that this new engine could be the answer to the Atom's underwhelming performance – so he bought Lagonda as well. With Lagonda he inherited the body stylist Frank Feeley, who had created those gorgeously curvaceous pre-war Lagondas.

Feeley set to work and came up with a handsome, flowing drophead on a modified Atom chassis: powered by the Atom's pushrod four-cylinder engine, it was called the 2 Litre Sports, and retrospectively it would be known as the DB1. The car you see below and right is one of just a handful left in the UK.

'FRANK FEELEY CAME UP
WITH A HANDSOME, FLOWING
DROPHEAD. RETROSPECTIVELY
IT WOULD BE KNOWN
AS THE DB1'

'THE DB2 WAS A CLEAN
AND MODERN DESIGN,
THE EQUAL OF ANYTHING
COMING OUT OF ITALY
AT THE TIME'

IN THOSE MAKE-OR-BREAK YEARS of the late-1940s, one significant event helped to kick-start Aston Martin back into its recovery phase. Technical director Claude Hill and test driver St John 'Jock' Horsfall persuaded David Brown to put in a last-minute entry for the 1948 Spa 24 Hours – at that time the pre-eminent longdistance race in Europe.

The prototype 2 Litre Sports chassis was hastily prepared with an open-winged body; so hastily that it was still being finished when it arrived at the circuit. Almost unbelievably, it went out and not only won its class but the race itself, defeating Chinetti's V12 Ferrari and a host of other 'big name' entries.

The Spa win gave Aston lots of prestige but didn't translate into many sales. The 2 Litre was expensive and its Claude Hill designed engine only a four-cylinder, so it was no surprise that only 13 were sold. Time to put that Lagonda twin-cam to use…

From a marketing point of view, six cylinders and double overhead cams were always going to win out over four bores and pushrods. The Lagonda engine didn't make it into the Feeley styled drophead but a six-cylinder racing prototype was built, in tandem with a pair that had the four-cylinder motor, all three of them wrapped in fully enclosed coupé bodies. After an abortive outing at Le Mans in 1949, the six-cylinder Aston acquitted itself at the Spa 24 Hours with a fine third overall – and effectively became the prototype for the first of the 'real' DBs: the DB2.

THE DB2 SET THE TEMPLATE for all that was to come. A handsome two-seater coupé, powered by a 2.6-litre version of the Lagonda twin cam, it had notably fine handling and strong performance for its day. Very early cars were adorned with useless 'washboard' louvres on the front wings but otherwise, as the later DB2 on the facing page shows, it was a clean and modern design, the equal of anything coming out of Italy at the time.

As a touring car, though, the DB2 lacked practicality: luggage had to be stowed behind the front seats. Enter the DB2/4, with vestigial rear seats into which you could squeeze up to two additional people; more significantly, there was an opening rear hatch for access to the load space. The DB2/4 certainly wasn't the first hatchback (Citroën's pre-war Traction Avant Commerciale is usually given the credit) but it was one of the pioneers.

Inevitably, the DB2/4 was less lithe than its DB2 progenitor – the headlamps had to be raised a couple of inches and it gained chrome bumpers – and the process continued as the DB2/4 evolved into the Mks II and III. The DB2/4 MkIII, which is usually simply called the DB MkIII, was the most radically different: compare the MkIII, above, with the DB2 on the left.

The DB2/4's bowler-hat-shaped grille was squashed down into a shape more like the one that would appear on the DB4, 5 and 6; likewise the dashboard instruments were grouped into a proper binnacle, rather than laid out on a slab of wood like place settings on a refectory table. More significantly, there were front disc brakes and a bigger, 2.9-litre engine. In standard form it put out 160bhp and in theory (if not in practice) you could order a super-hot 214bhp competition version.

The DB2 had been stretched to its practical limits, in every sense. It was time for a change: a new engine and a whole new car. Time, in fact, for the DB4.

»

FIRST, THOUGH, A QUICK DIGRESSION into what really interested David Brown – the racing side of things. Road cars were there to turn a profit, but his main reason for bothering to make them was so that he could go racing.

As his youthful exploits had shown, David was pretty handy with either 'bikes or cars and in his early days with Aston Martin was keen to have a crack at driving at Le Mans. 'I felt that, even at the age of 46, Le Mans was something I could handle and enjoy,' he later recalled, but the RAC thought otherwise and refused to grant him a competition licence. And, as one of his staff commented when Brown proposed racing in the Mille Miglia, 'If you get killed then we all lose our jobs!'

Fortunately David found the ideal person to manage Aston's competition interests in John Wyer, late of Watford garage Monaco Motors and the man who would go on to mastermind the Gulf Oil racing programme. Space doesn't allow their inclusion here but we should at least mention the DB3, DB3S and DBR1 race cars, which steadily upped the competition ante for Aston Martin during the 1950s until the company achieved an outright win at Le Mans in 1959, and the World Sports Car Championship the same year. The DB3S, in particular, is regarded as being one of the most beautiful road-racers ever built and achieved immortality of a different sort when it served as Terry-Thomas's crumpet-puller in the 1960 comedy School for Scoundrels.

Although the Le Mans win, achieved by Shelby and Salvadori in a DBR1, was the apotheosis of Aston Martin's competition efforts, John Wyer remembered that David Brown saw it as just another notch on his metaphorical bedpost. As the pair took off from Le Mans after the race, David looked down and said: 'Thank God we need never go to that bloody place again.'

ASTON MARTIN'S COMPETITION high point overlapped neatly with the introduction of its stunningly handsome new DB4 road car in late-1958, first of the trilogy – DB4, 5 and 6 – that, for most people, still represents the company's finest hour. Even if you discount the 'glamour factor' bestowed by Sean Connery wearing a tuxedo, this series of cars has everything going for it.

For a start, there was a new engine. The old Lagonda-based 3-litre had been pushed to the limits of development, but engineer Tadek Marek came up with a more-than-worthy successor: an all-new, 3.7-litre straight six. And this new engine went into an all-new body and chassis, built on the Superleggera or Superlight system patented by Touring of Milan, by which alloy exterior panels are wrapped around a network of small-diameter steel tubes. By race-car standards it wasn't that light – under that skeletal framework was a giant shoebox of a steel punt chassis – but it was good for a big grand tourer.

Most importantly, the DB4 looked supremely elegant. As is so often the case, the first-series DB4 was prettier than any of its descendants: early cars like the 1959 Series I pictured below right have an understated lightness about them that was compromised by the more dynamic, thrusting form of the slightly

721 HYK

'AS IS SO OFTEN
THE CASE, THE FIRST -
SERIES DB4 WAS PRETTIER
THAN ANY OF ITS
DESCENDANTS'

XH 871

longer, usually faired-headlight Series V and its DB5 successor – although the Silver Birch DB5 featured in rear three-quarter view opposite the DB4 would undeniably be more popular with the man in the street, for obvious reasons.

The DB4 went on to spawn a high-performance, short-chassis version – the GT – and an even more extreme derivation, the ultra-light DB4 GT Zagato, which was the archetypal Goodwood rival to a Ferrari GTO. The Zagato became so revered that it was revived as an official 'Sanction Two' limited production run in the early-1990s, using previously unallocated chassis numbers.

DB4 gave way to the DB5 in 1963, which will be forever associated with a saturnine Scot brandishing a Walther PPK. Not many people know, or indeed care, that Bond's car is in fact the prototype DB5.

SUPERFICIALLY SIMILAR, the DB6 of 1965 was significantly longer in the wheelbase than the DB5 and gained an upswept 'Kamm' tail. True aesthetes bemoan the compromise made to the original DB4's near-perfect proportions but the benefit was seen in improved high-speed stability, not to mention less risk of thrombosis for the legs of rear-seat passengers. Paul McCartney of popular combo The Beatles was a DB6 fan – he bought the example below (which is now owned by Aston Martin) and is reputed to have made the first-ever recording of the lyrics to Hey Jude inside the car, using its dash-mounted tape recorder.

On a more prosaic note, the DB6 MkII, which appeared briefly right at the end of production in 1969-'70, gained several user-friendly modifications: better seats, power steering and a lighter clutch, to name but three. It's tipped by experts as the one to have, especially since only 240 were built.

UNKIND SOULS WOULD SAY that the next DB model was a case of moving from the sublime to the ridiculous...

It is true that the William Towns-designed DBS, bigger and unashamedly transatlantic looking, has been the black sheep of the DB series for so long that many of them have already been sacrificed on the altar of parts donation for earlier cars.

But that is all very strange, because the DBS, particularly in its earliest, full-width stainless grille guise, is a very handsome car. The detailing may not be perfect – there's a heaviness around the sills, and especially the front and rear valances – but the car manages to carry its considerable bulk with panache.

'THE DETAILING MAY NOT BE PERFECT BUT THE DBS MANAGES TO CARRY ITS CONSIDERABLE BULK WITH PANACHE'

Received wisdom has it that the DBS's low ranking in the Aston pecking order is because, having been designed for an all-new V8 rather than the DB6 straight six it was launched with, it simply couldn't walk the walk to match its talk. The reality is that even the six-cylinder DBS is a quick car, and any deficiency in straight-line speed is compensated for by the handling benefits conferred by its new de Dion rear suspension, (chassis engineer Harold Beach had wanted to use a de Dion axle as far back as the DB4, but had been overruled on cost grounds).

The car in our pictures, a superb 1972 DBS V8, is what the DBS should have been from launch in late-'67. The new quad-cam V8 engine, designed – like the preceding straight six – by Tadek Marek, gave the DBS the punch it deserved. Aston Martin's road cars had reached a new level of performance.

Sadly, the inverse was true of the company. Aston Martin had always been just one of David Brown's interests and during the 1960s he had been distracted by another passion, ships and shipbuilding: he built up the Vosper-Thorneycroft business and this may have caused him to take his eye off the motoring ball. By the late-'60s the David Brown Group was losing money and David Brown started to think about cutting his losses.

That meant selling two of the businesses he had built up from nothing: David Brown Tractors and Aston Martin Lagonda. Both were disposed of in 1972, the car company (and its estimated £5 million debts) being taken on by a venture capital outfit called Company Developments. Five years later, Vosper-Thorneycroft was nationalised by the Labour Government; in 1978 David Brown left England forever and moved to the tax haven of Monte Carlo.

ASTON MARTIN DIDN'T DIE, of course. It would be fairer to say that it lurched from one bout of ill-health to another, passing through the hands of a bewildering number of financiers and entrepreneurs. The cars, which no longer wore the DB initials, were still prestigious and impressive but their sheer bulk had started to look rather antiquated to a new generation of buyers seduced by the lithe lines of a Porsche or Ferrari.

It was a long time before a fairy godmother appeared, in the unlikely shape of Walter Hayes, vice-chairman of Ford Europe. In the spring of 1987 Hayes happened to meet Victor Gauntlett, then-owner of Aston Martin Lagonda, on the Mille Miglia, and Gauntlett let slip that he'd really like to develop a smaller, higher-volume car than the V8 but lacked the capital to do it.

»

Hayes was a good friend of Henry Ford II and called round to Ford's British home at Henley when he returned from the Mille. 'Why don't we buy Aston Martin?' was his suggestion, and within a couple of months the deal was done: Ford would take a 75% stake in Aston Martin Lagonda, retaining Gauntlett as chief executive for three years.

But Ford had its eye on landing other, bigger fish, and soon after acquiring AML it reeled in Jaguar, too. Jaguar's problems were of a different magnitude to Aston's and the danger was that the Newport Pagnell firm's needs would be overshadowed by the more pressing concerns of its Coventry rival. The Jaguar deal brought one great benefit to Aston Martin, however: access to a whole new tranche of talent and technology.

The Jaguar parts bin could provide the basis of that higher-volume Aston desired by Victor Gauntlett. OK, so there was a danger it would be perceived as a rehashed Jaguar but, given the limited money on the table, Aston didn't have much alternative.

And the raw material was actually pretty promising. Jaguar had a 3.2-litre all-alloy straight six available, which could be supercharged to give it added oomph. The undeniably old, but fine handling, XJ-S could donate its chassis, while stylist Ian Callum came up with a superbly liquid shape that had echoes of the iconic DB4-6 shape yet was utterly modern.

An alloy-bodied, front-engined coupé with a supercharged straight six – it had the makings of a proper Aston, alright.

But what to call it?

REPUTEDLY, IT WAS WALTER HAYES who suggested the new Aston should be called the DB7. The well-connected Hayes was also a friend of David Brown's, and in 1993 invited the 89-year-old Brown to revisit Newport Pagnell for a celebratory lunch. When Hayes mentioned his DB7 idea, Brown revealed that there might be some DB7 badges lying about in a drawer somewhere – he remembered having had some made up in the late-'60s…

'NO-ONE BUYS A CONVERTIBLE FOR 150MPH-PLUS MOTORING... THAT'S FAR TOO FAST FOR ANYONE TO RECOGNISE YOU'

It's fair to say that not everyone liked the DB7. Some felt that the Jaguar connections were below the salt, while the car was also criticised for sounding uninspiring. But it did the job. It sustained the company through yet another difficult period and was Aston's biggest seller until the V8 Vantage arrived in 2005 and started selling in enormous numbers. The introduction of a 420bhp V12 for the DB7 Vantage in 1999 increased the car's credibility massively; as *Car* magazine shouted on its cover, 'the grand tourer reaches its peak'. The green coupé below is the last DB7 made and is from Aston's own collection.

The V12 went into the new 2001 Vanquish, the first Aston to be created with current chairman Dr Bez at the company helm, and one that marked the resurrection of the Bond association when it partnered Pierce Brosnan in *Die Another Day*. Like the film, the car was dramatic and very entertaining but not quite fully realised. Early cars had well-documented 'flappy paddle' gearbox problems – as Jeremy Clarkson pithily observed, it took two weeks for a

Vanquish to complete one lap of the BBC *Top Gear* test track – but once this had been sorted the Vanquish rightfully took its place as one of the best GT cars in the world. Fine car though it was, the Vanquish never quite escaped the shackles of sharing some interior details with its Ford relations. It took the arrival of the DB9 for Aston Martin to realise itself again as a unique brand.

The more observant among you will have noticed that the car below is a Volante, the name given to Aston convertibles since the DB6 of the 1960s. Initially the DB9 Volante was electronically limited to a mere 165mph top speed, because of worries that the soft-top might shred itself if subjected to the coupé's 186mph maximum, but that deficiency has since been rectified.

No-one buys a convertible for 150mph-plus motoring, in any case; that's far too fast for anyone to recognise you. The Volante is a car to be seen in, a fact that the producers of the hit ABC TV series, *Desperate Housewives*, were clearly aware of when they allocated one to the show's fiery-tempered Gabrielle.

»

PERHAPS THAT'S ONE TOO MANY references to popular culture, but the fact is that Astons have been enlivening the fictional world ever since James Bond drove a DB MkIII in the 1959 Ian Fleming novel Goldfinger. Aston enthusiasts therefore heaved a collective sigh of relief when the Bond film, *Casino Royale*, proved a worthy backdrop for the new DBS. The car itself went into production in 2007 and has since appeared in the 2008 Bond film *Quantam of Solace*.

The keyfob for the car shown above is labelled 'Hero 3', which signifies that it was one of three stunt cars built for *Casino Royale*. This one was clearly used for exterior shots only, since it has an incomplete interior with a truly massive roll cage. By the time Bond had crawled over this and squeezed himself under the steering wheel, the villainous Le Chiffre could have achieved world domination and be enjoying a nice cup of cocoa.

Some would-be buyers of the production DBS might need the cardiac defibrillator fitted to Bond's car when they learn the asking price that currently stands at just over £160,000.

SIR DAVID BROWN (he was knighted in '68) would have appreciated the engineering integrity as well as the opulence of today's Aston Martins. Although he later acquired all the trappings of the super rich – the polo ponies, the aeroplane, the big yacht in Monaco and the ex-model wife who was 48 years younger than himself – he lacked the superficiality of the true playboy.

Sir David liked living in the fast lane but only if he was the man in the driving seat. He was never just along for the ride. Sir David Brown died on September 3, 1993, only three months after he had been named President for Life of the company he built up as the result of answering a newspaper ad. It did indeed turn out to be 'A High Class Motor Company'.

» Thanks to Matt Clarke at Aston Martin Lagonda, the Aston Martin Owners Club (www.amoc.org) and Aston Martin Heritage Trust (www.amheritrust. org), Junction Eleven studios (www.junctioneleven.com), Robin Southward (DB1), Richard Dodkins (DB2 – which is for sale; see this issue's classified ads), David Crook (DB MkIII), Bryan Smart (DB4), Martin Hasker (DBS V8), and Aston specialist Desmond Smail, whose company restored the superb DB5 (+44 (0)1234 713083, www.djsmail.co.uk).

Cradle to Grave

Just after Aston Martin closed the doors at its Newport Pagnell factory after nearly 50 years of car production, John Simister took a DB4 and the last-of-line Vanquish on a symbolic journey to Aston's new home at **Gaydon** Photography: Matthew Howell

JULY 19, 2007. KENNY CLARKE, Aston Martin test driver and one of the company's longest-serving employees, drives the last-ever Aston Martin Vanquish off the line at Newport Pagnell. But this is no ordinary model-change; it's not like it was when the old V8 gave way to the Virage, or the DB5 was ousted by the DB6. This is the end. This Vanquish and that's it. No more.

The factory on the east side of Tickford Street, Newport Pagnell, Buckinghamshire, has closed. The collection of brick sheds and workshops behind the mock-Tudor cottage reverberates no more to the tapping of a panel-beater's hammer or the growl of a freshly fired-up V12 engine. That collection had grown organically from its founding in 1820 as Salmon and Sons, coachbuilder, through the facility's time as the Tickford coachbuilding firm (bought by Aston company owner

David Brown in 1954) and onwards from 1957, when Aston Martin's production moved there from Feltham, Middlesex, with a stopover in Yorkshire en route. But the modern world has left it behind.

The Aston Martins we know and love the best came out of the Newport Pagnell factory. The marque's first new model, in 1958, was the DB4, the car that set the tone and the style template for all Aston Martins to follow.

First and last, DB4 and Vanquish. Is there any common thread apart from the similar composition of any micro-particles of dust that might have lodged in crevices as the cars neared completion? Is there, fancifully, some sort of Newport Pagnell spirit absent from Jaguar-based DB7s made at Bloxham or the new Gaydon generation? I think we should find out.

»

This page
Bryan Smart's superb DB4 and last-ever Vanquish pose in front of 'Sunnyside', the old Salmon's cottage.

THE WHOLE HISTORY OF THE NEWPORT PAGNELL factory sits between these two cars. We've parked them outside the cottage, and not surprisingly everyone who walks past knows exactly what they are. Aston Martin was a significant employer here, and with the Works Service operation over the road it, still is.

A hundred employees lost their jobs at the closure, but 60 were given work elsewhere within Aston Martin – at Works Service; at the parts centre in nearby Wolverton; at Gaydon. Of the remaining 40, some were near retirement and everyone knew what was coming. Life goes on.

This is the Vanquish that Kenny Clarke drove off the line, chassis number 502593 and Newport Pagnell's final car. It wore the number plate V12 AML on the day, but now it's road-registered as KX07 OBB. Anoraks among us are pleased at the number's appropriateness, intentional or not. Under the current scheme KX is a Milton Keynes identifier, but under the old system it was issued by Bucks and was worn by many past Aston Martin company-owned cars. I lived in Bucks as a child and those BH, KX and PP number plates seemed thrillingly local.

And the Almond Green DB4? Built in 1959, it's an early Series One with frameless door windows and a particularly clean, pure look. Owner Bryan Smart is very fond of originality because it makes cars feel the way they were designed to feel. He's even carried this through to the choice of tyres, Avon Turbospeed crossplies. Should be interesting with the 3670cc straight-six's likely 200bhp; Aston Martin claimed 240bhp at the time but was as guilty as anyone of horsepower inflation.

Compare that with the 520bhp on offer from the Vanquish S Ultimate Edition's 5.9-litre V12. It's strange that, as cars get ever faster and more capable, the roads get ever slower and more fragmented. Maybe this £182,095 Vanquish S is an ultimate in more ways than one, for what use is there now for anything faster than this fastest-ever roadgoing Aston?

The M1 was also being built when Newport Pagnell started building DB4s. So traffic had to traverse the country on A-roads, one of which was the A50, which started at a junction with the A5 in Hockliffe, Bedfordshire, and wriggled its way right up to Cheshire. Most of it has been renamed, downgraded and chopped up into other route numbers now, and the rhythm of long-distance movement is long lost. It's fun to look at old maps, see where it went and retrace it today.

Tickford Street, nowadays the B526, used to be part of the A50. We leave the old factory and follow the old A50 back down to the M1, which it crosses at Junction 14 as the A509. But we're going to head north up the motorway, the venue in years past for many a high-speed test before transport minister Tom Fraser imposed an 'experimental' 70mph limit in 1965 after a spate of fog-bound accidents which had nothing to do with high speeds. Rival maker AC's vast M1 testing speeds with racing Cobras may have had something to do with it, too.

I'm in the DB4, and today the M1 is emphatically not as it was in those days before barriers and 'sheer volume of traffic'. There's a jam, of course, so I'm getting lots of practice with the DB4's ultra-precise four-speed gearchange and its lack of built-in guiding towards third that means you end up in the blind alley opposite reverse until you've learned the required lightness of touch. But what an untemperamental, docile engine this is. I'd expected something similar in feel to a Jaguar XK, yet this shorter-stroke, all-aluminium unit is revvier, friskier, somehow more modern. In triple-Weber DB4GT form it was good for 6500rpm, but the twin SU HD8s of this car aren't so generous in their airflow.

It's a lovely sight under the bonnet, though. Do you remember the Corgi model of the DB4, the first British die-cast with an opening bonnet? The minuscule twin-cam within seemed to fill the tiny engine bay, and the same is true of the full-size edition. It's a heck of a big

'See how slender the windscreen pillars are at the edges of the 'screen. There's air and space in here'

engine for 3670cc. No wonder today's racing Aston experts have got up to another litre out of it. The best part, though, is that I've wanted to drive a DB4 ever since I was given that model, and now I am.

We leave the M1 after sporadic traffic-gap bursts over 70mph, just so the DB4 can feel in character, and head along the A43 past Silverstone, all dual-carriageway nowadays with some roundabouts for extra amusement. You'd expect a DB4 to have heavy steering, but the

combination of this and the crossplies makes for an almost vintage feel, despite there being a steering rack between the front wheels. Go too quickly into a bend and the DB4 understeers lugubriously; the trick is to go in slowly enough for the front wheels to bite, then accelerate to settle the attitude and bring the tail round in the gentle, progressive oversteer that crossplies encourage. Do that and it all comes together, letting you exploit the DB4's relative lightness. At 1361kg, it's no

Far left
Cruising up the M1, which was being built at around the time Aston moved to Newport Pagnell.

heavier than today's compact hatchbacks.

Our drive involves time travel as well as road travel. The plan is to finish up at Gaydon, where today's Astons are made in a handsome, ultra-modern factory grander than anything the firm's owned before, a factory for the post-Vanquish era. But we're going via Bloxham, near Banbury, where a vital Aston sub-plot was enacted in the early Nineties. This involves a brief run on another one-time trunk road, the former A41 between Aynho and Banbury, which is now renamed the B4100.

The M40 has rendered that part of the old A41 redundant for heavy traffic, and now it looks much as it must have done when Aston made DB2s, except where it crosses the road that's supplanted it. The DB4 gets ever better as I learn its ways: you sit with a commanding view over the deep bonnet air-scoop, no wood in sight at your vision's edge but a fine array of dials in late-1950s Smiths and Lucas style dead ahead.

Three sets of heating and ventilation controls suggest cooling by

Below
DB4's 3670cc gives very different thrills to 5.9 Vanquish en-route to Vantage Business Park (top). Salmon's factory, below left, dates to 1820.

'The DB4 gets ever better as I learn its ways: you sit with a commanding view over the deep bonnet air-scoop typical of an early DB4'

committee, but the handbrake is a fly-off item (imagine getting that past EU Type Approval today) and the steering shows that there's no reason why a three-spoker should always have the vertical spoke at the bottom. And see how slender the windscreen pillars are at the edges of the wraparound windscreen. There's air and space in here.

The Bloxham factory, based around a former farm with some ancient buildings at its heart, is the Vantage Business Park now. TWR has left the place that once housed the Jaguar XJ220 operation and later, when in the space of a weekend the putative Jaguar F-type became the XJS-based Aston Martin DB7, contained the lines for the car that kept Aston alive.

The firm had been bought by Ford, and a new model was needed fast to stem the losses made by Newport Pagnell's Virage-derived cars. One was under development but it would have been too costly to make, so against the wishes of then-chairman Rod Mansfield, former head of Ford's Special Vehicle Engineering, the new prototype Jaguar was reworked

by designer Ian Callum into an Aston Martin. A new front-air intake and a pair of chrome-accented vents on the front wings were all it took; Callum has always maintained that the shape of one traditional British front-engined GT is never going to be much different from another.

This car was hardly a true Aston, although later V12 versions could claim more authenticity with their Aston-unique engines from which today's units grew. But it did the job and made the firm strong enough to justify its crucial post-Bloxham expansion into the new Gaydon factory.

I remember the DB7s lined up here at the launch, ready for the route to Goodwood and some hot driving tips from Peter Gethin, but today there are marketing, technology and light industrial businesses here. The people at the InTouch marketing consultancy are intrigued at the pair of Astons that bracket part of their building's unlikely car-making past.

The Vanquish. What a fabulous extravagance this car was, and is. While DB7s made the money, Newport Pagnell retained the glamour and the

Last Production Car
Vanquish S Ultimate Edition
Chassis No. 502593   19th July 2007

V12 AML

heritage and created the Vanquish with a little development help from Lotus. Designed, again, by Callum, it was the cultural bridge between Aston's past and its future, while the DB7 was the financial one.

It's based on a bonded-aluminium structure which previewed the one beneath the current DB9 and V8 Vantage: you can see the Lotus influence already. There's carbonfibre in here too, in the screen pillars and very visibly in the braided brace across the engine bay. This is the final version of the Vanquish S that appeared in 2004, with harder-edged dynamics and extra power, and part of what makes this one an Ultimate Edition (the 50th of 50) is an interior with very obvious stitching and gloss black detailing to go with the very slightly metallic black – is it in mourning? – exterior.

There was embarrassment at the Vanquish's launch in 2001 as clutches fried and the sequential-shift transmission misbehaved, but Aston Martin stuck with the idea and eventually made it work quite well. Not

Ferrari-well, but good enough. Wealthy owners could have their cars expensively converted to manual as of last year, but this final example sticks with the shift it was meant to have.

It's a bit perverse in operation, it must be said. You can't just start up, select a gear and go, so you'd better not be in a hurry. James Bond's Vanquish must have had special treatment from Q in Die Another Day, because he'd never have got away so quickly in a standard car. You switch on, wait for the gearshift control unit to sort itself out, select neutral by pulling both gloss-black paddles towards you, and only then will the push-button starter operate. At least you don't have to suffer the cheesy reminder of your car's 'power, beauty and soul' inflicted on you by the Gaydon cars' display screen on start-up.

It starts with a dangerous-sounding V12 yowl, harder and more menacing than a DB9's. And so it should: there's an extra 78bhp here. Into gear, minimal manoeuvring to keep the clutch from frying (it still » smells all too easily), and away I blast from the Vantage Business Park. The shift into second still requires care and a well-judged throttle lift, but the gearbox is a world away from the first incarnation.

This is a super-crisp, revvy, bombastic engine, which demands you keep your window open to hear its voice. To blip down two gears, hearing the wap-wap of the throttle's auto-blip, is to be in that heavenly aural place EU noise-limit police don't understand. The Vanquish is alive, pulsing, singing. There's a soul here which, I hate to say, makes the Gaydon cars seem a touch synthetic. It seems to be the soul of decades of handbuilt tradition, of craftsmen singing along with the radio, cracking jokes, doing things their own way. I suspect Gaydon, with its systems, streamlining and 6700-a-year production, can never reproduce that.

Is this all the wishful thinking of a mind inclined to favour the organic and human over the efficient, or is there something of substance here? I don't know, but in our world of fabulous cars it's what you feel that counts. And I do know I liked the last Vanquish I drove a lot more than the DB9 I drove on the same day, and that I like this one more again.

Why? Because of the transmission, I suppose, which makes it easier to enjoy the fabulously accurate, progressive and believable steering, huge grip and pointy wieldiness surprising in an 1835kg car. Never mind the pace: over 200mph, Aston reckons, and a lively 4.8 seconds to 62mph. Compare that with 140mph and around nine seconds to 60mph for the DB4, then the fastest four-seater on the planet. The DB4 is still brisk by today's standards but the Vanquish feels sensationally rapid.

Most of all, though, the Vanquish feels natural, at ease with itself, as if its characteristics are innate rather than applied to a neutral canvas. It even rides well, and has stupendous brakes. The last real Aston Martin? I don't think we can go that far, because history will be kind to the new generation, but there is still something slightly headstrong about it that doesn't quite fit with the Gaydon ethos.

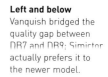

Left and below
Vanquish bridged the quality gap between DB7 and DB9; Simister actually prefers it to the newer model.

WE'RE AT GAYDON, BACK ON THAT OLD A41. Our two Astons are parked in front of the light stone headquarters building that fronts the factory. A new styling centre is being built to our left, positive signs of a positive future now that Aston is no longer controlled by cash-strapped Ford (without which there would be no Aston Martin today, don't forget). Neither car has anything to do with Gaydon, except that both of them heavily influenced what is now built here.

The DB4 looks oddly old-fashioned from the back but is the epitome of purity from the front and side. Its proportions, lost on the later, longer DB5, are perfect, its grille shape and wing vents have carried through to nearly every Aston since. By comparison the Vanquish is a bruiser, a taut skin over hefty haunches, a car which looks the way it drives. It's such a dramatic way to end the Newport Pagnell era.

Dr Ulrich Bez, Aston Martin's continuing chairman, comes out to view the scene. He's a man who shuns nostalgia but values heritage. 'The DB9 has the simplicity of this DB4,' he says, implying that the Vanquish hasn't. 'The difficult thing is to make a simple shape look right, because without decoration it is laid bare.'

That's the measure of the DB4's legacy and the shape that Carrozzeria Touring created for it. The Newport Pagnell factory is gone, but if you were to take a DNA swab of that new Gaydon styling centre you'd still find the genes of Newport Pagnell's first new car lurking within. Probably painted Almond Green.

'A new styling centre is being built to our left, positive signs of a positive future'

SWITCHING OFF THE LIGHTS AT NEWPORT PAGNELL

'It had been coming for a long, long time,' says Kingsley Riding-Felce of the Newport Pagnell closure. He runs both Works Service, where Aston Martins of all ages are serviced and restored, and the customer relations department, and has been with Aston since the precarious times of the mid-'70s.

'On the last day the guys were fantastic. There were lots of people there from the past, a broad cross-section including some former directors, and perhaps symbolically it was a sunny day between spells of rain. It was highly emotionally charged – it was not just the end of Aston Martin Lagonda at Newport Pagnell, but the end of the Salmons family business and Tickford.'

There was a family feeling at Newport Pagnell, built up by the hand-to-mouth way the company was run over the years. 'Victor Gauntlett was an incredible character. He always made it clear that we were at motor shows to sell cars and keep people in work, not just to have a presence. We worked very closely with the banks. And we always asked dealers to bank deposits from customers before 2.30pm on a Friday because we had to pay the workforce on Tuesday. It was a bit of a rollercoaster.

'A lot of people made sacrifices to keep the company going, such as taking low wages. What they created will always be with us. Aston Martins are cars for life – they can always be restored.'

In 50 years Newport Pagnell built about 13,000 cars, divided among 30 derivatives. Gaydon, on current form, can surpass that total in just two years. Makes you think. ⚠

» Thanks to Bryan Smart for helping us out on the day and lending his delightful DB4.

Left
While cars are no longer made at Newport Pagnell, Kingsley Riding-Felce continues to run Works Service there.

The BOND Astons

FROM Goldfinger TO Quantum of Solace

BMT 216A

Now pay attention: James Bond drove Aston Martins. Yes, he drove a lot more besides, but here's the story behind the ultimate Brit-built wheels that kept 007 one step ahead of the enemy

Words: Keith Adams Photography: George Bamford

JAMES BOND – it's just a name, and yet within those two seemingly innocuous syllables lies a wealth of adventure, intrigue and, dare we say it, darkness. No other fictional character of our times is quite so clearly defined – Bond is a tool to rid us of evil geniuses hell-bent on taking over the world, but he does it with a style that sets him apart from all others.

As the cliché goes, all women want him, and all men want to be him – and it's easy to see why: the tuxedoed anti-hero has the girls, the gadgets and most certainly the cars. It's a formula that clicked and, despite consuming six different lead actors and enduring a hiatus during the early 1990s, the film franchise has proved an unstoppable rollercoaster, continuing with the most recent of this 22-strong series *Quantum of Solace*.

But let's get down to the cars that Bond made famous. Rewind to 1953 and the arrival of Ian Fleming's first James Bond book *Casino Royale*. Clearly it's here that the secret agent's fine taste in automobiles was formed. Fleming wanted Bond to enjoy good cars – his first steed was fancifully described as a 1933 Bentley MkIV (later redated in the book *Moonraker* to 1930) with a Colt .45 in its glovebox.

When Fleming sold the motion picture rights to Albert 'Cubby' Broccoli and Harry Salzmann, 007's accessories took shape. Although *Dr No* lacked star cars, Bond's deft handling of his back-projected Sunbeam Alpine hinted at the excitement to come – excitement that took place mainly behind the wheel of an Aston Martin. »

'Britain might have shaken off
most of its post-war austerity, but
Goldfinger remained a heady
mixture of the exotic'

Aston Martin DB5
GOLDFINGER

Below
Undoubtedly 'The Most Famous Car in the World', and doubly precious, as the DB5 saw action in both *Goldfinger* and *Thunderball*.

'EJECTOR SEAT, YOU'RE JOKING!' 007 gasped. 'I *never* joke about my work,' Q humourlessly responded. It was at this moment that Bond, Q and MI6's Aston Martin DB5 were cemented into popular culture.

Although *Dr No* and *From Russia With Love* had scored well at the box office, 1964's *Goldfinger*, with its Q Branch-spec gadgetry, expansive sets and tricked-up Aston Martin, built on Sean Connery's portrayal of Bond and took 007 to the next level.

Britain might have shaken off most of its post-war austerity by then but *Goldfinger* remained a heady mixture of the exotic. And no more so than in the choice of wheels. The DB5 may have been selected by the film's production designer Ken Adam because it was the newest British sports car on the block, but it proved an inspired choice. In the film, MI6's Major Boothroyd – or Desmond Llewellyn's Q – flatly stated that Bond's Bentley had 'had its day', while introducing 007 to the delights of his DB5.

And what a car – Aston Martin must have been delighted by just how much of a starring role it was given. Like the Aston, those gadgets weren't in the book but, armed with a pre-production DB5 prototype to play with, the production team soon started to dream up the in-built armoury that endears the car to so many people to this day. Within six weeks, it was finished.

Although Connery's depiction of James Bond was edgy and brooding with controlled malevolence, the rather urbane DB5 suited him like a glove. It looked just as at home at the golf club as it did sweeping through the Alps dicing with Tilly Masterson's Ford Mustang, while tailing Auric Goldfinger's 1937 Rolls-Royce III Sedanca De Ville.

Now-familiar facets of the automotive landscape in the world of *Goldfinger* were actually rather novel in 1964 – and not just the homing beacon that might as well be a prototype satellite-navigation system. The Mustang was fresh on the street, as was the Aston – and for the average British filmgoer these cars were a world away from their Minxes and Oxfords. Quite right, too: would Bond have been taken seriously had he turned up at Goldfinger's factory in a Ford Zodiac?

There were actually two DB5s used in the making of *Goldfinger* – the first had all the gadgets, while the second was factory standard. After filming was completed, two more with all the toys were created retrospectively for publicity purposes, and it was then that the DB5 became known as 'The Most Famous Car in the World'. It was a suitable by-line for the vehicle that would go on to feature in *Thunderball*.

»

Aston Martin DBS
ON HER MAJESTY'S SECRET SERVICE

Above
This DBS is one of two cars used during the filming of *On Her Majesty's Secret Service*. It can be seen at The Cars of The Stars Museum.

'THERE'S NO NEED TO HURRY; we have all the time in the world' – a line delivered with such emotion at the end of *On Her Majesty's Secret Service* that it's difficult to believe the second James Bond never had a chance to reprise the role.

Controversial in many ways, *OHMSS* could have been the breaking of the Bond franchise: George Lazenby was drafted in to replace Sean Connery, and received mixed reviews when the film was released in time for Christmas 1969.

For a new start, 007 received a new Aston Martin company car – and the William Towns' DBS worked well with the overblown production values that make *OHMSS* so memorable.

Unlike in *Goldfinger* and *Thunderball*, where the Aston packed more weaponry than a Mafia convention, there were no such tricks in *OHMSS*. Its two appearances were as cameos – Bond was seen beach-drifting in the pre-title sequence, and then it was used as his wedding car at the end. Given the film's raison d'être was to introduce the

new Bond and was basically a melancholy tale, failing to stock the DBS with anything other than a bespoke glovebox added weight to the movie.

However, just like Brosnan's *Die Another Day*, as well as *Casino Royale* in 2006, Ford used the film to showcase its new products. 007's soon-to-be wife Teresa (memorably played by Diana Rigg) outwitted Blofeld's thugs (why do bad guys always drive a Mercedes-Benz?) in the snow using her Mercury Cougar. And that was before she'd seen off a fleet of suspiciously new Ford Escorts on a Swiss ice-racing circuit. As you do.

The passage of time has been very kind to car and film. Considered gauche and under-engined in the late-1960s, the DBS looks fantastic now. By the time *OHMSS* hit the screens, its maker was in financial trouble, and it would be the company's last Bond outing until deep into the 1980s. Troubled times lay ahead and Bond was starting to look like an anachronism. What he needed was a more suitable car – and it wasn't an Aston!

»

'Unlike in *Goldfinger* and *Thunderball*,
where the Aston packed more weaponry
than a Mafia convention, we weren't
treated to any car-related
tricks in *OHMSS*'

HYDRAULIC
OIL

GKX 8G

'The Vantage looks menacing in a way the more delicate DB5 never could'

Aston Martin V8 Vantage
THE LIVING DAYLIGHTS

Below
The Living Daylights
V8 Vantage looks the
business. This car was
used during filming and
now belongs to the Cars
of The Stars museum.

TIMOTHY DALTON'S portrayal of James Bond was a breath of fresh air when *The Living Daylights* hit the big screen in 1987. It's not that Roger Moore hadn't made the role his own; just that he had probably outstayed his welcome by at least two films. Cubby Broccoli actually wanted Pierce Brosnan for the movie, but contractual commitments meant that it couldn't happen, and Dalton was then drafted in for the part he had originally turned down back in 1968.

The producers decided a dose of traditionalism would be needed to maintain Bond continuity, and that meant the triumphant reunification of 007 and Aston Martin after an 18-year separation. His 1986 V8 Vantage (on 1985 'plates) was more than up to the task of taking up the baton from its forebears.

Packed with gadgets, the V8 jollies up the film on its first brief appearance at the fictional Blayden safe house. It's in open Volante form to start with, but the next time we see the V8 it's in Q Branch being 'winterised' – or having a Coupé roof fitted.

Once it's in downtown Bratislava, surrounded by battleship-grey buildings, the Vantage looks menacing in a way that the more delicate DB5 never could. On the run, the gadgets are put to good use: rocket launchers with a windscreen head-up display, retractable skis and spiked tyres are more than enough to shrug off the worst that the Tatran winter can throw up.

Like the Lotus Esprit used in the previous *For Your Eyes Only*, the Vantage ended its days self-destructing – but that was a cinematic illusion, as the film car remains alive and well and has pride of place within the Cars Of The Stars museum in Keswick, Cumbria.

Bond's flirtation with German cars arguably started here (although he first diverted from the Brit industry when he became a committed Saab 900 Turbo driver in the budget-constrained 1980s John Gardner novels) with a couple of blink-and-you'll-miss-it appearances of Audi 200 quattros, correctly overdubbed with a warbling five-pot soundtrack, in saloon and Avant forms. But his love affair with Astons wasn't over...

»

'Given that *Die Another Day* was the 20th Bond film, and crammed with references to previous episodes, the Vanquish was a fitting choice'

Aston Martin Vanquish
DIE ANOTHER DAY

CONSIDERING THE long-running association between James Bond and Aston Martin, it's disappointing to note that, following the series' hiatus between 1989 and 1995, 007's company cars in *Goldeneye, Tomorrow Never Dies* and *The World is Not Enough* were Q Branch-fettled BMWs.

Brosnan enjoyed a brief fling with his own DB5 at the start of his first film, *Goldeneye*, and it had been treated to a fair few gadgets of its own. As well as that, there were enough performance upgrades to allow it to dice with Xenia Onatopp's Ferrari F355GTS in the Alps…

But it wasn't until Brosnan's last Bond film, 2002's *Die Another Day*, that he was treated to an Aston Martin company car. Given that it was the 20th Bond film, and crammed with references to previous episodes in the series, it was a fitting choice.

Following the death of Desmond Llewellyn, the role of Q was taken on by John Cleese, who handed over the V12 Vanquish to Bond in his own inimitable style. When new-Q barked 'I never joke about my work' in response to a comment about the Aston's stealth

capability, you knew the circle had been completed.

Despite being a new-age Aston created in Ulrich Bez's iteration of the great company, there's something intrinsically right about the pairing of Brosnan and the Vanquish. For the first time, arguably, since *Man With The Golden Gun*, Bond was pitted against an equally well-kitted villain – and for the memorable car chase filmed in Iceland it was a Ford Premier Auto Group shoot-out. Vanquish and Jaguar XKR were pitched together, with the result being a slim victory for the car from Newport Pagnell.

Aston Martin supplied a pair of Vanquishes for the film, one of which featured a trick gearbox that meant it could run faster backwards than it could going forwards – a feature used to great effect.

In many ways, *Die Another Day*'s reliance on PAG products was over the top. At Gustav Graves' ice castle the car park is packed to the rafters with Volvos, Jaguars and Land Rovers – making it a *Stepford Wives*-on-wheels affair. Even Jinx's vehicle, a flame-red Ford Thunderbird, is a stablemate…

Aston Martin DBS

QUANTUM OF SOLACE

Below
DBS brings Bond up to date with a bang. This is one of two from *Quantum of Solace* that belong to Aston Martin.

SINCE 2006 and the *Casino Royale* reboot of the Bond universe, Bond's company car has been an Aston Martin DBS. Daniel Craig's 007 is different to all those who came before – uncompromisingly tough, but emotional. He wins his first Aston – a DB5 – in a poker game and, as a newly instated Double-0, the DBS comes next.

In the latest film, *Quantum of Solace*, Bond picks up from where *Casino Royale* ended, avenging the death of love interest Vespa Lynd (played by Eva Green). The DBS plays a bigger role, starring in a spectacular chase around Lake Garda for the pre-title sequence – Craig took Aston Martin's advanced driving course at Millbrook in preparation for the high-speed chase. During filming, three DBSs were used (Aston now owns two; Eon, the other), plus a handful of engineering development cars that would have had to be scrapped for legal reasons anyway.

The car pictured is the film's 'hero' car and, despite its greyness, the colour is described as Quantum Silver. James Bond and Aston Martin are now inextricably linked – and the association looks set to continue for years to come.

'In *Quantum of Solace*, the DBS stars in a spectacular chase around Lake Garda for the pre-title sequence'

BRITISH FILM INSTITUTE

WWW.DRIVEPAST.COM

Clockwise from above
Leaping 2CV from *For Your Eyes Only*; *The Living Daylights* saw Aston and 007 reunited; *Goldfinger* is where it all started; daring *For Your Eyes Only* poster caused controversy.

Top Ten offbeat Bond motoring moments
by Andrew Roberts

1 Bond films often provide excellent opportunities for the Mercedes-Benz spotter, from the W114 saloon in *The Man With The Golden Gun* and the 600 in *OHMSS* to the 250SE on Peterborough's Nene Valley Railway in *Octopussy*. However, the finest appearance has to be the fleet of black Ponton saloons in *Goldfinger*.

2 Fine examples of 'Rampantly Over-Acting Stuntmen In A Reasonably Priced Car' include *You Only Live Twice*, Toyota Crown; *The Spy Who Loved Me*, Ford Taunus 2.3 Ghia; and *For Your Eyes Only*, Peugeot 504.

3 Humble British vehicles plugged by their respective manufacturers include the Vauxhall PA Velox (*Dr No*), Morris Minor and Triumph Herald Convertibles (*Thunderball*) and the Leyland Sherpa partially consumed by Jaws in *The Spy Who Loved Me*.

4 In the early 1980s, Renault was closely associated with two Bonds: the 5 Turbo 2 with Sir Sean in *Never Say Never Again*, and the bisected 11TXE in *View to a Kill*.

5 The chase sequence with the Ford Mustang Mach I in *Diamonds Are Forever* (eight were provided) were shot in three separate locations – the streets of Las Vegas, the alley entrance in Universal Studios, and Pinewood for the pick-up shots.

6 Although Bond films are often compared with the Mini as being icons of the '60s, it wasn't until 1973 that 007 finally used one – the Moke taxi in *Live and Let Die*. This contrasted with the arch-enemies who favoured veritable fleets of Mokes in *You Only Live Twice* and *The Spy Who Loved Me*.

7 The Audi 200 quattro seen in *The Living Daylights* received a makeover from the German tuners Abt Sportsline – and is now probably rarer than an Aston Martin DBS.

8 In the novel *Goldfinger*, 007 chose an Aston Martin DB MkIII over the Jaguar 3.4 as his company car, but for the film the original choice was an E-type.

9 *Octopussy* boasts an electric rickshaw specially built at Pinewood Studios and capable of more than 70mph – partial compensation for an Indian-set scene that was apparently homage to *It Ain't 'Alf Hot Mum...*

10 Roger Moore may have described himself as a 'stunt coward' but for *Live and Let Die* he underwent three months of PSV training, and in some shots it really is Roger driving the AEC Regent. △

Thanks to: Deux Chevaux Club of Great Britain (2CVGB) Ltd, Aston Martin, The Cars of the Stars museum, JCB, Snowbusiness, and Martin Godward.

The Cars of the Stars museum, which supplied many of the Bond cars featured, is based in Keswick, Cumbria, UK. It also owns several other Bond cars, motorcycles, boats and film props and is open seven days a week (except December, when it's weekends only), 10am to 5pm. More details on +44 (0)1768 773757, http://members.aol.com/cotsmm/

Ten things you might not know about Bond's cars
by Andrew Roberts

1 In Ian Fleming's books, 007's original automotive love was his Bentley – 'One of the last of the 4.5-litre Bentleys with the supercharger by Amherst Villiers, he had bought it almost new in 1933 and had kept it in careful storage through the war' – but this is only reflected in *From Russia with Love*.

2 The Commodore Blue Sunbeam Alpine SII in *Dr No*, as used in the Jamaica scenes filmed in January 1962, was hired locally for the munificent sum of 10 shillings per day. It was a small price to pay for a slightly greater degree of glamour than was provided by the Hillman Minx saloon in the original 1958 novel.

3 Bond's Triumph Stag in *Diamonds Are Forever* was one of a ten-strong Triumph press fleet and the following year suffered the profound misfortune of starring in *Dracula AD1972*. At least in Hammer's epic it was spared the incongruous sound of an overdubbed Herald engine noise.

4 In *The Man With The Golden Gun*, the roads of Thailand seem to be dominated by lhd AMCs, from the red Hornet X and the gold Matador Coupe to the police's Matador sedans – despite the fact that the country drives on the left.

5 The Ford Escorts used in *OHMSS* also featured in a truly magnificent 1969 cinema commercial, narrated by Patrick 'King of the Voice-Overs' Allen.

6 The two buses bought for *Live And Let Die* were 1947 AEC Regents recently demobbed from London Transport prior to being shipped to Jamaica. Both of them had their roof severed at the main pillars in order to create the classic low-bridge stunt that enouraged so many joyriders in later years. In the event, only one was used.

7 The Aston Martin DB5 in *Goldfinger* was originally to be equipped with tail-lights that lifted to reveal a nail launcher. However, this rather nifty addition to the armoury was abandoned due to fears that small children might cause havoc by scattering handfuls of tacks on public roads in front of innocent motorists.

8 The Mustang and Goldfinger's Lincoln Continental were provided by those generous types at the Ford Motor Company in Dearborn. Strong men were seen to weep openly when the latter, Ford's premier car of the day, entered the crusher to be cubed by Oddjob.

9 Akiko Wakabayashi, the actress playing Aki, Bond's winsome chauffeuse in *You Only Live Twice*, could not actually drive and so half-a-dozen stuntmen had to pull the 2000GT convertible via a convenient cable.

10 The absence of a Bond car in *Live and Let Die* tallied with the additional absences of Q, and a briefing in M's office. Film makers were anxious to avoid comparison with Connery.

Simmonds
— EST. 1974 —

introduce the...

Superspoke
Steering wheel

The design brief for this wheel was to capture the classic aesthetic, whilst retaining our recognized top quality workmanship in providing a 14" wheel with a padded leather rim. The spokes are 5mm diameter stainless steel; symmetrically spaced for strength and looks.

Prices from £220 plus VAT for the standard black leather wheel

Boss* and fixing kit extra

*boss kits to fit many makes of vehicle; see simmondsshop.com for details.

Here at *Simmonds* we have the **desire to design.**
— EST. 1974 —

For the last twelve years we have been providing a design and manufacturing service to Morgan owners worldwide. Using traditional craftsmanship together with up to date technology, our dedicated small team have achieved bespoke solutions that satisfy our customers varied requirements. These are a small selection of our in-house designed components which have endured success in the Morgan Motor Car world, and due to popular demand we would like to offer them all classic car owners.

1
£105*

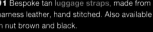
£145*

£98*

4
see above

#1 Bespoke tan luggage straps, made from harness leather, hand stitched. Also available in nut brown and black.

#2 Stainless steel rod mirror. Fully height adjustable mirror via a knurled thumb screw.

#3 Sheepskin lined double buckle bonnet strap, in hand stitched harness leather.

#4 Superspoke wheel, fitted to Morgan Roadster.

#5 Superspoke wheel with quick release mechanism, in two-tone leather.

#6&7 Chrome on brass Windwings with toughened glass and stainless steel hinges and fittings.

7
£325*

6
£325*

5
see above

*Please note: All prices are plus VAT and delivery

Simmonds of Malvern LTD   www.simmonds.uk.com   www.simmondsshop.com   info@simmonds.uk.com   Tel: +44 (0)1684 310111

Gentlemen's

RACERS

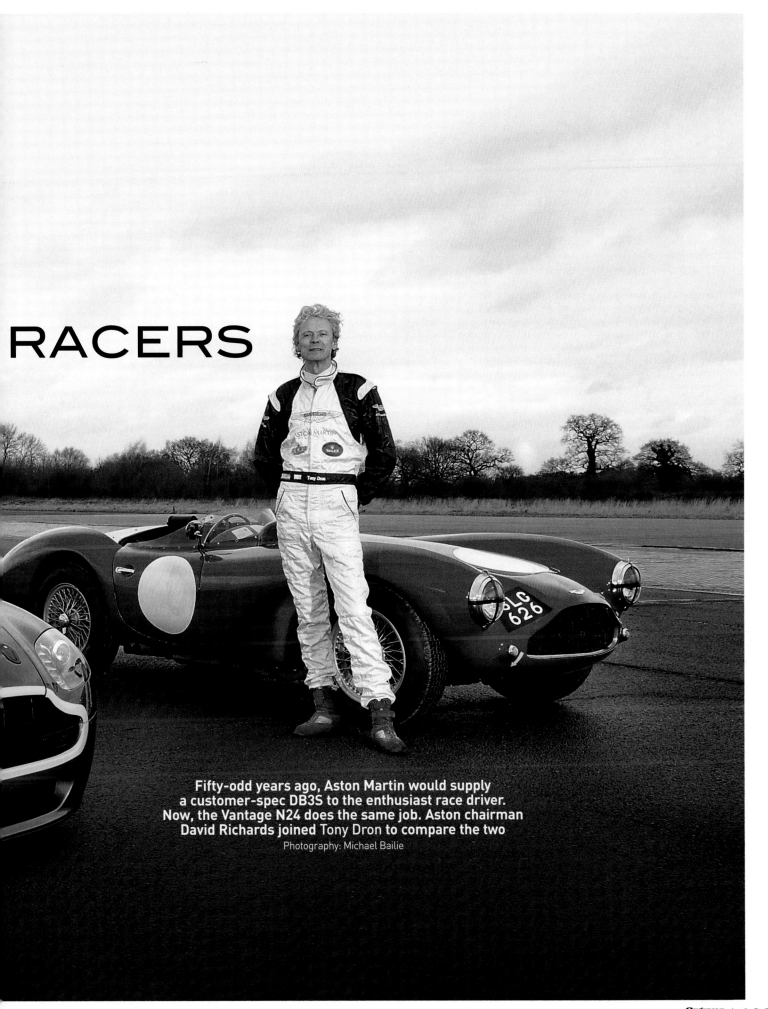

Fifty-odd years ago, Aston Martin would supply
a customer-spec DB3S to the enthusiast race driver.
Now, the Vantage N24 does the same job. Aston chairman
David Richards joined Tony Dron to compare the two

Photography: Michael Bailie

Above
Dron at speed in the DB3S – now running works spec, this car is good for 140mph and has excellent aerodynamics for the period.

1955 Aston Martin DB3S

SPECIFICATIONS

Engine
2922cc in-line six, dohc, three sidedraught twin-choke Weber carbs

Power
180bhp @ 5500rpm (racing models up to 240bhp @ 6000rpm)

Transmission
Four-speed manual, rear-wheel drive

Suspension
Front: trailing links and triangulated upper arms, torsion bars
Rear: sliding block de Dion axle, trailing arms, torsion bars

Brakes
Discs front, drums rear (racing models: discs all round; early cars had drums all round)

Weight
c880kg

Performance
0-60mph c6.6sec
Top speed c140mph

DON'T WRITE IN TO TELL ME that the financial world is in turmoil and new car sales, especially of this kind, have dropped through the floor – we've heard all that but, as it happens, sales of this sort of car are holding up very nicely so far, thank you. Aston Martin Racing, operated by Prodrive, sold all the N24 racers it could produce and has in recent months launched its replacement, the Vantage GT4, which is little changed. Prices start at £96,645. Production of this built-to-order model runs at one car per week and Prodrive expects to complete about 50 in its first year. If you order one now, you will probably have to wait three months.

As for the 1955 DB3S, also seen here, this car too was sold recently for a price rumoured to be in excess of £2m, which sounds madly high to me, but then what did I ever know about money? We got to see it before it headed off to its new home in a Swiss museum, and a surprise invitation to drive both it and its modern counterpart set me thinking.

Back in 1955, when this DB3S 'customer racing model' was produced, Aston Martin enjoyed the secure patronage of that great industrialist, David Brown. It was a famous high point in Aston history for a company which has, since the marque was founded in 1922, had many dedicated and passionate owners, some wealthy and some less so. It's only a few decades since Aston enthusiasts looked on in agony as one financial crisis followed another. Even in the good times, this precious jewel of the motor industry sometimes appeared perilously vulnerable as a trading concern.

It's been a very different story in recent years but, through thick and thin, Aston Martin under changing managements always retained a special

integrity in its products – a consistent byword for high-performance, high-quality motor cars. Things leapt forward dramatically in the era of Ford ownership, which saw healthy expansion thanks to untold investment in talented management and engineers as well as loads of cash. Since Ulrich Bez started running the business, clear planning has seen Aston Martin emerge as a real force in this rarefied market sector.

Apart from the prestige and pride of ownership, there has always been a certain magic in the Aston Martin driving experience. That has been my experience anyway, not just of the great racing classics but also of standard V8 road cars down the years. It certainly applies to these two 'customer racing models', spanning half a century and featured here at Prodrive's Warwick test track.

David Richards himself, chairman of both Prodrive and Aston Martin Lagonda, has turned out to join in the fun on this December day, grinning like a schoolboy after a largely sideways session on the track with the DB3S. 'I'd forgotten what fun these things are,' he says as we stand by the cars for some static pictures, adding slightly ruefully: 'I sold mine long ago for much less than they're worth today but I love being with the old Aston guys – they're real fun too.'

At time of writing, Richards' Prodrive company has been running Aston Martin Racing, in partnership with the factory, for five years. Before he shoots off to his next appointment, I seize the chance to fire a few questions while the cameras are clicking. Yes, Subaru's withdrawal from the WRC was a slight surprise. 'Can the Honda F1 team survive?' I ask.

'I've got a meeting about that this afternoon,' he says, but the tone gives nothing away. His desire to be a force in F1 is known but he's been on record since, saying he'll be ruled by his head and not his heart. Turning to the Vantage N24 beside us, he mentions that Prodrive made sense of things in short order, getting the build and development programmes sorted out in its inimitable style.

The car does look fabulous and I'm more than eager to drive it. Like »

'The DB3S is renowned for its beauty and benign handling, if not its outright grunt'

Above
Vantage N24 is lighter and more powerful than standard Vantage: it has now been superseded by the GT4, which has a 4.7- rather than a 4.3-litre V8.

the DB3S 'customer' cars of the 1950s, this is the standard customer-racing car of today. This one, a 2006 N24 formerly used by PalmerSport, has been brought back into Prodrive's possession as a test vehicle to develop some bigger brakes, needed for the 4.3-litre N24's replacement, the new 4.7-litre GT4.

Based on the Vantage V8 road car, N24 and GT4 racers are suitable for many events worldwide including, new for 2009, the Aston Martin GT4 Challenge category in the popular Britcar series. They are also ideal track day machines, and it might become possible to drive them to circuits using public roads. Until now this was illegal but Prodrive has been seeking Single Vehicle Approval (SVA) – which would add around £3000 to the GT4's price. With no need to buy a trailer or transporter, the premium might well be worth it.

The N24 name, by the way, commemorated the success of the prototype in the Nürburgring 24Hrs in 2006. Handbuilt to full racing specification in a dedicated area at Aston Martin's Gaydon factory, the latest GT4s emerge around 300kg lighter than standard road cars. That's a massive change but there's much more to it than merely replacing heavy glass with clear polycarbonate and stripping out unwanted trim and sound deadening. Bodyframes are modified to accept such items as pneumatic jacks and are also reinforced to withstand hard circuit use. The suspension is suitably beefed up too.

Dan Sayers, Prodrive's GT4 product engineer, has been in charge of GT4 development from the beginning. His background is mainly in rally engineering but he knows his stuff on circuits. In moving forward from the N24, understeer was identified as a problem, so for the GT4 the front camber has been increased slightly and the front springs and anti-roll bar have been softened. The rear anti-roll bar has been made rather stiffer. Further handling improvements were achieved by fitting new, fully-adjustable rear dampers.

**2006/'09
Aston Martin
Vantage N24**

SPECIFICATIONS

Engine
N24: 4300cc V8, four valves per cylinder, fuel injection. GT4: 4735cc

Power
N24: 410bhp @ 7500rpm
GT4: more than 420bhp

Transmission
Six-speed manual or optional semi-auto, rear-wheel drive

Suspension
Front and rear: double wishbones, coils, anti-roll bar

Brakes
Cast-iron discs, four-pot calipers

Weight
c1330kg

Performance
Not stated but much faster than standard Vantage V8's 0-60mph in 4.7sec and 180mph top speed

Despite the huge reduction in weight, both N24s and GT4s are still getting on for a tonne-and-a-half of very quick racing car. The grip from the big tyres is prodigious, too, so stopping them demands extraordinary braking ability – and that has become more of an issue now with the GT4's slight increase in performance.

Negotiating a path through the test car's rollcage and entering the stripped-out interior is slightly daunting but, once in the seat, I feel extremely comfortable. Thanks to plenty of room for my tall frame, I am at home straightaway. Starting up, engaging the SportShift transmission and pulling away is as easy as with any good road car. Out on the circuit, it is instantly obvious that this is a proper gentleman's racer, a very civilised machine. The engine howls in the proper style, it leaps forward along the straights and the braking performance is nothing short of fantastic for a modified road car.

There are smooth sections and some slightly bumpy areas on this test track but the Aston is never upset once, not even over some awkward wet patches following a spot of rain. The handling balance belies the terrific performance and it's surprisingly easy to drive very fast indeed with minimal steering input. This is the sign of a very well-developed car, of course – the difficult trick is to make it go that bit faster than anybody else can.

When I discuss it afterwards with race driver Lars Sexton, a resident Prodrive engineer and test driver, he confirms my view: 'You need precision to get the best from it. The temptation, because it works so well, is to overdo it – braking too late and belting into the corners too fast – but if you ease back just a little and drive it precisely, it goes even faster.'

I couldn't agree more, saying that I've found the same principle applies almost universally, even when racing the old stuff.

'Well,' says Lars, smiling, 'we had some of the old Aston historic racing guys here, trying the N24, and they were sawing away at the wheel, not getting it right at all!'

Above
Interior features lightweight mouldings, except for the standard facia, which is simply retrimmed in Alcantara; engine is little changed except for free-flow filters and exhaust.

'It's surprisingly easy to drive very fast indeed – the difficult trick is to make it go that bit faster than anybody else can'

'All I can say to that,' I reply, grinning, 'is that they can't have been the quick guys from historic racing.' But I don't doubt him for a second.

Having parked the mighty N24, it is time to turn the clock back 54 years and get aboard the legendary DB3S. One of the great gems in Aston Martin's history, the DB3S is renowned for its beauty and benign handling, if not its outright grunt. The chassis, a major advance on the DB3, was designed by the talented but secretive Willie Watson and the body came from the faultless hand of Frank Feeley. Light, tiny and slippery through the air for its time, the DB3S made the most of its straight-six 3-litre engine, partly thanks to the excellent traction of the de Dion rear axle. At the peak of development, it produced 240bhp – good for about 140mph.

Apart from 11 works team cars, there were a further 20 customer cars built to a tamer state, giving about 180bhp, and this example, DB3S/110, was one of them. A 1955 car, not registered until March 17, 1956, its early history is unknown. Certainly, it was not raced until 1975 when it tackled a Silverstone club race. Familiar in more recent historic events, the specification has been improved to that of a works racing DB3S but its fundamental originality has been respected.

Below
Frank Feeley-designed aluminium body tightly wraps tube frame with de Dion and 3 litre straight six; this car, DB3S/110, is one of 20 customer examples built.

After the comfort of the N24, I feel pretty cramped in the small open cockpit but the driving position is good enough. The pedals, however, have been arranged to make heel-and-toe changes impossible for tall drivers, a major drawback in such a machine. At speed, even over bumps and wet patches, the superb handling of a good DB3S inspires instant total confidence. Sliding easily on those skinny tyres, it can be chucked about with careless abandon but, as with the modern racer, it's much quicker when driven neatly. It's easy to see how this delightful thoroughbred embarrassed more powerful opponents in its day, at least when it came to the tight corners. Mr Richards was quite right: responsive, light and easy, it's enormous fun to let rip with a DB3S.

At the end of a great day, I reflect that Aston Martin is probably stronger now than at any previous point in its history. Yes, we know very well that new car sales are in terrible shape but my sincere feeling is that Aston Martin Lagonda Ltd has got the muscle and the quality of product to take the inevitable hit of this wretched recession, and come out fighting.

Thanks to Coys for arranging the DB3S: www.coys.co.uk.

'David Richards is grinning like a schoolboy after a largely sideways session on the track with the DB3S'

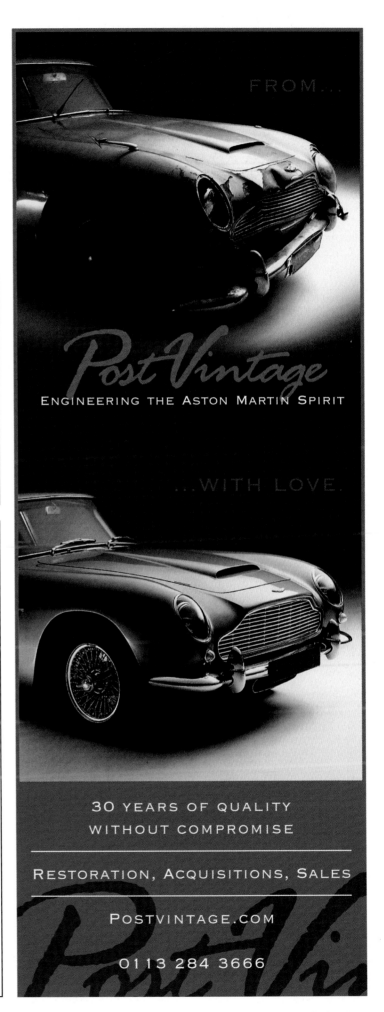

Culture shock

There's more to Florida than Disneyland.
We bluffed our way among the beautiful
people at the world-class Amelia Island
Concours d'Elegance – by arriving in
the Aston Martin DBS

Words: Richard Heseltine
Photography: Mark Dixon

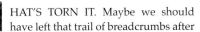

HAT'S TORN IT. Maybe we should have left that trail of breadcrumbs after all. Randomly scrolling through the menus without first checking the manual has rendered the satnav mute, the on-screen display now resembling a Rorschach rendition of Hattie Jacques. It's dark, foggy, more than a little damp, and the twisted, gnarled Spanish oaks lend the backdrop a 'let's go for a walk down by the old deserted graveyard' horror movie vibe. Welcome to Amelia Island, Florida. Beautiful by day, impossible to navigate at night. Especially if you're directionally – and technologically – impaired.

It seemed like the perfect gig: drive Aston Martin's flagship DBS to what is arguably the best concours in North America, before heading to Miami via a few work-related get-togethers. Soak up the atmosphere, mingle with the beautiful people (before striding off at a mighty clip once they rumble us) and regress to childhood with all the 007 connotations. Does the DBS stack up as a proper GT and will those US johnnies be susceptible to the latest V12 model in the marque's canon?

Like you need to ask. Having eventually got our bearings, we're greeted on day two with the soon-to-be-familiar query of 'Is that the new V12?' by everyone on the reservation, from van drivers to car park attendants. That and 'Are you lost?' A reasonable assumption, but here one motivated more by the California licence plate.

The Aston certainly belongs in this exclusive enclave. The two-day build-up to the main Sunday concours consists largely of meet 'n' greets and seminars from the great and the good of racing and hot rodding's glorious past. Those and tyre-kicking opportunities proffered by established blue chip brands and wannabes alike. Nowhere but outside the Ritz-Carlton on Amelia Island can the juxtaposition of a Spyker C8 and a Paris Hilton lookalike with the legend 'Angel' emblazoned in gold on super-tight hot pants appear normal. It's that kind of place. No cultural imperiousness on our part, you understand, more a sense of slack-jawed wonderment. You've got to see it to not believe it. »

'IT'S ALL TOO HARD NOT TO BE SEDUCED BY SOMETHING THAT LOOKS AND SOUNDS *THIS* GOOD. FERRARI SHOULD BE FRETTING'

And everyone is incredibly friendly. So when visiting from London, a city that the mass media will have you believe requires a stab vest and tin helmet to traverse safely, this naturally comes as a shock. It's almost as though you're being pummelled by politeness, which is really rather nice. Everyone wants to be here, the boorish egos that blight many highbrow car events having seemingly been left at the door.

Saturday's RM Auctions sale lends a little light relief from the new stuff, with a fabulous array of arcane Americana among the many European classics. Unfortunately, all hopes of bagging a Dual-Ghia for a song evaporate in a picosecond. Same too for the rather fabulous Touring-bodied Hudson Italia – on Borranis – and one-off '54 Packard Panther-Daytona dream car, as penned by Dick Teague (the man who gave the world the AMC Pacer). Bidding is buoyant(ish), even if interest in Ferrari 250GT Californias appears to be waning, a high – and unaccepted – offer of just shy of $2m being some way short of the £5.6m RM knocked out the ex-James Coburn car the previous year.

Altogether more entertaining are the reactions to auctioneer Peter Bainbridge's vowel-contorting delivery. His almost theatrical air of bombast is persuasive, one local claiming: 'Every time I hear that limey talk, I feel like I should stand to attention.' A point lost on his mojito-swilling companion: she's busy clicking her sparkly heels together while staring transfixed at a man with a parrot on his shoulder.

And then the big day arrives. As the early morning mist clears, the precisely manicured lawns of The Golf Club of Amelia Island play host to 150 or so classics running the gamut of forgotten etceterinis to cutting-edge hot rods. Many of them are still queuing up as the concours opens at 9am; a surreal cavalcade of Bohman & Schwartz-bodied Cadillacs, vocal four-cam Porsche sports-racers and a Mercedes-Benz W196 streamliner on the back of a flatbed vying for your attention.

Founded by sometime racer, finder of significant 'lost' cars and Cannonball Run veteran Bill Warner, and now in its 14th year, this event is a must-visit for all car lovers.

Even if you hate concours events and feel that all classics look better for a little road rash, you'll be surprised by the standards of preservation as well as restoration on display here. From one of the least disputed styling masterpieces in motoring history – the Phantom Corsair – to a gloriously unmolested OSCA MT4, there's something for everyone.

Each year, the organising committee tries to outdo itself with new and inventive classes. There can be few other events where a gaggle of American Bantams, that uniquely American take on the Austin Seven, flanks a dozen '50s Indy dinosaurs. And that's before you factor in everything from an ex-Björn Waldegård Porsche 911 Safari rally veteran (as campaigned on Sears' own-brand whitewalls…) to a Georges Irat; multi-hued, front-wheel-drive 1930 Ruxton to Fiat *Otto Vu* Supersonic.

By midday, the place is packed. Hotter than hell, too, the wool and fire-ants-weave jacket proving a dumb choice after all. Judges look crimson-faced in their constricting blazers and ties, but at least they're being chauffeured around in golf buggies, with one of their number prompting millimetre-perfect avoidance techniques on our part. But the wheelman in question is Johnny 'Lone Star JR' Rutherford so it's all cool and groovy: he's a great guy. And, as obits go, 'Pasty white hack dies in freak low-speed accident with triple Indy 500 winner' has a certain ring to it.

Elsewhere, this year's guest of honour David Hobbs proves chatty, laid back and gracious. With much of this prolific racer's back catalogue on display, from Penske/Sunoco Ferrari 512M (gorgeous, if not a winner in period) to Group 4 BMW M1, via F5000 Lola T310 and Gulf Ford GT40, all that's really missing is a Morris Oxford with a Hobbs Mecha-Matic transmission – his first competition tool. There aren't many on the East Coast, we imagine, or anywhere else for that matter. »

'THE ASTON'S CIVILITY IS THE BIG DRAW. THE NEW TOUCHTRONIC PADDLE SHIFT IS A REVELATION'

There has to be a winner, though, and this year's Best in Show award ultimately goes to the barking – and smoky – 1931 Voisin C20 Demi-Berline from The Munder Collection. On an entirely personal level, wish fulfilment arrives courtesy of hot rodding superstar Dean Jeffries and his extraordinary Mantaray. Nominally based on a Maserati GP car chassis (which one remains a mystery), this Ford small-block-powered, asymmetrically sculptured device still appears out of this world 45 years after it won big at the Oakland Roadster Show. Effortlessly friendly, Jeffries seems genuinely touched by the reaction to his – and the 'ray's – appearance, saying: 'Thanks to this car I've been able to see the world. I've taken it everywhere, even Egypt. I love showing it, and I love the fact that people still want to see it.' As do we, Michael Douglas' stunt double (yes, you read that correctly) proving to be an absolute gent. One who's owned a Ford GT40 Spider for the better part of 40 years, too. Lucky man.

Then comes the highpoint of the trip: riding in the rear of the Aston as Mark the snapper and publisher Geoff head for 'nearby' Fernandina Beach for dinner. Though nominally a 2+2 (the back seats are optional), the DBS isn't remotely comfortable for rear-ferried passenger. Not even if you're on the stumpy side. The meal is soured by the knowledge that the whole process has to be repeated later. Alcohol helps, mind.

Day four and it's off for a meeting at the Collier Collection in Naples, the drive consisting of endlessly straight roads, the flatness of topography providing an ideal place for a few high-speed passes. You would imagine. Unfortunately, the sheer number of nonagenarians blighting the blacktop, allied to the quantum volume of fuzz, reins in temptation. And when free of hectoring commuters, middle-lane bandits and on to some private roads (your honour), the Aston disappoints slightly. It's a lovely car, really it is, but the DBS just doesn't feel particularly quick: certainly not 0-60mph in 4.3 seconds and on to 191mph quick, although we suspect that's down to the ECU throttling back to cope with US low-octane petrol. At 150mph, though, it's rock solid, and undramatic enough for the wingman to make hotel reservations on his mobile without hyperventilating.

The Aston's civility is the big draw. The ride quality is surprisingly supple and the new Touchtronic paddle shift a revelation. With memories of the rubbish system that came free with the Vanquish not entirely exorcised, we expected it to be easily confused but it's a cracker. It's an exceptional auto and there's no baulking once it's hot.

On arrival at Naples in early evening, the designated driver screws up (again) with a tour of every dead end and industrial unit in town before we finally make it to the hotel. Fortunately the primal scream therapy lasts only as long as the time it takes for us to get to the bar. Another day, and there's little driving save for an evening visit to the downtown area. A brief one as it transpires: it's St Patrick's Day and there are only so many green wigs and inflatable shamrocks we can stomach. So we retire to the hotel to watch '80s B-movie crashfest, The Junkman.

Up at half-past dark, then follows the long and achingly-boring drive along Route 41 to Miami. Florida is much like you imagine Norfolk will be given a few more decades of global warming – flat and humid, with funky fauna and bloodsucking insects the size of pterodactyls. Sticking religiously to the speed limit, and staring at the horizon, we have plenty of time to ponder what, precisely, constitutes a flag-burning meeting? That, and whether it would be ethically acceptable to stuff a Chrysler 392 into a Toyota Prius.

On arrival in rain-lashed Miami, it's time to hand back the car. And with some regret, too. Although perhaps not bowled over by its outright urge, we identify the DBS as a proper gran turismo; one that we would happily give garage space to had we the necessary £159,043. Few cars of this type engender such an overwhelmingly positive response from bystanders and other road users, and it's all too hard not to be seduced by something that looks and sounds this good. Ferrari should be fretting. △

Left
Was there ever a cooler-looking XJ-S? Line-up of Bob Tullius Group 44 racing Jags and Triumphs was impressive, especially for visiting Brits.

Clockwise from above
Indy display celebrates the glory years; from the sublime to the ridiculous; Brock Yates (centre) and Johnny Rutherford (right) see the funny side.

Aston Martin
AT LE MANS

Over 100 Aston Martins have competed in the Le Mans 24 Hours since the 1920s. With one win to date, the latest generation of LMP1 cars (below), could just add to that tally

Words: Richard Heselline Photography: George Bamford
Archive pictures: Jarrotts, Aston Martin

It's a race that is both enduring and to be endured, whichever side of the pitwall you're standing. As one of the last truly great motor sport classics yet to be neutered or corrupted, Les Vingt-Quatre Heures du Mans still entrances all who make the pilgrimage each June. Whether a fan or a competitor, you don't so much root for an entry to prevail, you root for it to survive. Le Mans can be a fickle mistress, one who doesn't always play nice.

Just ask any driver armed with an Aston Martin. Ever since the first works effort rolled up at the Circuit de la Sarthe 80 years ago, only to return to Blighty with a brace of DNFs, this legendary marque has experienced its fair share of heartbreak. Over 100 Aston Martins – or derivatives – have attempted the 24 Hours, yet the triumph tally remains static at just one outright victory. As a comparison, Jaguar »

Left from top
Aston's first appearance at Le Mans, 1928 – LM1 (no. 25) and LM2 (26) both retired; DB2 of Abecassis/Shawe Taylor finished fifth in '51; refuelling the Clark/Keen DB2 in '52 – it came seventh.

Far right
Connaught drivers Tony Brooks and John Riseley-Prichard had their first works Aston drive in DB3S/8 at Le Mans in '55, but retired with mechanical trouble.

has won seven times.

Thing is, for so much of its history, the marque has threatened to vanish into irrelevancy – or worse – but somehow has always hung on in there. Same too, for its involvement in the great race. Most of Aston Martin's outings over the last five decades have been down to plucky enthusiasts whose impoverished inventiveness has often maintained the marque's presence, even if their efforts haven't always been rewarded.

But this calamity-prone manufacturer is now independent again (although this may soon change), and run by a cabal of racing men. It shows. In recent years we have been treated to a resurgent brand that has taken on the GT elite for bragging rights – and won. And now, even more tantalising, comes the prospect of a challenge for overall spoils with a proper sports-prototype.

We can only hope. It's been quite a wait for a second triumph, especially as Aston Martin's lineage at Le Mans stretches back further even than the inaugural 24 Hour race of 1923. The town lent its name and its roads to Grands Prix as far back as 1906, and in sixth place at the end of the 1921 event was B Marshall in Bunny, Aston Martin chassis B2. Seven years later, the marque debuted in the 24 Hours with LM1 and LM2. The former retired having met with a ditch after 31 tours, its sister lasting until the 19th hour, when a gearlever snapped off. There was,

however, one small consolation: the equipe trousered the Rudge-Whitworth prize of 1000 Francs for having the fastest 1 1/2-litre car over the opening 20 laps.

Some 23 team cars would emerge between 1928 and 1936, the marque scooping fifth place and class honours during its next showing at Le Mans in 1931 (AC 'Bert' Bertelli/CM Harvey) with LM6. This would prove a regular finishing spot, with Driscoll/Penn-Hughes steering LM9 to a category win a year later, and Newsome/Widengren in LM10 in 1933 to make a fifth place/class triumph hat-trick for the marque. There would be further successes, Skeffington/Murton-Neale guiding LM20 to – quelle surprise – fifth place and a class win in 1937, but from 1938 there would be an 11-year hiatus before Aston Martin again appeared in the endurance classic.

By which time it had undergone another changing of the guard. In 1947, David Brown famously spotted an advertisement in The Times for 'A High Class Motor Business' and assumed control. A year later, he followed through by acquiring Lagonda, principally to secure its new in-line 'six'. Once inserted into the splendid new Frank Feeley-penned DB2, a three-car works team descended on Le Mans in 1949 to showcase the firm's brave new world, backed up by two privateer pre-war 2-litre cars and a lone DB1. Tragedy struck the factory squad when Pierre Maréchal perished after crashing at Maison Blanche. There would be

little glory that year. But there was some reason to be cheerful. Much of this was down to the arrival of John Wyer as works competition manager. Inheriting a trio of drivers, he set about recruiting more for a tilt at the 1950 race. Eric Thompson was one of them.

'I got to know John when he was MD at Monaco Motors, which had run my HRG at Le Mans in 1949,' recalls the supremely affable 89-year-old. 'When he joined Aston's, he already had Charles Brackenbury, George Abecassis and Lance Macklin. John had a gift for pairing up professional drivers and amateurs like myself. For me Le Mans was lovely, as you got so much seat time. It certainly beat Shelsley Walsh…'

Not that his works career got off to a flying start: 'For 1950, we had three cars and I was down to drive with Jack Fairman. Unfortunately he had a coming together with a truck on the drive down and was injured. The car wasn't going to be fixed in time either, so I drove a development hack known as 'the sweatbox' with John Gordon. We were out quite early on with a broken crank. The others went very well and finished first and second in class [and fifth and sixth overall].

'A year later, we were back with three cars [joined by two privateers]. I was teamed up with Macklin, who was very much the coming man at the time. That year we had a fairly uneventful race and finished third overall and won the 3-litre class.'

'IN 1955 THE TRIO OF OPEN CARS, INCLUDING CHASSIS DB3S/8, PICTURED HERE, RETIRED THROUGH ACCIDENT DAMAGE AND MECHANICAL WOES'

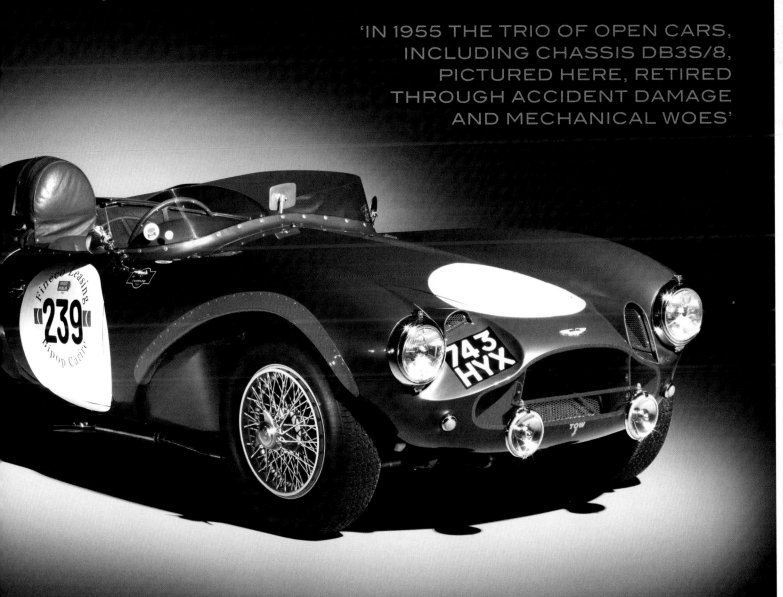

Left from top
DB3S of Abecassis/ Salvadori looked fabulous but failed to finish in '60 due to clutch failure; car no. 25 of Parnell/ Collins retired when Parnell (in car, bottom) crashed at Tertre Rouge.

Right
DBR2/1 had its first race outing at the 1957 24 Hours, driven by Peter and Graham Whitehead. It ran for a while in seventh place before the gearbox lost its oil.

With the arrival of former Auto Union man Eberan von Eberhost in November 1951, Aston Martin upped the stakes. As chief engineer, he conceived the slab-sided DB3 in time for the 1952 event.

'There were three cars, and the one I shared with Reg Parnell was an experimental coupé; we were out before long,' says a deadpan Thompson. 'It was too heavy to be competitive, and for the following year we had the DB3S which was a much better car but none of us finished the 1953 race.'

Although the chassis was essentially borrowed from its predecessor, the DB3S was lighter and smaller. But rather than concentrate on honing just this one model, the competition department embarked on a raft of new projects, which served only to sidetrack the big push. A supercharged straight-six was instigated, as was a twin-plug head. The Feeley-designed coupé was certainly a looker, and cleaved the air more cleanly than the open car, but without any noticeable rise in velocity (only rear-end lift).

Lastly, there was David Brown's own pet project, the ill-starred 4.5-litre V12 Lagonda sports-racer. Thompson was lumbered with this white elephant.
'I was teamed up with Dennis Poore, who was another good amateur, but it was obvious to me that none of the professional drivers would touch the thing.
I don't have terribly fond memories of it.' Which is understandable, as he crashed

'A THREE-CAR WORKS TEAM – INCLUDING THE 3.7-LITRE DBR2 SHOWN HERE, CHASSIS DBR2/1 – PARTICIPATED IN 1957; IT LEFT WITH NIL POINTS'

out on lap 25. It was a disastrous race for Aston Martin. Both of the factory DB3S coupés were eliminated in separate incidents, while the remaining trio of open cars (including chassis DB3S/8, pictured here, and driven by Brooks/Riseley-Prichard) retired through accident damage and mechanical woes. By the time the following year's running rolled around, the DB3S had reached the end of its development cycle, although Peter Collins and Paul Frère still splashed their way to second place in a race that entered notoriety following Pierre Levegh's apocalyptic accident in the Mercedes-Benz 300SLR.

Some months earlier, Aston's newly appointed chief racing designer Ted Cutting had been handed a brief to produce a replacement for the DB3S. Lack of time meant the new strain had to be created around the existing – and proven – straight-six.

There was no talk of selling replicas to privateers, though: this was strictly a works effort. The 3-litre DBR1 debuted in prototype form in 1956, and ran near the front for 22 hours before retiring; in second place at the flag were Moss and Collins in a DB3S, just ten miles behind the victorious Ecurie Ecosse Jaguar D-type. A three-car works team, including the 3.7-litre DBR2 shown here – chassis DBR2/1 – participated in the 1957 running and left with nil points, Tony Brooks having been lying second in an ill car before turning turtle at Tertre Rouge. A class win for a French-entered DB3S was scant reward.

But this result did go to prove the august model's worth and never more so than in 1958, when the three factory DBR1s stumbled and it was left to brothers Peter and Graham Whitehead to maintain Aston's honour with another second-place finish. Distracted by a half-hearted stab at Formula One, the marque didn't appear a likely bet for 1959 either. As usual, Stirling Moss was the hare, dicing with Jean Behra's Ferrari Testa Rossa in the early stages. But team tactics effectively dictated that Moss' race was run with 19 hours to go.

The fancied challenge from Maranello effectively evaporated by midday on the Sunday as the leading Ferrari of Hill/Gendebien dropped out, supposedly »

Right from top
Before the start in '54 – DB3S no. 21 of Whitehead/Stewart would crash out; the Whitehead brothers' DB3S came second in 1958, as it had in 1955; DBR1s line-up in 1959, the year of Aston's 1-2.

743 HYX

due to 'fuel starvation'. With four hours to go, Carroll Shelby and Roy Salvadori throttled back the lead DBR1 and ran an eventual 324 laps to head the sister car of Paul Frère and Maurice Trintignant to a triumphant one-two finish. And having realised his ambition, and also conquered the World Sportscar Championship, Brown pulled the plug; from now on racing would be the sole preserve of privateers, albeit some more privateer than others.

Although the DBR1 landed a brief reprieve, Salvadori claiming third overall with Jim Clark under the Border Reivers banner in 1960, Zagato's take on the DB4 soon became the weapon of choice in place of the regular GT. But it wasn't enough for some dealers who wanted an official motor sport programme, the French concessionaire doing most of the lobbying.

Yielding to pressure, Brown and Wyer announced a single-car effort for Le Mans, 1962. Comprising parts robbed from the DB3S, DBR2 and even the Lagonda Rapide, the resultant Design Project 212 featured a 4-litre DB4GT-based straight-six and another Feeley-

produced outline. With no development to speak of, the handsome coupé nevertheless made an instant impression. With a strong driver line-up of Graham Hill and Richie Ginther (then team-mates at BRM), the former led early on and was lying second after five hours, only for a cracked oil pump pipe to hasten retirement.

Encouraged by this performance, Brown instigated the construction of three more Project cars for the '63 season. DP215 was effectively a development of DP212, with a new box-section chassis and revised suspension, and intended to run as a prototype. Two sister cars were built for the GT class and allocated DB4GT chassis in an act of Ferrari-esque homologation chicanery. This brace of DP214s – with their Mulsanne-friendly silhouettes and lightweight frames borrowed from the DP215 – bore little resemblance to any production Aston.

Not that it really amounted to anything. Phil Hill led briefly in DP215, only to abandon the car with transaxle issues. Bruce McLaren's race ended after his DP214 blew its engine at Les Hunaudières, covering the track with oil and causing a pile-up that claimed the life

Right
Appropriately numbered as 007 and 009, two DBR9s were entered for the 2008 Le Mans.

IN ASSOCIATION WITH

JARROTTS

of Alpine driver Bindo Heinz. The third entry lasted until 2.10am before being eliminated by piston failure. Brown pulled out of front-line motor sport once again, this time for good.

Enter the barren years. In 1964, both DP214s were sold to Dawnay Racing. Michael Salmon and Peter Sutcliffe drove one in that year's 24 Hours and were holding eighth place on the Sunday morning before being disqualified. It would be a further three years before Aston Martin would again be represented. And then only as an engine supplier, the new Tadek Marek-designed V8 being raced in 5-litre form (although the exact displacement has long been debated) in the back of Team Surtees' Lola T70s. The Polish-born designer was apparently less than keen that the engine be campaigned.

The net result was humiliating failure: the lead car of John Surtees and David Hobbs ground to a halt after just three laps with a holed piston, reputedly due to overheating caused by the new – and untested – Lang Heck bodywork. The sister car was in-and-out of the pits before retiring for good, two-and-a-half hours in. An inglorious start for an engine that would become a fixture at Le Mans for the better part of 30 years.

»

Right from top
The two DP214 project cars (here at Goodwood) both retired at Le Mans '63 with piston failure; Robin Hamilton kept Aston faith in '77 with RHAM1 and '82 with Group C Nimrod.

'THE DBR9 IS A BEAUTIFUL CAR, BUT IT'S THE NOISE THAT'S MENTIONED MOST – PEOPLE REALLY ENJOY THE ASTON'S SHRILL V12 SOUND'

If only intermittently. With Brown no longer at the helm, Aston looked unlikely to see out the '70s, serial ownership making a competition programme unthinkable. It was only down to the efforts of marque specialist Robin Hamilton that Aston returned to La Sarthe. Using a 1969 DBS as a starting point, the former Rolls-Royce apprentice modified the car out of all recognition for an attack on the 1976 race. That never materialised, although he sweet-talked riot gear firm SAS to partially sponsor a stab at the 1977 running.

Joined by former autocross star Dave Preece and veteran Michael Salmon, Hamilton hustled Le Petit Camion (as it was dubbed by French fans) to 17th overall and third in the GTP class. A return visit two years on with twin turbos resulted in a dizzying fuel consumption and scorched pistons.

Undeterred, Hamilton pushed ahead with a new sports-prototype after tapping Lola's Eric Broadley for input. The resultant Nimrod emerged in time for the new-for-1982 Group C formula with partial backing from Aston's latest saviour, Victor Gauntlett. With the works car vying with Viscount Downe's privateer entry at Le Mans, both ran steadily in the race. If only briefly. The factory Nimrod driven by Bob Evans, Geoff Lees and Tiff Needell was eliminated in a huge accident caused either by a tyre shredding or rear bodywork acting as an air-brake, depending on whom you ask.

Evans recalls: 'It wasn't a bad car but it wasn't a great one either. You knew it was never going to be competitive as it was too slow and too heavy, but it was early days. It was all very *Boy's Own*. Tiff was lucky to escape unhurt from his shunt, though. I remember him saying afterwards, "I always wondered what it was like to turn left at 210mph. Now I know."' The Downe car meanwhile limped home minus a cylinder to seventh overall.

At the end of the year, Hamilton headed Stateside in an effort to save the project, the Viscount's squad producing its own radical rework. But there would be no further finishes, other Aston-powered challengers from EMKA and Cheetah never troubling the dominant Porsches (although the former led for a lap in 1985).

There would be a Group C swansong, however. In 1989, Aston Martin was officially represented in the World Sportscar Championship, the Max Boxstrom-designed AMR1 featuring a special 32-valve version of the enduring V8. Managed by Richard »

Below
AMR1 was a last hurrah for Tadek Marek's long-lived V8; it finished 11th overall in 1989, but rule changes killed it off.

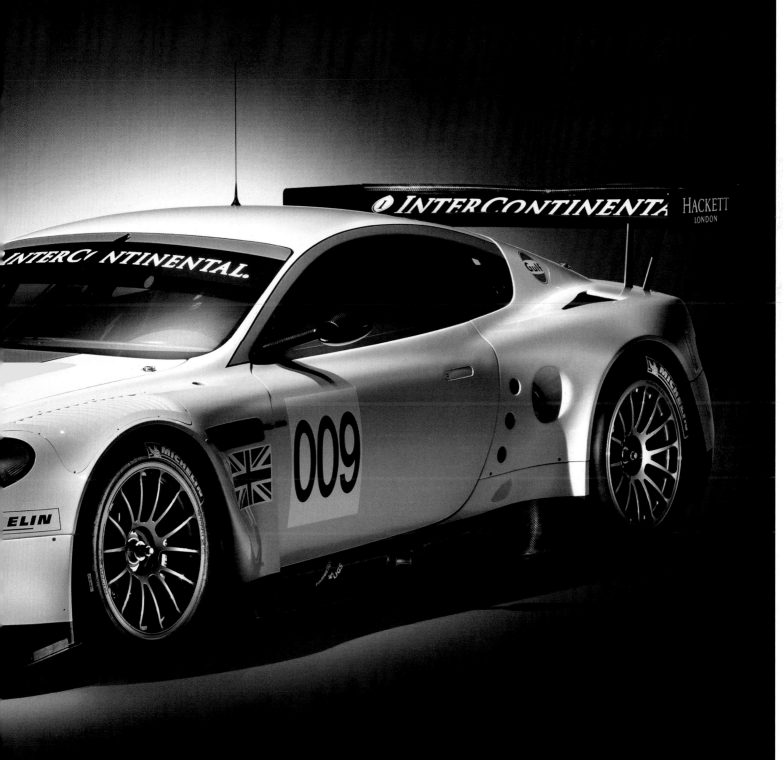

'THE AMR1 FEATURED A SPECIAL 32-VALVE
VERSION OF THE ENDURING V8, BUT THERE
WOULD BE NO AMR2 – THE FIA CHANGED
THE ENGINE RULES'

'AGAINST EXPECTATIONS, THE GULF-LIVERIED B09/60 PROVED GENUINELY COMPETITIVE AT THE 2009 LE MANS'

Williams, and with a raft of talented drivers on the roster, all looked rosy. But, despite an 11th place finish in that year's 24 Hours, and altogether stronger showings later on in the season, there would be no AMR2. Williams recalls: 'It was a five-year programme, with the central goal being to win at Le Mans. Ford bought the majority shareholding in Aston in 1987 but there was no interference.

Then the FIA changed the engine rules to 3.5-litre normally-aspirated units. We were up against Jaguar within the Ford family, and Jaguar got access to Cosworth's motor, rather than us. AMR2 was already progressing, and we'd tested a lot of components, but that was it. We were done.'

There was little cause for cheer during a barren 1990s (unless you count the Synergie-built DB7LM that failed to qualify in 1995. We don't). Fast forward to July 2004 and, for the first time in 40 years, there was something approaching a sustained competition programme. Aston Martin Racing, owned wholly by Prodrive, was established to take the fight to the hitherto dominant Pratt & Miller Chevrolet Corvettes. With GT success in the following year's Sebring 12 Hours, the DBR9 proved its worth and claimed its first Le Mans class win in 2007.

Aston talisman Darren Turner was on the driving strength and has his own thoughts on why the British challenger – nowadays fielded exclusively by privateers – remains so popular with race goers: 'The car has always had a great following at Le Mans. Some of that comes from the aesthetics because the DBR9 is a beautiful car, but it's the noise that's mentioned most when you talk to people out there: all these cars sound different but most people really enjoy the shrill V12 sound of the Aston.'

A bellow that is only amplified in the current Lola-Aston B09/60. This sports-prototype takes advantage of new rules that give production-based engines a power break in the premier LMP1 category (it uses a 6-litre unit from the DBR9). While very much a privateer 'Charouz Lola' for its maiden outing, works involvement was altogether more conspicuous for the 2009 running.

And, against expectations, the Gulf-liveried prototypes proved genuinely competitive even if fourth place was as good as it was ever likely to get. And from here? Aston Martin remains one of the most emotive names out there, one that remains inextricably linked with sports car racing despite the occasional – and protracted – hiatus. △

Thanks to Matthew Clarke at Aston Martin for his help with the photography of the Aston Martin Racing DBR9.

V12 TO LE MANS

In 2009, Aston Martin went mob-handed to Le Mans in search of glory across three separate racing categories. Octane came to town in the new V12 Vantage to see how they got on
Words: Nick Trott   Photography: Nick Dimbleby

IT'S THE MORNING AFTER THE 'BIG ONE'. Circuit workers peel Rolex stickers from the concrete barriers opposite the Le Mans pitlane, forklifts remove assorted detritus and bleary-eyed mechanics go to work preparing the race cars for transit back to their assorted HQs around the world.

The pitlane has never been so busy – not even during the weekend when the race teams did battle for the skyscraper-esque trophy awarded to the winner of the world's greatest endurance race. We stand and watch this theatre of disassembly for an hour or so before a biblical rainstorm saturates the circuit.

It's the rain that was forecast for Sunday morning but never came. It's the rain the Aston Martin race team were hoping for; the great leveller that would've put the knee-wobblingly beautiful V12 Lola-Aston Martin LMP1 back among the all-conquering (and rule-favouring) diesels from Peugeot and Audi.

Above left
Bonnet vents mark the V12 out from its V8 brother – not that this lot have noticed.

'The Vantage leaves 12-cylinder music hanging in

Aston Martin did not win the Le Mans 24-hour race on the 50th anniversary of their only outright race victory – but they gave it a bloody good go.

Rewind three days and the centre of Le Mans is crammed with race fans desperate to get a glimpse at their heroes during the 'Parade des Pilots'. Every nook and cranny of the medieval city centre is filled with people. Flag-waving children perch themselves on dad's shoulders, brave teenagers climb trees and everybody has a camera at the ready to catch the moment and publish it on YouTube.

A brilliantly entertaining spectacle of race-weekend showmanship, the driver parade and the accompanying supercar parade gives race fans the opportunity to see the drivers up close and drool at an eye-watering convoy of Paganis, Ferraris and other assorted hyper-chariots. And to make things even better, *Octane* is about to drive an Aston Martin V12 Vantage in the supercar parade.

We're following a Koenigsegg and a McLaren-Mercedes SLR 722S. Neither driver seems particularly keen on sacrificing a layer of clutch plate for the good of the fans so the V12 Vantage spends the majority of the parade leaving great yelps of 12-cylinder music hanging in the air and one or two long streaks of tyre rubber on the tarmac. 'It'd be rude not to,' said a pleading British fan through our open window. Later, the Koenigsegg driver responded to the same plea… and cooked his clutch so severely that a bitter stink emerged from its bowels for hours afterwards.

The V12 Vantage is adored. Lower, faster and costlier than the standard V8 Vantage, the V12 packs the 510bhp 6-litre engine from the DBS into the smaller Vantage platform. The results could be catastrophic – a short-wheelbase chassis plus a mighty V12 engine anyone? – but Aston Martin has yet again proved its engineering prowess by delivering a beautifully-resolved supercar that's part Nürburgring slayer and part long-distance GT. The duality of the V12's character cannot be underestimated. Track-focused Pirelli PZero Corsa tyres deliver race-car grip and handling but a leather and suede interior, combined with a decent ride ensure that roadtrips are comfortable and relaxed. And how about this for practicality? For our trip to Le Mans, we managed to pack the following in the V12: a two-man tent, two sleeping bags, two inflatable mattresses, two pillows, two overnight bags, three rucksacks, two large bags of snacks and two beach towels. On the way back, we even managed to squeeze in a couple of bottles of champers too – and all this in a car with a top speed of 190mph and a 0-62mph time of 4.2seconds.

At 14:50 on Saturday we're perched at the fast Tetre Rouge corner waiting for Luca Di Montezemolo – Ferrari's chief and guest starter of this year's race – to wave the flag to signal the start of the 77th Le Mans 24-hour race. The atmosphere is charged, the weather a scorching 28°c and the noise deafening from the 234,800-strong crowd. Di Montezemolo waves the flag and 55 cars charge towards the Dunlop Bridge with the Peugeot taking the lead from pole position.

In the pits, the dramas are unfolding already. Audi privateer driver Narain Karthikeyan will not contest the race having »

he air and some long streaks of rubber on the tarmac'

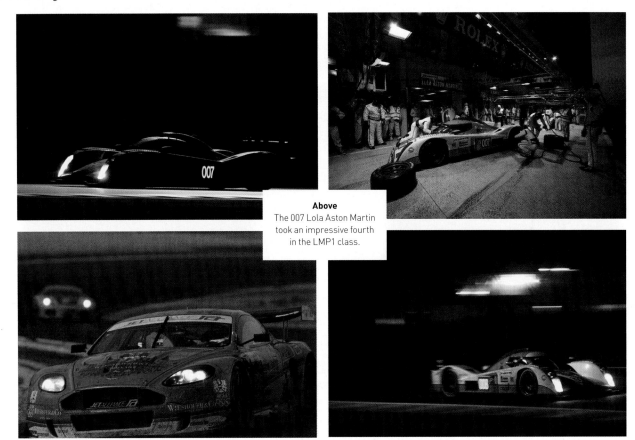

Above
The 007 Lola Aston Martin
took an impressive fourth
in the LMP1 class.

'There's a flute-like wail from the Gulf Astons'

dislocated his shoulder while jumping over the pit wall moments before the start and the sole Lamborghini in the race has yet to leave its pit-garage. The GT1-class Jetalliance Aston Martin DBR9 has returned to the pits due to malfunctioning electronics and 12 laps later Harold Primat drives the 009 Lola Aston Martin into the garage with suspected alternator drive belt problems. A moment later two Peugeots collide in the pits.

On track, the remaining Peugeots whistle eerily around the 8.46-mile circuit, its near-silent V12 turbodiesel contrasting vividly to the Aston's naturally-aspirated petrol V12. The diesel makes a hushed whoosh compared with the flute-like wail from the blue and orange Gulf-sponsored Astons.

The piercing shriek from the Aston is no coincidence either – early versions of the Lola Aston Martin featured periscope exhausts that emerged above the rear bodywork but Aston Martin's road car division asked the race team to tune the system to sound more like their V12 street cars. Dutifully (and rumour has it, reluctantly) the race team repackaged the pipes and joined the two banks of six into one exit just below the rear wing. Funnily enough, when Aston Martin Racing analysed the data after fitting the new exhaust, it emerged that the sonically-tuned version actually produced a smidge more power too.

At 16:32 the Jetalliance Aston Martin DBR9 competing in the GT1 class stops on track with more problems – this time a fuel pump failure. The car is stranded near the Porsche Curves tantalisingly close to the pitlane but it will take driver Lukas Lichtner-Hoyer over an hour to bring it back to the pits. The works 009 LMP1 Aston Martin suffers further issues when at 19:20 it spends six minutes in the pits as the team attempt to cure a water leak in the cockpit. It rejoins last in the LMP1 class,

43rd overall. At the front of the field, the 007 and 008 Aston Martins are still pushing hard with the 008 car climbing to as high as third. However, the 009 car driven by Stuart Hall collides with a Radical at 8pm. The location of the accident couldn't be more unfortunate; it occurred directly underneath Aston Martin's hospitality box.

A safety car is deployed while the wrecked Radical is removed from the track, then four hours later the stewards exclude Hall from the rest of the event for his part in the accident. Teammates Primat and Kox are forced to contest the remaining 15 hours of the race, alternating every three hours.

More troubles arrive for the Aston Martin Racing squad when at 22:00 the 008 car driven by double GT1-class winner Darren Turner gets swiped by a Corvette. The Aston comes off worse and heads to the pits for the first of many visits to cure a vibration issue. At midnight – and just as fellow works driver Stuart Hall is being excluded – Turner hands over to former F1 star Jos Verstappen. Making his Aston Martin debut, former LMP2 Le Mans winner and F1 driver Verstappen runs fast and hard but two further unscheduled stops for a gearbox then a brake issue effectively put the 008 car out of contention.

As 01:00 approaches we return to our base – the brilliantly named 'Team Langoustine' campsite – and spend the next three hours discussing the finer points of the V12 Vantage with our knowledgeable and friendly neighbours. 'DBS or V12 Vantage?' was the deeply philosophical question we mused until around 03:00. Beer was not involved. Much.

It's a fair question. The DBS and V12 Vantage use the same engine and their outright performance is virtually identical. Perhaps the best way to communicate their subtle dynamic »

Clockwise from left
Exhaustion, anticipation and then elation as fourth and 13th-placed Lola AMs cross the line together.

Pos	B. #	Cla	Name	Si
1	9	LMP1	Peugeot 908 Hc	
2	8	LMP1	Peugeot 908 Hc	
3	1	LMP1	Audi R15 TDI	
4	007	LMP1	Lola Aston Mart	
5	11	LMP1	Oreca AIM	
6	7	LMP1	Peugeot 908 Hc	
7	14	LMP1	Audi R10 TDI	
8	16	LMP1	Pescarolo Judd	
9	15	LMP1	Audi R10 TDI	

'The V12 doesn't broadcast wealth like a Ferrari'

differences is to describe the DBS as a GT with race car performance and the V12 Vantage as a race car with GT credentials. The DBS is bigger too and packs a greater visual punch on the road. However, despite the allure of the Bond-car connection, all our friendly camping buddies would chose the more focused, punchier V12 Vantage over the DBS. Tellingly, most would chose the V12 over its Lamborghini, Porsche and Ferrari rivals too.

We fall asleep listening to the glorious chorus of the remaining Le Mans racers reaching the half-way mark in the 24-hour classic. We wake at sunrise, or 'happy hour' as 008 Lola Aston Martin driver Anthony Davidson describes it. 'The car is in its sweet spot at around 05:30-06:00. The air is cooler so the engine is performing strongly and the light is better so you can take advantage of that extra performance.'

Davidson, a former F1 driver with Minardi, BAR-Honda and Super Aguri, is revelling in the moment – back at one of the greatest circuits in the world and driving for one of the most famous marques in motoring. He reveals that as soon as Aston Martin Racing announced its plans to enter the 2009 race with a LMP1 prototype he was on the phone immediately to the team, asking for a seat in the new car. Wish granted, Anthony's superb driving skills, tireless work ethic and talent for development dovetail perfectly with the seemingly indefatigable Aston Martin Racing team. Few doubt it will be the last time Davidson drives for Aston Martin.

At 09:50 an eerie silence falls over the circuit. The cars have slowed, which means the safety car has been deployed. A few seconds pass before an image of a car embedded deeply into a tyre wall is shown on a big screen. We notice a flash of baby blue, then orange then… oh no, it's an Aston. Harold Primat, driving the 009 car, has crashed at post 115b (Porsche Curves). He's OK, but an ambulance takes him to the circuit medical centre. The organisers, the ACO, report that exhaustion may have been a factor after the exclusion of the third driver (Hall) but Primat reveals later that the cockpit had started to steam up and fill with water, a precursor to a leak that saturated the rear tyres and caused the accident.

With three hours to go, Tomas Enge is leading the Aston Martin attack in fourth place overall in the 007 car. Earlier, team-mate Stefan Mucke set an astonishing 3:26.632 lap – the fastest petrol car on track and a time just 2.3 seconds slower than the Peugeot of Nicolas Minassian.

Aston Martins competed in three classes during the 2009 Le Mans 24-hour race. In LMP1, the 007 Lola Aston Martin finished a superb 4th place overall. Car 008 finished 13th, crossing the line in a crowd-pleasing formation with the 007 car while 009 returned to the pits on a flatbed truck. Despite reliability woes at the beginning of the race, the Jetalliance DBR9 clawed its way back to 3rd in class at the finish. And us? We retired early on Saturday morning with overfuelling issues (too much beer) but returned to the race later in the day to enjoy the 3pm finish.

The V12 Vantage spent much of the weekend being photographed and filmed by an enormously passionate crowd. It keyed into the spirit of this year's event like no other car present; stylish, desirable and yet inherently classy, in these tough economic times the V12 doesn't broadcast wealth in quite the same way as a Lamborghini or Ferrari and yet matches its rivals for performance and trumps them for practicality and comfort. A superb car for a superb occasion. Roll on 2010. ⚠

Aston Martin
THE FUTURE

Just when you thought Aston Martins couldn't get any more powerful or beautiful, along comes the One-77. But the innovation doesn't stop there, plans are afoot for a four-door Aston and a Lagonda SUV

Words: Nick Trott

One-77:

Time-travel 20 years into the future and the Aston Martin One-77 will be seen as the car that set the precedent for all subsequent Aston Martins. The frustratingly slow release of information on the car – from the first tantalising sketches released from Aston Martin in 2008 to the prototype displayed at the 2009 Geneva Motor Show – will be forgotten and the true totemic quality of the car will be understood. Today, its £1.2milliom price tag and 700bhp engine grab the headlines; tomorrow we will study the carbon fibre chassis, the CNC parts and rakish styling and celebrate this car's status as the grandfather of modern Aston Martin.

Of course, it's hard to think about the future when this epic car has yet to see production. But when any of the main architects in the One-77 speak, they speak equally of the car as it is now and of the next generation of Aston Martins.

Ian Minards, Aston's director of product development, says the One-77's engineering 'will signal the direction we want to go in with Aston Martin' and 'we're going to show you that although we're developing a £1.2million supercar we're actually thinking about the next generation of Aston Martin.'

Director of design Marek Reichman concurs and adds that the evolution of the Aston Martin design language begins with the One-77. 'You'll start

Below
Like all great Aston Martins, the One-77 is designed to be driven and drooled over in equal measure.

to see the form language has more tension in it, it has more hard lines, the softer lines are refined even further.' Then to allay any fears about Aston Martins turning geometrical and ugly, Reichman adds, 'but an Aston Martin will always be beautiful.'

So what does the One-77 hide beneath its 'tension' lines that has so excited the public and press since its unveiling earlier this year? To start with, the bonded-aluminium 'VH' chassis common to Aston Martin's current line-up is replaced with an immensely strong and light carbon fibre monocoque. Like the formidable Lola Aston Martin LMP1 Le Mans racer, this tub improves performance and safety by being simultaneously strong yet light. The downside? Manufacturing complex carbon fibre structures is a time-consuming and costly exercise and better left to specialists, which is why Aston Martin has formed a technical partnership with Canadian-based Multimatic – a world-leader in carbon composite technology – to build the chassis.

Unlike the Le Mans car, the One-77 has its V12 engine positioned at the front – albeit closer to the centre of the car than any previous Aston Martin. Indeed the motor rests some 257mm aft of the front wheel centre line, which promises progressive, stable on-limit handling characteristics.

Aston Martin looked closely at the similar front-engine/rear-wheel drive/carbon chassis combination featured in German DTM race cars and applied many of the same principles to the One-77, especially with regards to the suspension. Like a DTM car, double wishbones are used with pushrods connecting the suspension movement to a set of inboard and horizontally

Below

The 'tension' of the One-77's lines can only be equalled by parking a car worth £1.2million at the supermarket.

mounted coil-over spring/damper units.

Perhaps the most awe-inspiring sight when you peer inside the engine compartment of the One-77 is not the V12 motor but the sublime blocks of machined aluminium that grip the coil-overs. The craftsmanship displayed in these high-grade aluminium parts goes some way towards justifying the One-77's dizzying price tag.

The One-77's fully adjustable dampers feature advanced dynamic suspension spool valve technology (DSSV). Used in the highest-levels of motorsport, these valves permit damper adjustments to be made without removing the units from the car. The One-77 will be the first road car to use DSSV technology.

And what of the engine? Like the chassis, Aston Martin has chosen to work with a third-party specialist to bring the best out of the motor – and this time its long-term partner Cosworth that has been entrusted with the task. 'Our brief to the engine team was for them to take the 6-litre V12 as far as it could go, both in terms of output and weight reduction,' explains Chris Porritt, One-77 programme manager. Porritt, a class winner with chief executive Dr Bez at the demanding Nürburgring 24-hour race, says the target is for a power output of 'no less than' 700bhp with a 10% reduction in engine mass.

'Incredibly,' continues Porritt, 'Aston Martin and Cosworth engineers achieved a mass reduction of some 25%. It's an awesome accomplishment.' Awesome indeed: with more than 700bhp and slippery aerodynamics by Marek Reichman and his team, some engineers are speculating the One-77

'With more than 700bhp and slippery aerodynamics, some engineers speculate the One-77 will top 220mph'

will top 220bhp. Zero to a rather more pedestrian 60mph will be achieved in around 3.5seconds.

Furthermore, the One-77's 7.3-litre engine may not only be the ultimate evolution of the 6-litre V12 found in the DBS, DB9, V12 Vantage and forthcoming Rapide, it could also be the last. A very suitable sign-off.

Other technical highlights from this extreme engine include a dry-sump oil-system that is mounted 100mm lower than any previous Aston road car and a recalibrated stability control programme. A new six-speed gearbox is fitted – a sequential clutchless manual activated with paddles behind the steering wheel rather than a traditional automatic gearbox – and the gearbox and rear-wheel drive transmission system feature strengthened internals to cope with the extra power and torque.

So, with test drives not planned until later this year, how will the One-77 steer? Dr Bez is very clear on this issue; the car was designed to be used and not locked away in a hermetically-sealed garage. 'Customers are already asking me if they can drive this car and whether it will be reliable. They all want a car they can drive. I say that of course it will be reliable – it will make the 8000km durability testing at the Nürburgring like all our other cars. It will be driven fast and it will be driven at its maximum speed.' Dr Bez goes on to

promise that no other car will match the One-77 for its combination of aesthetic beauty and outright driveability – not even the formidable, and similarly-priced, Bugatti Veyron.

The last piece of the One-77 jigsaw is the extraordinary amount of personalisation available to the customer. 'This car does not have options in the traditional sense, it's more that the owner participates in the process of the development,' says Dr Bez. Each customer will be given the opportunity to fine-tune the suspension set up with experts including Chris Porritt, and even decide the speed in which they want their One-77 to change gear. Dr Bez likens this to tweaking the EQ on your hi-fi to get the exact sound you desire. Incredibly, even the exhaust note can also be tuned to the driver's requests.

Just 77 of these astonishing cars will be manufactured and 'no more,' says Dr Bez. The starting price is around £1.2million and although Aston Martin will not admit as much, it is thought all 77 are accounted for. Expert driver tuition is also provided to each customer in the hope that not one of the 77 will meet a costly end.

The question is – where next for Aston Martin sports cars? Look closely at the styling of the One-77, the carbon chassis parts, the position of the engine and the suspension and you start to get some clues. The next Vantage, DB9 and DBS will be astounding, just like their grandfather.

Lagonda:

'The Lagonda concept is a vast luxury car with SUV proportions'

Below
The ultimate in school-run Kudos? Mooted Lagonda would be several classes above road-blockers from BMW, Audi and Porsche.

The Lagonda name has been dormant since 1993 when Carrozzeria Ghia built the sleek and elegant Vignale concept. The Vignale car could not have been more different from the wedgy Lagonda of the 1970s just as the latest concept to bear the Lagonda name could not be more different from the Vignale.

The new Lagonda, first shown at the 2009 Geneva motor show in March, will be the first of a new breed of Aston Martins not to carry the famous Aston Martin wings badge. The car – or should it be sub-brand? – will be known simply as Lagonda. Aston Martin is an authentic, pure sports car but Lagonda is something else.

Something else indeed. The Lagonda concept is a vast luxury car with SUV proportions and, rumour has it, a new V12 engine. The transmission is equipped with an automatic gearbox with four-wheel drive (another first for Aston Martin Lagonda) and it will sit four in considerable comfort. Designer Marek Reichman was keen to create a shape with clear lineage back to Lagondas of old, stating that 'the clear delineation between cabin, shoulder and flank is strongly reminiscent of the powerful and evocative lines of the 1930s era Lagondas, in particular the V12-engined version of the LG6.

Further details are sketchy, but a rumoured tie-up with Mercedes-Benz for use of chassis and engines has been mooted, as is a range extension including a smaller SUV. The business plan for Lagonda, according to Chief Executive Dr Bez, is to triple the global dealer network and 'take the company into new and emerging markets around the world.'

'We wanted to make the most beautiful four-door car in the world'

Rapide:

First shown as a concept in 2006, the four-seat Aston Martin Rapide will be the first of the 'new' Astons shown this year.

Based on the VH bonded aluminium chassis architecture, the Rapide takes the DB9's glorious aesthetic and teases out two more doors. It could be a disaster – a stretched limo Aston – but Dr Bez is adamant that the car's styling is balanced and beautiful. 'The proportions must be perfect,' he says, 'if we couldn't achieve this then we wouldn't have made the car.'

Quoting the 1938 Phantom Corsair prototype and Cisitalias as the key influences, director of design, Marek Reichman adds, 'we wanted to make the most beautiful four-door car in the world.'

Currently undergoing the final stages of endurance testing, the Rapide is becoming an increasingly familiar sight at both the Nürburgring and the roads around Aston's Gaydon HQ. The engine is Aston Martin's venerable 470bhp 6-litre V12 mated to a 'Touchtronic' automatic paddle-shift gearbox delivering power to the rear wheels. Luxury features are thought to include a glass roof, bespoke fitted luggage and a hi-spec Bang & Olufsen stereo.

The Rapide will be manufactured at a new production plant in Graz, Austria – the first time an Aston Martin has been manufactured outside the UK. The facility, run by Magna-Steyr, has been designed to closely model the Gaydon factory and blends a modern production line with traditional hand-finished elements.

The first cars will be shown in September with deliveries starting in early 2010.

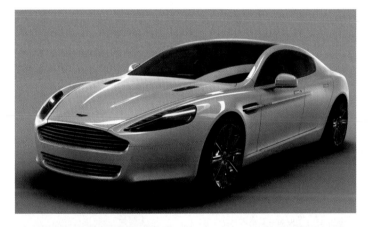

And now for something completely different...

Cygnet:

From ugly ducklings...

No, it's not April 1. This really is Aston Martin's radical new take on supplying supercars with a conscience...

ASTON MARTIN to produce a city car? Has the world gone mad? Well before you raise your Montblanc and fire off a strongly worded missive to David Richards take time to properly consider the Cygnet concept...

Based on the radical Toyota iQ Aston's urban-friendly supermini will be marketed to existing Aston Martin owners only, encouraging them to enjoy the benefits of a small yet luxurious back-up car when using the supercar is simply not appropriate... or convenient.

Called the Cygnet (in deference to the 'ugly duckling' slurs that will no doubt come its way) the new car is easily the most radical departure of Aston Martin's long and turbulent history. But for those worried that this new venture will dilute the marque's core values take solace in the fact that it is expected to sell for a luxurious £20,000 – roughly twice the price of the base Toyota.

The Cygnet is certainly a novel approach to the thorny issue of environmental damage facing supercar manufacturers; no doubt producing 2000 Cygnets a year will help Aston Martin lower its average corporate emissions. In addition this new venture is potentially a clever shot across the bows of competitor premium superminis, such as MINI and the Mercedes-Benz A-Class, which would previously have found their way into the lives of Aston Martin owners looking for city cars.

Whether or not the fur-lined, chisel-fronted Toyota iQ will find its way into the hearts of DBS, One-77 or Vantage customers remains to be seen but, if nothing else, it will be interesting to watch.

Here's a new twist on Aston Martin ownership: the company is working on the Toyota iQ based Cygnet concept, the ultimate second car for those who love their Aston, but also regularly pound the city streets...

Below
Clever marketing, a radical vision of the future, or cynical dilution of the Aston Martin brand? Cygnet has already sparked controversy.

Given the Works

Aston Martin's Works Service department has been looking after Aston customers for decades – and it has some good news for beleaguered 'wedge' Lagonda owners Words & photography: Mark Dixon

IT'S HARD TO IMAGINE NOW, but a farmer of my acquaintance used to take his 1950 Land Rover back to the factory at Solihull whenever it needed a service, right into the 1970s. He reckoned it was worth the trip up from Hertfordshire to make sure the job was done exactly right. (He still has the Landy and it's still running well, so maybe he has a point.)

Try the same thing these days and you'd be laughed out of the Lode Lane gatehouse, but there is another venerable British marque that still welcomes customers with open arms. Aston Martin's Works Service in Newport Pagnell is the place to go if you want your Aston to be overhauled, repaired or restored by the people who really, really know what they're doing.

Aston Martin has had a dedicated service department since the 1930s (right). Originally based at Feltham in Middlesex, servicing and repair facilities were moved to Newport Pagnell in 1955, where they faced the old Salmon's coachbuilding house known as 'Sunnyside' – a name in keeping with its pre-war suburban

ambience. Apart from a modern glass-and-steel façade, Works Service's buildings are also pleasingly traditional in style: think WW1 aircraft hanger crossed with Victorian red-brick factory.

At time of writing, older cars rub shoulders with modern descendants, but the facilities are about to undergo a shake-up which will see the different departments separated into four areas: the main workshop; a crash repair shop; a special vehicles section to deal with one-offs and conversions; and a 'heritage' building for restoring classic Astons.

At the time of our visit, every kind of Aston from DB4 onwards could be found somewhere on the premises, not to mention oddball rarities such as one of only two Ogle-bodied V8s (this one being converted from right- to left-hand drive) and a DB7 Zagato. But most surprising was just how many wedge-shape Lagondas were in for attention.

'Love it or hate it, the Lagonda probably saved the company in the 1980s,' points out Kingsley Riding-Felce, the dapper director of Works Service. 'It was in production a long time – 1978 to 1990 – and we built 637 of them, so it was a relatively good seller for Aston Martin. Many of our customers have owned these cars for years and years.'

Besides its UFO looks, the Lagonda's defining feature was its impossibly futuristic digital dash, introduced at a time when pocket calculators and Casio watches were vying for schoolboy attention with Top Trumps and the Boomtown Rats' latest single. The dash has been a perennial source of grief to later owners (for reasons of reliability rather than looks) and must have discouraged scores of would-be buyers in recent times.

Help is now at hand, though. Electrical engineer David Dillow, who has worked at Aston for 30 years, grew tired of receiving 3000-volt shocks every time he had to fiddle around at the back of a Lagonda dashboard. He came up with a brilliant solution: flat-panel LCD units to replace the miniature television screens installed in mid-'80s cars.

Three types of 'digital' dash were fitted during Lagonda production. The first was a red LED display, used from launch until 1984. This was superseded by the CRT (cathode ray tube) screens for a couple of years, which were in turn replaced by VF (vacuum fluorescent) displays in the

'WE REALLY DO TRY TO LOOK AFTER OUR CUSTOMERS AND THE LAGONDA DASHBOARD CONVERSION IS A CASE IN POINT'

late-'80s. It's the CRT that gives the most trouble, according to Dave.

'The screens are basically mini televisions and suffer from the same kind of faults you get on a domestic TV,' he explains. 'If the battery voltage fluctuates – when you switch on the headlights, for example – the picture is prone to jumping and things like the vertical hold can drift out of position. They were installed before the windscreen was fitted in the build process and adjusting the settings is a nightmare. Modern LCD screens take up virtually no space and run at a much safer voltage.'

If you actively dislike the digital display, working or not, there is another option – fit conventional analogue instruments into a custom-made facia. Works Service has converted several Lagondas to take round V8 dials and it's currently doing the same for a Japanese customer.

The registration plates have been temporarily removed from this Japanese car but foreign numbers are a common sight at Works Service: a few cars sport Monaco's chic blue-on-white plates and there's a Lagonda outside that's wearing, appropriately, a Saudi plate.

Kingsley Riding-Felce is convinced that it's not just the quality of workmanship that explains why customers ship their cars such distances to Works Service. 'This business is all about relationships,' he explains. 'For the customer, it's about having personal contact with the people who actually work on your car. We really do try to look after our customers and the Lagonda dash conversion is a case in point. At our projected price of £3000-3500, we won't be making much of a profit but our main objective is to support the car owners in the field.'

Aston Martin Works Service, Tickford Street, Newport Pagnell, Buckinghamshire MK16 9AN, +44 (0)1908 619264, email worksservice@astonmartin.com.

Every ASTON

All the Aston Martin greats right up to the present day – plus a few you might not have heard of
Words: Russ Smith, Matthew Hayward, Richard Gunn

1920 – 1925
Sports/Super Sports

Production of the Sports officially started in 1920, although development work began almost five years earlier. The early years mainly revolved around motor sport, and it wasn't until 1923 that cars were actually on sale to the general public. The Sports was highly advanced though; using four-wheel brakes, and a fully-floating rear axle, it was a natural competition winner – but it was obvious the car would need more power to win at an international level. After this realisation, the Super sports was put into production. This uprated Sports had an engine like no other, and it gave the Aston Martin race-winning performance. The four-cylinder twin-cam 16-valve engine produced 55 bhp, easily enough to dispatch the competition. Production of both models ended in 1925 when the company went into receivership, having sold approximately 50 cars.
Power: 55bhp
Top speed: 90mph

1927-1932
First Series (1½-Litre)/International

After the company was saved in 1927, Aston Martin pressed ahead with the new 1½-litre. Building on its competition experience with the earlier Sports/Super Sports, the 1½-litre was launched at the 1927 Motor Show. Following a year of competition use, Aston Martin made a multitude of changes to the original design, such as a dry sump and lower bonnet line, re-launching it under the new name of 'International'. Originally impressing the motoring press, the International was fast, refined and easy to drive, but the over-inflated price didn't do it any favours in the long run. 129 'First Series' cars were produced before production switched to the Second Series in 1932.

Power: 56bhp
Top Speed: 80mph

1932 – 1934
Second Series (New International)/ Le Mans

Aston Martin set about making this car much more profitable than the 'First Series'. As well as cutting production costs, they also cut the sale price of the New International to £475. With a great result at Le Mans in 1931, Aston Martin offered a 'Le Mans' upgrade to the international chassis. This featured a high compression engine, which pushed the power up from 60bhp to 70bhp. Sales of the Second Series were steadily increasing, and it was the Le Mans that people wanted, especially after the introduction of the tourer-bodied Le Mans Special.

Power: 70bhp
Top Speed: 85mph

1934 – 1936
Third Series (Mk II)

As the name suggests, the Mk II was not an entirely new car. The basic idea behind the Mk II was to develop the Second Series into a more usable, yet faster car. Using a new balanced crankshaft assembly, and a few other minor modifications to the 1½-litre engine saw the power output rise to 73bhp, although the top speed was unchanged at 85mph. The car was available with a number of different bodies, including a tourer, two-door saloon and a drophead coupé.

Power: 73bhp
Top Speed: 85mph

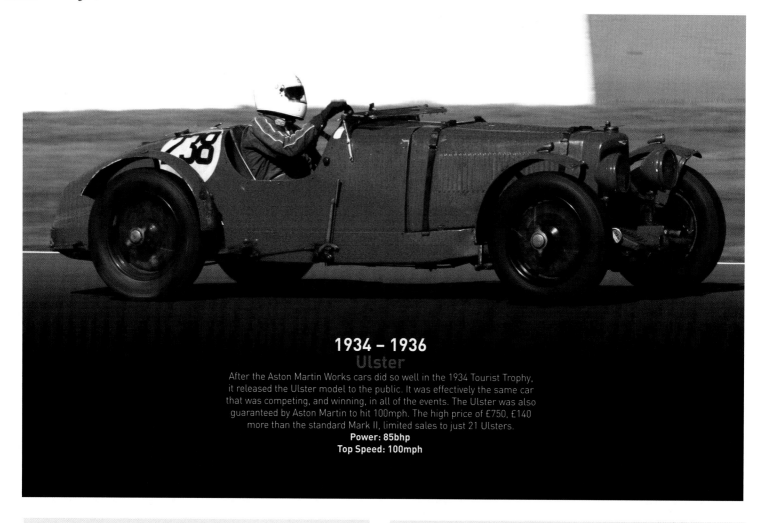

1934 – 1936
Ulster

After the Aston Martin Works cars did so well in the 1934 Tourist Trophy, it released the Ulster model to the public. It was effectively the same car that was competing, and winning, in all of the events. The Ulster was also guaranteed by Aston Martin to hit 100mph. The high price of £750, £140 more than the standard Mark II, limited sales to just 21 Ulsters.

Power: 85bhp
Top Speed: 100mph

1936 – 1940
2-litre Speed/Type C

The 2-litre speed model was completed just in time to compete in the 1936 Le Mans 24 Hour, but the race was cancelled at the last minute. In the first two years of production, just 15 2-litre Speeds were produced. The 'new' engine was not actually new, but using the 1.5 as a starting point, the bore and stroke were increased, and domed pistons were fitted, giving the 2-litre an impressive 110bhp. In 1938, it was decided that the eight leftover Speed Chassis would be used to create something a lot more modern looking. The Type C didn't go down well with Aston Martin enthusiasts, and the last one sold in 1940.

Power: 110bhp
Top Speed: 95mph

1937 – 1939
15/98

After many years of churning out race-winning competition cars, this was Aston Martin's first attempt at a more relaxed, mass-produced tourer. Two different body styles were available: the four-door Saloon and the two-door Tourer, both bodied by next-door neighbour E Bertelli. The 2-litre engine was proven on track with numerous race wins, but coupled with the heavy Bertelli-built bodyframe it was slow. The original planned production run of 100 cars was soon slashed to 50, and owing to slow sales, the original launch price of £595 was reduced to £495 during 1938 to try and shift the remaining stock.

Power: 98bhp
Top Speed: 82mph

Est. 1927

Renowned Worldwide for the Manufacture and Restoration of Veteran, Vintage & Classic Wire Wheels

- Alloy, stainless steel, chrome and silver-painted wire wheels designed to suit a variety of British Classic Cars

- New alloy wire wheels - aluminium rim with stainless steel centre, spokes & nipples

- Highly polished stainless steel wire wheels available from stock

- All chrome wire wheels manufactured using chromed stainless steel spokes & nipples

- Bolt-on wire wheels available for your modern classic

- Most wheels are now tubeless

- Up to three years warranty

- Supply, fit and balance wire wheels with tyres

- Extensive range of wire wheel accessories held in stock

- In-house Workshop to build and restore Vintage and Veteran, including alloy, wire wheels

- Official distributors for Blockley tyres and Classico tubes

UK Sales
Charles Americanos
(T) 01753 598 384
(F) 01753 547 170

Export Sales
Isabella Zethofer
(T) +44 1753 598 382
(F) +44 1753 773 443

Vintage & Veteran
Norman Bradshaw
(T) 01753 598 386
(F) 01753 547 170

Motor Wheel Service International Ltd.
Units 1-4 Elder Way, Waterside Drive, Langley, Slough, Berkshire, SL3 6EP, UK
Tel: +44 (0)1753 549360 Fax: +44 (0)1753 547170 E-mail: info@mwsint.com Website: www.mwsint.com

Our online database contains wire wheel and accessory fitment details for hundreds of vehicles.
Just go to **www.mwsint.com** and select **Fitment Guide** from the menu.

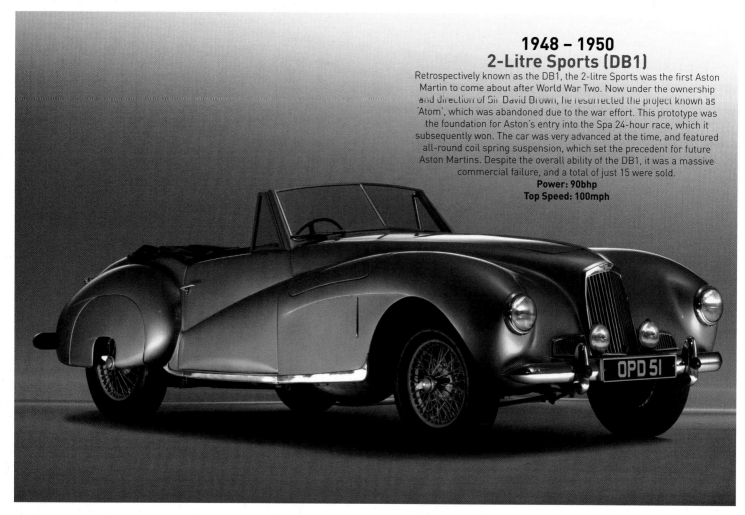

1948 – 1950
2-Litre Sports (DB1)

Retrospectively known as the DB1, the 2-litre Sports was the first Aston Martin to come about after World War Two. Now under the ownership and direction of Sir David Brown, he resurrected the project known as 'Atom', which was abandoned due to the war effort. This prototype was the foundation for Aston's entry into the Spa 24-hour race, which it subsequently won. The car was very advanced at the time, and featured all-round coil spring suspension, which set the precedent for future Aston Martins. Despite the overall ability of the DB1, it was a massive commercial failure, and a total of just 15 were sold.

Power: 90bhp
Top Speed: 100mph

1950 – 1953
DB2/DB2 Convertible

While the Aston Martin 2-Litre of 1948 has become retrospectively known as the DB1, the DB2 of 1950 was the first to officially wear the initials of Aston owner David Brown. The chassis was largely the same as the 2-Litre, but the curvaceous fastback body with an imposingly long bonnet was fresh and graceful, and would inspire Aston's styling path for the next two decades. The 2.6-litre twin-cam engine was a W O Bentley design for Lagonda and initially proved temperamental. It eventually settled down to endow the DB2 with impressive performance for the era, especially when in 121mph Vantage form from 1951.

Power: 105bhp
Top Speed: 116mph

1953 – 1957
DB2/4 / DB2/4 Convertible

The '4' tacked onto the end of the DB2's title denoted that this reworking of the theme could now fit four people inside – at a squeeze. The 2+2 seating was made more habitable by a higher rear roofline and opening rear window. However, the extra weight meant that performance was down, so Aston Martin boosted capacity to 3-litres in 1954, taking power to 140bhp. The Mk II of 1955 incorporated a rear end restyle and a tougher rear axle, and also introduced the incredibly rare notchback hardtop version, of which just 34 were made.

Power: 125bhp
Top Speed: 119mph

1957 – 1959
DB Mk III Coupe

It may have been the third series of DB2/4, but Aston Martin dropped the 2/4 nomenclature for its 1957 to 1959 range of saloons and dropheads. The most noticeable change was a more tapering front end topped off by a neater front grille, but vertical rear lights were also fitted and the body generally tidied up. Mechanically, the engine rose marginally in capacity but was made a lot stronger and more powerful at 162bhp. Aston Martin claimed 214bhp was possible with the competition-tuned triple carb version of the engine, but this was probably somewhat exaggerated. Front disc brakes standard from late 1957.

Power: 162bhp
Top Speed: 119mph

1958 – 1963
DB4/DB4 GT

The definitive, and most-loved Aston Martin shape was born with the DB4 of 1958. It was massively over-engineered with a hefty steel chassis and new all-alloy 240bhp double-overhead camshaft engine of three litres (but capable of being expanded well beyond this level if needed). What really grabbed the headlines though was the DB4's Superleggera bodywork. Designed by Italian coachbuilder Touring, the stunning lines were formed of aluminium panels laid over a frame of steel tubes, making the sportscar very strong but also lightweight. From 1958 to 1962, there were five series of DB4s, adding power, length and height to the original formula.

Power: 240bhp
Top Speed: 140mph

1960 - 1963
DB4 GT Zagato

Even though the Zagato was fully road legal, its real home was out on the track, most obviously the Le Mans 24-hour race. Only 19 DB4 GT Zagatos were built, using the shorter DB4 Chassis and a lightweight Zagato body. The uprated DB4 engine produced 314bhp, which gave the Zagato world-beating performance in 1960. The Zagato is arguably the most desirable Aston Martin ever made, and undoubtedly the most valuable.

Power: 314bhp
Top Speed: 154mph

1963 – 1966
DB5/DB5 Volante

Had not a certain James Bond 007 turned the DB5 into the most famous car in the world, this DB4 evolution might have gone largely unnoticed; originally, it was just going to be known as the DB4 Series 6. However, *Goldfinger* and *Thunderball* made stars of both the car and its maker. Four litres of potent power – 282bhp as standard, 314bhp if pumped up to Vantage spec – and long, lean looks with cowled headlamps meant that the legend was largely justified. Disc brakes were now on each wheel, all but the very earliest cars had five gears, less entertaining were the automatics.

Power: 282bhp
Top Speed: 141mph

1965 – 1970
DB6/DB6 Volante

The 'proper' DB-series reached a graceful end of life with the DB6 of 1965 to 1970. A longer wheelbase meant it could seat four people, although only the two up front would have any real comfort. The higher roofline, split bumpers and more aerodynamic Kamm tail were the main identifying points from what had gone before. Civilised extras were offered in the form of power steering, air conditioning and a limited-slip differential and, as was the Aston way, there was a more powerful Vantage version, this time boasting 325bhp. In 1969, the Mk II appeared, characterised by flared wheelarches and a fussy fuel injection system as an option.

Power: 325bhp
Top Speed: 148mph

1967 – 1973
DB S/DBS-V8

A new stylist – William Towns – meant a completely new look for Aston Martin, with 1967's DBS shifting its focus from Italy to America with its arresting muscle-car stance. Able to accommodate four passengers, the DBS was designed for V8 power, but Aston's eight-pot wasn't ready in time. So the DBS was something of a stopgap, using the same 4-litre engine of the DB6 with the usual option of an uprated Vantage version. However, all that extra weight knocked performance back; a DBS could only offer the same kind of speeds as a DB4. Although the V8-endowed model was available from 1969, the six-cylinder continued until 1973 as the entry level Aston.

Power: 282bhp
Top Speed: 140mph

1972 – 1990
V8/V8 Volante

If the Sixties was Aston's golden era, then the Seventies saw the glow fade. David Brown sold the company in 1972, resulting in the DB initials being dropped and the front end of the V8 cars being restyled with single headlamps, a smaller grille and a few more curves. The engine's troublesome fuel-injection system was soon dropped in favour of four Weber carburettors, plus a gaping bonnet scoop to clear them. The company's lack of cash meant that the V8 would have a long existence; with many detail changes and updates, it survived until 1990, an unprecedented lifespan for a top-flight luxury sportscar.

Power: 320bhp
Top Speed: 146mph

1974 – 1976
Lagonda

In 1974, the elegant William Towns styled DBS was given 4 doors and a slightly longer wheelbase, creating the Aston Martin Lagonda. Another difference was the far-from-attractive Lagonda style grille. This was the first car since the 1961 Rapide to wear the Lagonda badge, but it was not a success. This can be blamed on the 1974 oil crisis, which seriously limited the appeal of any V8 powered super saloon, let alone one that would rarely see MPG in the double figures. During the two years of production, only seven were sold.

Power: Not Quoted
Top Speed: 149mph

1977 – 1989
V8 Vantage/V8 Vantage Volante

With 1977 the Queen's Silver Jubilee year, Britain seemed keen to celebrate all that was best about itself, so what better time for the Aston Martin V8 Vantage to be launched? Hailed as 'Britain's first supercar,' the 5.3-litre V8 was breathed on so hard that an incredible 438bhp was unleashed. The dash to 60mph took just 5.4 seconds, with 170mph the ultimate speed. Visually, the car could be distinguished from its calmer stablemates by a blanked off grille and bonnet scoop. 1978's Oscar India variant adopted a small boot spoiler and a smoother bonnet, with the car continuing in this form until 1990. The rich person's Ford Capri is an apt description.
Power: 438bhp
Top Speed: 168mph

1977 – 1990
Lagonda

The '70s was an eccentric decade, and even Aston Martin wasn't immune to the craziness. Behold the strangely glorious Lagonda, launched in 1977, the same year that *Star Wars* hit cinemas (and looking like it should have starred in it). Outside, the car – on a stretched V8 chassis – was an uncompromising razor-edged wedge shape by William Towns, inside it was a technological tour-de-force of touch-sensitive switches, digital displays and futuristic gizmos. These electronics were its weak point, for the Lagonda soon became known for being unreliable as well as for its astonishing looks. Simplification followed, allowing the wedge to stay in production until 1990. Utterly mad, yet also endearingly British.
Power: 280bhp
Top Speed: 143mph

1986 – 1989
V8 Zagato

Looking to reignite a successful past relationship, Aston Martin returned to Italian coachbuilder Zagato in the mid '80s for a strictly limited edition version of the V8. The plan was for Zagato to come up with an exotic body which could be fitted to a lightened, shortened chassis. But the result divided opinion; gone were the luscious curves of Zagato's Aston revamps of '60s and in their place were brutal straight lines and angled edges, with an extensive use of flush-fitting glass. Critics found it hard to get over the resemblance to contemporary Japanese sports coupes, but, with only 83 of these distinctive machines ever built, they are amazingly valuable today.
Power: 432bhp
Top Speed: 186mph

1989 – 1999
Virage/V8 Coupe

After 20 years of the V8 saloon shape, even Aston Martin was forced to concede that it was time for a change. Enter the Virage, the final blast of the original V8 concept. A bold and imposing new body was designed by Royal College of Art tutors John Hefferman and Ken Greenley, and slotted over the existing V8 chassis (albeit with a relocated rear axle). A US tuning company had fun boosting power to 310bhp, although the car needed this extra muscle to cope with its additional weight. Despite the old-fashioned underpinnings, the car still looked sufficiently sleek and modern to revitalise Aston Martin for the '90s.
Power: 330bhp
Top Speed: 157mph

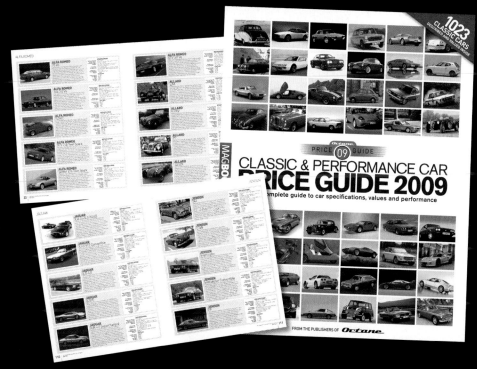

1993 – 1999
Vantage
As with previous Aston Martins, the temptation to tweak the Virage formula for even higher performance was strong, and the Vantage name was applied to the Virage model in 1993. Although visually alike, the Vantage body was reworked so that only the doors and roof were the same as before, giving it a more purposeful and powerful stance. Naturally though, the best changes were kept for under the bonnet, where bolted-on twin superchargers gave an enormous 550bhp. That was enough to propel this two-tonne car to 200mph, with 60 coming up in just 4.2 seconds. Later Vantages had 600bhp to play with.
Power: 550mph
Top Speed: 186mph

1993 – 1999
DB7/DB7 Volante
Ford's outright purchase of Aston Martin brought fresh optimism and security. Nothing symbolised this new hope more than 1994's DB7. Designed using Blue Oval resources, the chassis evolved from that of the Jaguar XJ6...but the many changes and stunning Ian Callum-penned body meant that it was much, much more than a re-skinned Jag, although the close resemblance of the later Jaguar XK8 did steal some of its glory. The supercharged 335bbhp 3.2-litre six-cylinder engine was also new, the first six-pot to appear in an Aston since the DBS of 1967. The DB designation also harkened back to the past, a tribute to honorary life president David Brown.
Power: 335bhp
Top Speed: 165mph

1999 – 2003
DB7 Vantage/DB7 Vantage Volante
Previous Vantage versions had usually just increased the output of a type's existing engine. 1999's DB7 Vantage went a radical step further, it had an entire new engine dropped in. And what a powerhouse; a new 6-litre 48-valve V12 unit of 420bhp, making the Vantage more than a match for any of its European supercar rivals. In fact, so desirable was the Vantage that sales of the six-cylinder DB7 promptly dried up, forcing it to be dropped by the end of 1999. A 2002 offshoot was the V12 GT (or GTA when sporting an automatic transmission) which offered 435bhp and other performance and cosmetic tweaks.
Power: 420bhp
Top Speed: 185mph

2001 – 2007
Vanquish/Vanquish S
Launched in 2001, the Vanquish was the flagship of Aston's line-up. Aston Martin decided to fit the Vanquish with a semi-automatic paddle-shift gearbox. The gearbox was criticised for being slow, but it was ultimately user-friendly, and the shift speed was improved in 2005 with the introduction of the Vanquish S. The S also upgraded a few of the original Vanquish's shortcomings with an uprated chassis package, and a substantially more-powerful V12 powerplant. A 6-speed manual gearbox was made available in 2007 when the run-out Vanquish S Ultimate Edition was launched.
Power: 450bhp
Top Speed: 196mph

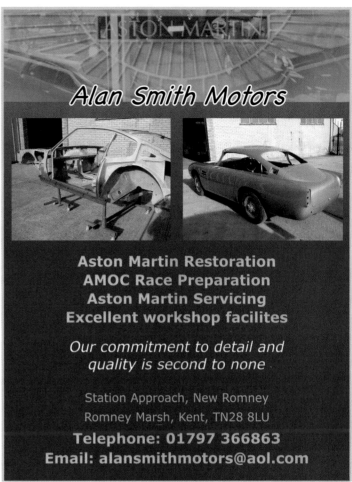

2002 – 2004
DB7 Zagato/DB-AR1

Created specifically for the US market, the DB-AR1 (American Roadster 1) was an extremely limited edition, Zagato styled roadster. It is heavily based around the DB7 Vantage, and it shares the same 6-litre V12 engine. All but eight of the 99 DB-AR1s built were sold in the USA, costing a mere $226,000 when new, but even at that price owners had to make do without a roof. The similarly styled DB7 Zagato came first, and was identical to the AR1, other than the fact it used a slightly-shortened DB7 Chassis, and had the trademark Zagato double-domed roof, harking back to the DB4 Zagato.

Power: 435bhp
Top Speed: 185mph

2004 – Present
DB9

Successor to the highly successful DB7 range, the DB9 is available in both coupé and Volante form. The car shares its 6-litre V12 engine with the more expensive Vanquish, but it was designed to be a production friendly, mass-production model securing the future of the company and directly rivalling the Ferrari F430 and Porsche 911 at the same time. Using a similar gearbox to the Vanquish, Aston Martin managed to improve the responsiveness and shift time, giving the DB9 a much more positive driving experience.

Power: 450bhp
Top Speed: 186mph

2005 – Present
V8 Vantage/V12 Vantage

With the Porsche 911 directly in the line of fire, Aston Martin came up with the V8 Vantage. The most affordable Aston Martin in the current line-up, the modern day Vantage offers the chance of Aston ownership to the masses, relatively speaking. In early 2009 the V12 Vantage joined the ranks alongside the V8. The combination of a lightweight aluminium body and V12 engine means that the V12 Vantage is in a league with rivals such as the Porsche 911 GT3, Lamborghini Gallardo and the Audi R8 V10.

Power: 380bhp
Speed: 174mph

2007 – Present
DBS V12

Featured in 'Casino Royale' and 'Quantum of Solace', the DBS really is James Bond's car of choice. Superseding the Vanquish as the flagship Aston (and Bond Car), the DBS brings much more aggressive styling to the table, and a manual gearbox – something the Vanquish was criticised for lacking. Using a development of the 5.9-litre V12 found in the DBR9 race car, it packs a real punch. 510bhp propels the DBS to 60mph in 3.8 seconds, continuing on to 194mph. The DBS Volante was unveiled at the 2009 Geneva Motor Show, and is built alongside the DBS coupé at Aston Martin's Gaydon factory.

Power: 510bhp
Top Speed: 188mph